Above: Savoy/ABC Birkenhead in 1938.

🄰 🄱 🄲 The First Name in Entertainment

Front cover: ABC (ex-Empire) Mile End in 1984 (photograph by Allen Eyles).

Savoy Northampton in 1936.

A B C

THE FIRST NAME IN ENTERTAINMENT

ALLEN EYLES

CINEMA
THEATRE
ASSOCIATION

Distributed by
BFI PUBLISHING

BRITISH FILM INSTITUTE

bfi

BFI PUBLISHING

First published
in September 1993 by the
Cinema Theatre Association
5 Coopers Close
Burgess Hill
West Sussex RH15 8AN

Distributed by
BFI Publishing
British Film Institute
21 Stephen Street
London W1P 1PL

The CINEMA THEATRE ASSOCIATION was formed in 1967 to promote serious interest in all aspects of cinema buildings, including architecture, décor, lighting, music, film projection and stage facilities. The Association campaigns for the preservation and, wherever possible, the continued use of cinemas and theatres for their original purpose, and maintains an archive of historical material. Visits to cinemas and theatres in the UK and overseas are regularly organised, as well as lectures, talks and film shows. The Association publishes the magazine *Picture House* and the bi-monthly *CTA Bulletin*, a members' newsletter. (Enquiries/Membership Secretary: Bill Wren, Flat 30, Cambridge Court, Cambridge Road, Southend-on-Sea, Essex SS1 1EJ.)

The BRITISH FILM INSTITUTE exists to encourage the development of film, television and video in the United Kingdom, and to promote knowledge, understanding and enjoyment of the culture of the moving image. Its activities include the National Film and Television Archive; The National Film Theatre; The London Film Festival; The Museum of the Moving Image; the production and distribution of film and video; funding and support for regional activities; Library and Information Services; Stills, Posters and Designs; Research; Publishing and Education; and the monthly *Sight and Sound* Magazine. (Membership details: Membership Department, South Bank, London SE1 8TL.)

ISBN: 0-85170-430-1

Typeset by
InterMedia Graphic Systems
Lewes, East Sussex

Printed in Great Britain by
The KPC Group
London and Ashford, Kent

Contents

Acknowledgements

I am very grateful to the members of the CTA Committee who kindly agreed to read the text in an earlier draft for their comments and information – Richard Gray (chairman), David Trevor-Jones (vice chairman) and Keith Skone (publications manager) – and to the CTA's president, Tony Moss, for his contributions to the text regarding ABC organs and for other observations. John Fernée also read portions of the text closely and made some valuable observations. I am greatly indebted to Elain Harwood for uncovering biographical details of W. R. Glen and for her suggestions regarding the text.

My further thanks are extended to other CTA committee members: Tim McCullen for contributing elusive data, and Bill Wren for resolving a specific query; to the CTA's archivist, Brian Oakaby, for welcoming me to the Archive; and to Peter Loftus for his valuable reminiscences of working for ABC and dispatch of vintage ABC programmes; to Pat Billings in Dublin for looking into the Irish connection; to Ian Riches, for his comments on ABC in the early multiplex era; to Edward J. Stevenson (former chief projectionist whose association with ABC dated back to the Twenties); to Tommy Sinclair (who introduced me to Edward J. Stevenson in the box of the ABC Toledo Muirend circa 1977); to Ronald Grant and the Cinema Museum; to Peter S. Haigh, former editor of *(ABC) Film Review*; to Ray Wallis, Vanessa Jenkins, the late John Osborn, and Metro-Goldwyn-Mayer Cinemas; and not least to Battersea Reference and Local History Library, Lavender Hill, for the unfailing helpfulness of its staff and its excellent opening hours.

I am grateful to Alan Ashton, Paul Clements, Derek Phillips, E. Walkden and Bob Wood for their helpful response to the first mention of this project in the *CTA Bulletin*, and to Carol Gibbons for her past generosity to the Cinema Theatre Association which has made publication of this book possible.

When I asked in the *CTA Bulletin* for information regarding the post-ABC history of specific sites, I was deluged by letters and phone calls, all most welcome, from Fred Burgoine, Brian Cooper, Ben Doman, Peter Douglas, John Duddy, Dave Fleming, Dan J. Ford, A. G. Frost, John Gibson, Mervyn Gould, Bob Grimwood, Brian Hall, Donald Hickling, Gerald E. Hooper, Brian Hornsey, T. Louden, Tom Pate, Rev. Stephen Pugh, Andrew Richardson, Gil Robottom, J. A. Smallwood, Gary Stevens, Mike Taylor, Alan J. Towers, N. Walley, Harry Whiteside, Adrian R. Whitewick, Trevor Wicks, Ned Williams, W. H. Willis and Giles Woodforde. Their contribution has made me feel reasonably happy about the thoroughness of the cinema listings.

Lastly, my love and thanks to my wife Lesley who provided practical support when it was most needed.

On behalf of the Cinema Theatre Association, I dedicate this book to the memory of Gordon Coombes, former ABC executive and a staunch friend of the society. We are fortunate to have as source material many of his career reminiscences in *Picture House* articles, but his further contribution would have been substantial.

Introduction

Associated British Cinemas had a particular place in my childhood cinema-going in the Fifties. There were three new programmes released every week onto the major circuits: ABC, Odeon and Gaumont. I lived at Tooting Bec and then nearby at Streatham in South London, an area where ABC cinemas were thick on the ground. Although they were not called ABCs then but had different names – Regal, Mayfair, Ritz, etc. – I was made aware that they were part of a circuit just as much as the Odeons or Gaumonts, and experience soon showed that they screened a good proportion of the best new films. (I did not go as far as attending the Saturday morning shows, which would have made me an ABC Minor expected to sing the Minors song.)

While the cinemas built for the circuit did have a recognisable style, most ABCs were taken over and could only to a degree be made to conform to the circuit look. ABC cinemas had a common decorative scheme of pastel shades – light blues and pinks – with highlights picked out in gold, "spray" light fittings, *ABC Film Review* on sale in the foyers, Pathe News and Pearl & Dean advertising on the screen – and the triangle logo that was prominently featured in press advertising and street posters, on the screen in the titles prefacing the trailers, and most conspicuously mounted on the front of the cinemas in red and blue neon with the name of the theatre inserted in green. (It was not until the Sixties that most of the names were changed to "ABC". By then, the logo had changed as well.)

What further gave the circuit its identity was the films it showed. ABC cinemas had first call on the output of Metro-Goldwyn-Mayer and Warner Bros. as well as the productions of the parent Associated British Picture Corporation (most of which seemed to star Richard Todd). (It was, of course, possible to see ABC circuit releases in other cinemas in areas where ABC were not represented, but in my case these were some distance away at Clapham Junction and Upper Norwood.)

The chances are that anyone seeing Warner Bros. and Metro-Goldwyn-Mayer pictures before the Seventies, especially anyone living in the London area, viewed them in an ABC theatre – probably with trailers for more MGM or Warner pictures the following week. The distinctive hues of Metrocolor and particularly WarnerColor (too often grainy, with purplish blues where black should have been) were also part of going to the pictures at ABCs. So accustomed did I become to seeing these companies' new films in ABCs that it was very disconcerting to hear the lion's roar when the curtains opened in an Odeon or Gaumont – although the odd film would escape to the opposition. Just as unsettling later on was to see the Paramount and Universal trademarks on an ABC screen when those studios first switched to the circuit.

I have fond memories of ABC because the Regal (later ABC, now Cannon) Streatham was, without my particularly realising it, my favourite circuit house. I always felt more at home there than at the Odeon Astoria or the Gaumont at Streatham: the Odeon Astoria seemed old-fashioned and too lofty while the Gaumont, although wonderfully modern after its post-war reconstruction, was usually empty and "cold". The Regal seemed more comfortable and less formal: it had (and still has) that spacious, inviting entrance hall, its auditorium was nicely proportioned and pleasantly decorated while its cheaper seats (in the days when the stalls was divided into different price areas) still placed me a good distance back from the screen with excellent sightlines, its CinemaScope installation was superior to that at the Odeon Astoria, and its

Author's favourite of the Fifties: Regal Streatham in 1938
photographs. It is the three-screen Cannon in 1993.

mostly elderly usherettes were never officious except perhaps in their efforts to sell the *Film Review*.

Cinema buildings began to interest me as I saw them closing down and disappearing. The big ABCs were not at first affected but I was drawn out of curiosity to see inside the modern Regal Twickenham when that was announced as closing. As a direct result of my afternoon visit, the youthful audience at a packed screening of the Steve Reeves adventure picture *Hercules Unchained* suffered a momentary interruption to their viewing pleasure. I had introduced myself to the manager who was, despite a somewhat military-like bearing, most welcoming. He showed me round the building with special enthusiasm for an enclosed outdoor passage where he administered a thick ear to unruly youngsters before throwing them out. And he arranged for me to make my first visit to a projection box. There the chief showed me the equipment and invited me to feel the weight of the anamorphic (Cinema-Scope) lens he was about to fit to the projector showing the second reel of *Hercules Unchained*, telling me not to drop it as it was worth several hundred pounds. Engrossed in talking to me, he suddenly realised he had left it too late to fit the lens in time for the change-over. He explained that he would have to let the screen go dark for a moment. I can still hear the massive roar of protest that seeped into the projection box from that crowded matinee audience – and how it seemed to come from miles away so that it was not at all menacing. My apologies if you were there that afternoon.

In later years when I began writing about cinemas, a company executive, the late Gordon Coombes, kindly provided a letter of access to ABC properties and it is due to that open sesame that I viewed many of the more distant ABCs, often just before they closed down. The Cinema Theatre Association also arranged many trips that included ABC cinemas, the first to the vast ABC Bournemouth which had not then been subdivided. However, I cannot pretend to have seen the circuit as thoroughly as I would have liked for the purpose of this book, even if there is little space for individual theatres.

Constraints of time, money and a deadline have precluded more research, such as a visit to Scotland to pursue the early life of John Maxwell and the early history of Scottish Cinema and Variety Theatres, or interviews with veteran managers.

About to close: Regal Twickenham in August 1960. (Photograph by Allen Eyles.)

This newspaper photograph of the Regal Twickenham during demolition provides some record of the auditorium's appearance. (Courtesy of Brian Cooper.)

I have given some priority to documenting the programming of ABCs, in the belief expressed above that the particular films shown were a key part of the ABC experience.

I hope that this book provides a broad impression of the company's activities, of most aspects of circuit policy and operation – although others, such as showmanship, catering and kiosk sales, screen advertising and ABC Minors shows, could have done with detailed exploration. I hope that local historians can provide more detail on these in relation to particular theatres, and interview past managers and staff. There are a disproportionate number of references to London-area cinemas as these are the ones I knew best and the ones easiest to research (I would have liked, for instance, to spend more time in newspaper files looking at the way ABC operated in more of the key cities).

I would be glad to hear from anyone who can elaborate on the history of ABC. The pages of the Cinema Theatre Association's magazine *Picture House* are a means of continuing the history of ABC, while the bi-monthly *CTA Bulletin* will provide an up-date on developments at the surviving ABC cinemas.

1 | John Maxwell

Associated British Cinemas and its sister companies in distribution and production were one of the unqualified success stories of the British film industry in the Thirties, and of British business in general during a difficult decade. The Associated British group grew larger and larger, making profits and paying dividends every year, without any of the financial crises that attended its main rival, the Gaumont-British Picture Corporation. Making money from cinemas was not difficult but it indulged in film production successfully, i.e. without losing money – a skill which eluded Gaumont-British and which was not even attempted by another, later competitor, Odeon.

Associated British Cinemas claimed to be the second largest cinema circuit in the world in 1937, and was certainly far ahead of the Gaumont and Odeon chains (which were then, of course, under separate ownership). At its peak, ABC sold nearly six million tickets a week. With the best spread of cinemas, screening a generous proportion of the best Hollywood pictures, and with a well-established triangular trademark, the circuit was known to almost every filmgoer.

Like Odeon with Oscar Deutsch and Granada with Sidney Bernstein, the company owed its success principally to the drive, perseverance and financial perspicacity of one man. In the case of ABC, it was a dour, tough, canny, fair-minded and honest Scotsman named John Maxwell. In the early years of ABC, Maxwell seemed to revel in the limelight and his photograph was widely reproduced in the trade press and opening programmes. It is possible that he regarded it as necessary to become a public figurehead while ABC was becoming established but, from the mid-Thirties onward, he retired from public view, although he enjoyed the fruits of his success, travelling to the studios in a Rolls Royce and smoking the best

John Maxwell. (BFI Stills, Posters and Designs.)

The original Prince's Springburn, Glasgow, circa 1930: probably the first cinema operated by John Maxwell.

Govan Cinema, Glasgow, circa 1930: believed to be one of the first picture houses built by Maxwell.

cigars. Maxwell, like Deutsch, was primarily a financier and there was a trade joke that if you put them in the same room you would have together the two men who knew least about actual cinema management.

Born in 1877 (or possibly late 1876), John Maxwell had built up a steady practice as a family solicitor in Glasgow in 1908. According to Alan Wood in his biography of J. Arthur Rank, *Mr. Rank*, Maxwell had "the respect for learning often found among Scots; as a young man he would sit down to study in the evenings, with the old-fashioned purpose of improving his mind. He was also interested in politics and stood for Parliament (unsuccessfully) as Liberal candidate at Motherwell." A few years after Maxwell's death, an old colleague, Arthur Dent, remarked: "He was undoubtedly the most knowledgeable of men to enter the film industry, and was as shrewd as he was wise. He knew films like a sage knows its onions, and had a cultural background unequalled in the business. Few people at that time suspected that by sheer force of character he would one day change the face of film history..."

Maxwell first observed the commercial possibilities of film exhibition when engaged as a solicitor to handle the legal aspects of one or two cinema deals. His initial cinema venture was as a partner in the hiring of the Pollokshaws Burgh Hall to show films (Pollokshaws, three miles southwest of the city centre, was then a borough in its own right. The Burgh Hall was still standing in the mid-Seventies, used for dances.) By 1912, Maxwell had taken a financial interest in a small rented picture house, believed to have been the original Prince's at Springburn, a district of Glasgow. In 1912, he began acquiring existing cinemas as well as sites for new ones in partnership with James Wright and an accountant, William H. Jack.

In 1914, while a senior partner of the solicitors Maxwell, Hodgson and Co., his film interests amounted to ten or eleven existing cinemas in Glasgow, Perth, Montrose, Arbroath and elsewhere, and the building of the Shawlands Cross Picture House and another cinema at Govan.

These various enterprises were merged in 1917 into one company called Scottish Cinema and Variety Theatres Ltd. By 1920 SCVT had twenty cinemas, but it did not enlarge substantially after that until ABC was formed, with SCVT as an autonomous unit.

Instead, Maxwell involved himself in film distribution and production. In 1922, he joined forces with Arthur Dent to set up Waverley Films, initially providing the financial backing as a "flutter". This company acted as a regional distributor handling the output of Wardour Films in London. It became the largest Scottish distributor and eventually acquired Wardour Films itself, retaining the Wardour name.

In 1925, Maxwell moved to London and set about expanding his film interests south of the border. Under his leadership, Wardour released the output of the giant Ufa concern in Britain until Gaumont-British took it over from April 1928.

Savoy Cinemas Ltd. was registered on 31 March 1924 with £5,000 in £1 shares. This was a Maxwell company with a London head office that initially held the Savoy Bradford and soon expanded its holdings to include the City Leeds and Picture House Chorlton-cum-Hardy (both of which were promptly renamed Savoy), Prince of Wales Liverpool and Elite Bordesley Green, Birmingham. J. E. (James Edward) Pearce was the managing director, while David A. Stewart, a former variety agent who had joined Maxwell in the early years of SCVT (or, according to one source, as far back as 1913), was in charge of the Scottish circuit.

With a footing in exhibition and distribution, Maxwell now took a giant step into production. He joined British National's board in January 1927 after Wardour had arranged to distribute its output in Britain. Then, just three months later, he and other directors of British National turned it and its Elstree studio into the base for a new company, British International Pictures. Encouraged by new legislation requiring distributors and exhibitors to take a certain percentage of domestic films that promised a wide showing for BIP pictures in Britain itself, Maxwell boldly set about producing films that were aimed at the international market. In August 1928, he acquired a controlling interest of fifty-one per cent in the First National Pathe distribution company in Britain while maintaining Wardour Films as a separate distributor. He hoped to gain access to the American market for his British productions through First National.

A notable new director, Alfred Hitchcock, made a series of pictures under contract to BIP, including *Blackmail*, which he began shooting as a silent film in February 1929. After BIP acquired sound equipment in April 1929, Hitchcock reshot various sequences with spoken dialogue. *Blackmail* opened on 28 July 1929 as Britain's first talking picture, while the silent version was released later to cinemas that had yet to install sound. (Another BIP picture, *Kitty,* opened earlier but its sound sequences had been added in America.)

Maxwell's more costly productions were *Moulin Rouge, Piccadilly* and *Atlantic*, all directed by E. A. Dupont. *Atlantic* was not only the first full-talkie made in Europe but it was shot in English, German and French versions – the first multi-lingual film and a big hit (later multi-lingual ventures were not as successful). Maxwell even persuaded George Bernard Shaw to release his play *How He Lied to Her Husband* for filming by BIP, and posed with Shaw as he signed the contract for a publicity photograph.

Maxwell would continue in production to the end of the Thirties, but he soon lost the services of Alfred Hitchcock and the films that came from BIP (or the Associated British Picture Corporation, which replaced BIP in 1937) were more notable for their number (and helping his cinema circuit's quota requirements) than for their quality. It is clear that Maxwell abandoned his ambition to become a force internationally (and it seems likely that he concentrated on the cinema chain as a consequence). While there were some huge domestic hits like *Blossom Time* (1934) with Richard Tauber, the most artistically ambitious of Maxwell's later films resulted from backing Erich Pommer and Charles Laughton in their Mayflower productions of *Vessel of Wrath* and *St. Martin's Lane* (both 1938 releases) and *Jamaica Inn* (1939), the latter marking Hitchcock's return to Elstree but resulting in a box-office disappointment that closed down Mayflower.

Maxwell's biggest achievement by far was in building up the Associated British Cinemas circuit.

2 | The Beginning of ABC

Associated British Cinemas started life in 1928 as a subsidiary of BIP. It was first registered as a private company at the end of January with a capital of £50,000 and J. E. Pearce as managing director. Registration as a public company followed on 26 November when it had a capital of £1 million for establishing a circuit of about forty cinemas, J. E. Pearce still being the managing director. BIP held two-thirds of the ordinary share capital and its shareholders had first option on the rest. ABC was one of a number of large scale ventures launched in 1927/8 and followed the example of the Gaumont-British Picture Corporation in marrying film production, distribution and exhibition to make a large integrated concern.

ABC began as an amalgamation of three existing exhibition circuits already controlled by John Maxwell. One was SCVT, the company which Maxwell had built up in Scotland over many years. ABC took a ninety per cent interest and it continued as a separate entity under the control of David A. Stewart until 1947. SCVT had many cinemas in Glasgow: three in or near the city centre (the huge Coliseum, the Kings at Charing Cross and the Theatre de Luxe) plus six in the suburbs (the Empire, Gaiety and Palace at Clydebank, Govan Cinema, Picture House Shawlands Cross and Prince's Springburn). Near Glasgow were the La Scala Motherwell and Plaza Wishaw. In Edinburgh, SCVT had the Haymarket Picture House and the Savoy, plus a site for a new cinema. Around Scotland, SCVT were also represented in Arbroath (Palace), Dumbarton (Pavilion), Dumfries (Playhouse), Dundee (Palace), Gourock (Pavilion), Kilmarnock (King's), Kirkcaldy (Opera House and Pathhead), Methil (Gaiety), Montrose (King's) and Rosyth (Picture House).

Another part of ABC consisted of Savoy Cinemas. In the Birmingham area the company held the centrally located Select in Station Street, the Elite Bordesley Green and the New Palace Summerhill Road (plus, possibly, the Bordesley Palace). In the Manchester area, there was the Gaiety plus the Savoy at Chorlton-cum-Hardy. Other cinemas were the Bath Assembly Rooms, Grand and Westover Bournemouth, Savoy and Regent Bradford, Pavilion and Queens Cardiff, Broadway Hammersmith in West London, Savoy Leeds, and Prince of Wales Liverpool. In addition, Savoy had sites for huge cinemas in Brighton and Dublin and was planning the reconstruction of the Regent Birmingham and the Whitechapel Pavilion.

Lastly, there was the Favourite Cinemas group of four cinemas, which was already linked with Savoy, operating from the same London address. This quartet comprised the two Blue Halls in Hammersmith, West London; the Olympia Liverpool; and the Empire Newcastle.

These three circuits gave ABC a starting strength of forty-three (or possibly forty-four) properties, plus five schemes in different stages of development (of which all but that for the Whitechapel Pavilion were soon realised).

Before the end of 1928, ABC had put in an offer for the ninety-two halls of the giant PCT chain, the major nationwide circuit at the time. This followed a Gaumont-British bid for the company. Maxwell's offer divided PCT's directors, who eventually decided to sell to G-B. But the Maxwell intervention forced G-B to pay five shillings more per share.

Maxwell turned his expansionist eye elsewhere and within a few weeks ABC had paid Mortimer Dent and Joseph Cohen approximately £250,000 for eleven cinemas that formed part of their C.D. Circuit – eight in the Birmingham area (Gaiety Coleshill Street, Metropole Snow Hill, Astoria Aston, Aston

BIP's talkie sensation Blackmail *at ABC's Broadway Hammersmith, West London, in 1929.*

The Regal Glasgow, a newcomer of 1929.

Cross Picture House, Adelphi Hay Mills, Olympia Darlaston, Plaza West Bromwich, and the not-yet-opened Edgbaston Picture House), plus the Empire Crewe, White Hall Derby and Hippodrome Nuneaton.

In 1929 ABC opened three cinemas – the Ritz Edinburgh, Regal Glasgow (a thorough conversion of an existing building) and the Savoy Dublin – and the Greenock Picture House was reconstructed into the Regal. These properties are discussed more fully in Chapter 4. In July 1929, ABC made a new £1 million share issue to enable further expansion of the company.

It was during this year that ABC took over (either completely or through a controlling interest) several small companies that each added added one or two cinemas to the circuit. These brought in pairs of cinemas at Clifton, Bristol (the Triangle and the more valuable Whiteladies, both of which may not have been physically operated by ABC until 7 April 1930), the Potteries (the Capitol Hanley and the Majestic Stoke-on-Trent), the Manchester suburbs (the Claremont Moss Side and Premier Cheetham Hill) and Blackpool (the Princess and Hippodrome). Other acquisitions gave the circuit a central Bristol cinema, the King's, plus the Beau Nash Bath, Regent Chatham, Picture House Doncaster, the very recently opened Lido at Golders Green in North London, the Empire Rotherham, Olympia Newport, both the Star and Theatre Royal at Preston, Prince's Leicester, New Coliseum Whitley Bay, and major cinemas in Great Yarmouth and Norwich, both called the Regent.

In October 1929, Maxwell added seven in a take-over of Cinema Proprietors Ltd. from Leon Salberg and Sidney W. Clift: the Alhambra Moseley Road, Palace and Picture House Erdington, Robin Hood Hall Green, Original Saltley, plus the Orient Aston (a Chinese-themed cinema under construction) and the New Empress in Nottingham. The company had been formed in Birmingham with £300,000 capital at the same time as ABC but the owners decided to take a quick profit and start all over again. Besides the Orient, they were originally expected to contribute a new cinema planned for Saltley but instead retained this and opened it as the Rock in 1934 (it became part of Sidney W. Clift's Clifton circuit).

With the take-over of Cinema Proprietors, Maxwell had laid the foundation of ABC's huge strength in Birmingham.

The SCVT part of the circuit made significant advances in Glasgow. Besides opening a key first-run house, the Regal, in the city centre, the company also added the Grosvenor Hillhead and Picture House Dennistoun, the Phoenix, the Arcadia Bridgeton, and two at Shawlands, the Waverley and Camphill Picture House, to add to its existing theatre there. Elsewhere in Scotland, apart from its new Edinburgh and Greenock theatres, the company gained second houses in Dundee and Motherwell, the Plaza and New Century respectively, and entered Falkirk by taking over the Grand Theatre.

In Manchester, ABC gained a controlling interest in the centrally located and large Theatre Royal, although J. F. Emery still remained a director and Famous Players Lasky continued to lease the property until its new Paramount opened in October 1930. A £250,000 deal with Ada Kenyon in July 1929 added the Playhouse Miles Platting, Ardwick Picture Theatre, Casino Rusholme and New Royal Ashton New Road to the ABC circuit. (Indicating the feverish pace at which cinemas were changing hands, Ms. Kenyon had only recently bought the Ardwick and Casino for around £70,000.)

In London in February 1929, John Maxwell had become chairman of Madame Tussaud's and its cinema at Baker Street was booked by ABC, although it never became part of the ABC circuit. Maxwell wanted a proper West End presence to showcase the films that were being made by BIP and so ABC bought Hyde Park Cinemas Ltd., the company headed by Arthur Gilbert which had leased the vast new Regal Marble Arch from A. E. Abrahams since its opening in November 1928. The Regal had started spectacularly with the talkie sensation *The Singing Fool*, starring Al Jolson, and had been hired by Maxwell for the very first showing of BIP's first talkie, *Blackmail*, at a late night trade screening on Friday 21 June 1929. ABC took over the cinema on 28 September 1929 and Maxwell had a special showing of the new BIP sound spectacular *Atlantic* there on 14 November. However, following its initial success with talkies, the Regal soon proved to be a financial headache, expensive to run and located at the periphery of the West End.

Seeking a more central London showplace for BIP productions, Maxwell took the trade by surprise when he persuaded Oswald Stoll to lease the Alhambra Theatre in Leicester Square for a year at a rent of approximately £1,000 per week.

Orient at Six Ways, Aston, Birmingham, seen in 1946: a cinema taken over during construction and opened by ABC.

The Edgbaston Birmingham. Queues outside for the 1935 BIP release Abdul the Damned *and a view of the auditorium circa 1935 showing landscape panels on the side walls and projection from beneath the balcony.*

Until then, this celebrated music hall had only occasionally featured films, but Maxwell's proposal was too lucrative for Stoll and his fellow directors to refuse. It was here that *Atlantic* opened on 23 December 1929. The Alhambra proved such a big success during the year, with the American anti-war film *All Quiet on the Western Front* running a massive fourteen weeks, that Stoll tried to continue the film policy after BIP left. (In time, Oscar Deutsch would make an even more generous offer for the Alhambra so that he could replace it with the flagship theatre of the Odeon circuit.)

Maxwell also leased a live theatre in New York, the Cohan, to showcase BIP product in North America, but the losses were so heavy that by December 1930 he was trying to sell the remainder of the lease and the Cohan Theatre had stopped showing films by early February 1931.

Back home, still in 1929, the ABC chain expanded in the London suburbs with an arrangement to acquire another Arthur Gilbert concern, Suburban Super Cinemas Ltd., which leased three more cinemas from A. E. Abrahams. This brought the Palladium Brixton, Queen's Forest Gate and Coronation Manor Park into the ABC fold (although they may not have been actually operated by ABC until 26 May 1930).

3 | ABC in the Thirties: The Take-Overs

It is clear that, from the late Twenties, numerical size became the primary measure of a circuit's importance and John Maxwell was intensely eager that ABC should beat its major rival, Gaumont-British. ABC's growth in numerical terms during the Thirties came principally from its acquisition of existing cinemas (the aspect that is covered in this chapter) but it also had its own architectural department, headed by W. R. Glen, which designed a considerable number of large, well-planned and, for the most part, well-sited cinemas (see next chapter) that delivered a disproportionate part of the circuit's profits.

Maxwell took direct control of ABC's expansion by supplanting J. E. Pearce as managing director in late 1930 (Pearce then ran the small London-headquartered subsidiary, Associated Irish Cinemas). As Maxwell was also the chairman and ran the company profitably, his authority was unassailable. In the early years of ABC and BIP, he seemed to enjoy personal publicity – or else considered it essential to promote confidence in the young organisation. But from the early Thirties onwards, he did not show up at the opening of new ABC houses which were, in most cases, inaugurated with a minimum of pomp and ceremony (the company was usually represented by general manager Arthur S. Moss). But he took a very close interest in what was going on, from the purchase of sites and drawing up of plans to checking out existing cinemas that might be suitable additions to the circuit.

Many entrepreneurs in the process of building up small circuits received irresistible offers from Maxwell, sold what they had already achieved, and usually started all over again with the proceeds. (In opening the Edgbaston Picture House and the Orient Aston Cross, ABC completed the expansion projects of two separate Midlands chains Maxwell had acquired.)

In August 1930, Maxwell arranged to buy A. E. Abrahams' remaining cinema interests, a poor batch that consisted of the Rialto Bermondsey, the Hippodromes Rotherhithe and Willesden, and a controlling interest in the Kinema (later Lido) Ealing and Grand Gillingham. However, Maxwell seems to have had second thoughts about the Rialto and Grand as they were taken over by the young Eric Rhodes (see *Picture House* no. 12, Autumn 1988). ABC was most interested in the Hippodrome Rotherhithe which was still a silent cinema, closing it for two months' redecoration and re-opening with talkies. (Abrahams was one of those soon back in the cinema business, putting up the new Regal Edmonton.)

ABC seems to have acquired more than twenty cinemas in 1930 while opening only three newly-built ones. Some, like the Burnley Palace, were music halls that ABC converted to cinemas. Others, like the Poplar Hippodrome and Shoreditch Olympia (bought jointly in yet another take-over from Arthur Gilbert, here operating as Olympodromes Ltd.), had already gone over to films but had all the disadvantages of being the wrong shape of auditorium. On the other hand, the Capitol Winchmore Hill was a very recently opened Lou Morris enterprise designed by a leading architect, Robert Cromie, but one that was far too large for its location and never very profitable to operate. But there was also the well-located Capitol Wallasey, plus the quite modern Ritz at Bordesley Green to strengthen ABC's grasp on Birmingham. Further take-overs of this period included the Belmont Anfield, Scala Birkenhead, Capitol Barking, Grand Mansfield, Grainger Newcastle, Palladium Bolton, Broadway East Ham, Empire Derby and Grand Warrington, plus two more in Scotland: the Rialto in Glasgow's Cathcart district and the Picture House Falkirk.

In or around 1931 (a year in which only four new cinemas were opened three of them in Scotland), ABC moved into Bootle (Gainsborough), Tipton (Regent), Croydon (Hippodrome), Lowestoft (Marina), Blackburn (Savoy), Darwen (Olympia), Torquay (Burlington, plus a site for a new cinema), Dover (Plaza), Northampton (Majestic), Lincoln (Picture House), Sheffield (Hippodrome), Hull (Rialto), Llandudno (Cinema), Reading (Central, a major acquisition), St. Helens (Capitol), Stockport (Hippodrome), Southsea (Gaiety), Higher Broughton (Rialto) and Wednesbury (where the Rialto, already closed for substantial improvements, was re-opened by ABC). In London, the circuit now had the Walthamstow Dominion, while in the Glasgow area it added the Hippodrome Oatlands (which was improved and renamed Ritz) and in the Liverpool suburbs it now operated the Popular Anfield and the very new Commodore Bankhall. Then there was a second house in Leicester (the Melbourne), two more in the Potteries at Longton (the Alexandra Palace and Empire), and the circuit's first in Northern Ireland when it converted the Royal Hippodrome Belfast from music hall to films.

By May 1931, with its new theatres and take-overs, ABC was registering more than 1.75 million admissions weekly (or approximately 91 million annually) and had more than 230,000 seats overall. This compares with weekly admissions of over 1.25 million, a yearly total of 65 million, and some 165,000 seats in the first half of 1930.

While opening only four new theatres in 1932, ABC seems to have added more than twenty existing properties (it has not been possible to link every take-over to a precise year). The company purchased the Hippodromes at Ipswich and Norwich plus the Playhouse Colchester from Federated Estates. There were more Liverpool additions (mostly from W. Gordon) – the Grosvenor and Garrick at Kirkdale, the Mere Lane Super Cinema at Everton and the Homer in Great Homer Street – while across the Mersey it started booking films for the Regent Tranmere as a prelude to later purchase. In Manchester, ABC took the Queen's Openshaw and the huge La Scala near the town centre at All Saints' where an ornate exterior and foyer gave way to an awkward, plain auditorium. In London, the Islington Empire and Camberwell Palace were now under ABC management. Other additions to the circuit around this time included the Regal Bolton,

Albion Castleford, Theatre Royal Chorley, Commodore Southsea, Trocadero Tankerton, Majestic Blackburn, two more in Bristol (the Empire and Park St. George) and a further house in Wales (the Castle Super at Merthyr Tydfil).

In Maxwell's haste to expand, ABC had taken on many properties (including several of its most recent acquisitions) that were loss-making and difficult to manage. Often these were the dregs of packages that provided worthwhile theatres and meant that ABC had more outlets than it needed in some locations. In Torquay, for instance, the Burlington was of little value once ABC had opened its Regal, but the older property had been part of the deal by which the company had gained the new cinema's site. Five of its many Birmingham cinemas were also a problem: the Metropole Snow Hill, Astoria Aston, Elite Bordesley Green, Picture House Erdington and Empire Stirchley.

In an attempt to deal with this problem, Maxwell created a subsidiary, Regent Circuit Ltd., in May 1933, to be run at arm's length by Ralph S. Bromhead, who had been ABC's assistant general manager under Arthur S. Moss. As Bromhead recalled (in a 1981 interview with the author): "Regent was a sort of throw-off of the ABC – all of their worst cinemas, their losing cinemas. And Mr. Maxwell said, 'We'll put them all together and book them on a special basis and see if we can stem the losses.' So we had offices in Regent Street [Heddon House]. We had a small organisation of, speaking from memory, roughly thirty rather poor theatres, most of which were at rather exorbitant rents, and we did stem the losses a bit." (Somewhat confusingly, five of the Regent cinemas in the Liverpool area were soon purchased by a completely separate local company called Regent Enterprises, which had earlier sold the Commodore Bankhall to ABC and would sell other properties to the circuit.) ABC's Regent circuit does not seem to have been a great success as it was disbanded and the cinemas returned to direct ABC control in 1935, although Bromhead's departure to County Cinemas in November 1934 may have been a factor.

With so many problem theatres, ABC moved more slowly and added very few properties to the circuit during 1933 and 1934, while only eight new theatres were opened. During 1933, ABC moved from offices in Heddon House, Regent Street, to 30-31 Golden Square, near Piccadilly Circus, which would become its permanent headquarters, and the parent company BIP renamed itself the Associated British Picture Corporation.

Around 1933, ABC took over the recently opened, enormous Mayfair at Tooting, South London, as well as the Picture House a short distance away in Balham. In North London, the circuit moved into a former live theatre, the Bedford at Camden Town. Far more significantly, it acquired the three most important cinemas controlled by Ralph Specterman's companies: the Commodore Hammersmith, Capitol Forest Hill, and Prince of Wales Lewisham. The Commodore, a vast cine-variety house with 2884 seats and standing room for 252 inside the auditorium, became the most important London suburban house on the circuit, helping to excuse the lacklustre takings of the Capitol Forest Hill. ABC also did another deal with entrepreneur Lou Morris, who made a specialty of building and selling theatres, by which he disposed of the Princess Dagenham, opened in November 1932. Outside London, ABC added the Central Canterbury (put into the Regent circuit) and the Empire Huddersfield.

In 1934, ABC took a lease on the Rialto Coventry Street in London's West End, regaining a central West End showplace to supplement the somewhat remote Regal Marble Arch. On the southern fringes of the London area, the Majestic Mitcham and the Regal Purley were acquired. Around Birmingham, three more cinemas were added – the Tivoli Yardley and the Pavilions at Stirchley and Wylde Green, Sutton Coldfield. Two other newcomers – the Pavilion Oswaldthistle and Palaseum Stepney, East London – were consigned immediately to the Regent circuit, leaving one to puzzle why ABC wanted them as they seem to have been acquired individually.

ABC returned to the acquisition trail with a vengeance in 1935 and 1936 at the same time as its pace of new theatre openings accelerated. These were years of keener competition as other circuits like County, Union and the fast expanding newcomer Odeon jostled to acquire existing buildings and find sites to construct their own new cinemas.

According to trade myth, ABC and County conducted an exchange of theatres – County swopping the Regal Canterbury for the Golders Green (Temple Fortune) Orpheum – but, as the take-overs seem to have happened a year apart,

there is unlikely to have been any connection.

ABC was always in the market for the odd single property. It took over the as-yet-unopened Roxy Blackheath under rather macabre circumstances, the original owner having hanged himself backstage from an iron staircase. This opened in February 1935.

Although a small acquisition numerically, the take-over of the three huge Forum cinemas in the London area at Ealing, Fulham Road and Kentish Town from Herbert Yapp in March 1935 was a major coup. This came just a few weeks after the purchases of the large Carltons at Islington and Upton Park from Clavering and Rose, and of W. C. Dawes' Modern Cinemas, a small but valuable inner West London circuit comprising the Queens Bayswater, Prince of Wales Harrow Road, Palace Kensal Rise and Royalty North Kensington. There was no doubt that ABC had become a major force in the London area.

Two other London properties followed that year: the Golden Domes Streatham and the Rex Stratford. The Rex had been an elaborate reconstruction (by architect George Coles) of an old variety theatre for Sokoloff and Pearl, only opened in November 1934. Business had been somewhat disappointing in the summer of 1935, creating discord between the two partners and putting them in the mood to sell. W. 'Bill' Cartlidge, then the youthful manager of the theatre, has recalled in his autobiography Maxwell's personal involvement in sizing up the theatre for an ABC take-over one Friday night when there was variety on stage as well as films: "...two gentlemen, one of whom I recognised as the great John Maxwell, strolled into the theatre. Both Sokoloff and Pearl were in the office at the time and, although they said nothing to me about expecting visitors, it was quite apparent that all had been pre-arranged. Mr. Maxwell and his friend, who later turned out to be Sam Byer, the private negotiator who did a lot of buying for Mr. Maxwell, went into the auditorium and saw most of [a comedy] act. It was one of the few times that I ever saw John Maxwell break into a laugh. He came back into the office and asked how much money we had taken that night. With the directors' permission I told him and he was very impressed. Mr. Maxwell was asked whether or not he would like a drink and he replied saying that if we had some whisky it would be very nice. I think it greatly appealed to his Scottish sense of

Forum Ealing (architects: J. Stanley Beard & Clare with W. R. Bennett) in 1934 photographs. This notable ABC acquisition of 1935 is alive and well as a three-screen MGM cinema in 1993.

humour when I opened the safe and produced a bottle; he thought it a very funny place to keep whisky."

Still in 1935, the spread of Birmingham theatres increased to take in four more substantial suburban properties: the Regal Handsworth, Royalty Harborne, Crown Ladywood and The Oak Selly Oak.

The purchase of the Granadas Dover and Hove from Mistlin and Lee significantly strengthened ABC's position on the South Coast, where other acquisitions were the Astorias at Brighton and Cliftonville in the break-up of veteran exhibitor E. E. Lyons' last circuit following his death. Although ABC already had the enormous Savoy in Brighton, the large Astoria would prove to be a worthwhile off-circuit cinema. Late in the year, ABC took over W. D. Buck's two Southampton cinemas, the Atherley Shirley and Broadway Portswood, keeping the Broadway and letting the less desirable Atherley go to an independent a few years later.

A curiosity of 1935 was the Pathe Cinema Car, a compartment of a LNER train which showed films and had its own ticket-selling attendant. But it seems doubtful that ABC were directly involved and it is more likely to have been an arrangement between the railway and Pathe Equipment.

The death of Walter Bentley, another veteran exhibitor with South Coast interests, led to the sale of his circuit. While Union acquired his properties in Eastbourne and Folkestone, ABC gained the important city centre Elite Nottingham, the Elite and Scala Middlesbrough, and the Empire Stockton-on-Tees.

1935 also brought a significant increase in Liverpool area representation as ABC took over the Granada Dovecot, Regent Knotty Ash and Carlton Tuebrook as a group, as well as the Regent Crosby, Regal Norris Green, Astoria Walton, and a less imposing batch from Regent Enterprises: the Popular Anfield, Victory Kirkdale, New Coliseum Paddington, Regent Tranmere and Coliseum Walton (plus the Popular Derby in the Midlands).

Scottish opportunities were not being neglected and ABC could now claim ownership of the Tower Helensburgh and two in Glasgow: the delightful Spanish-style atmospheric Toledo at Muirend and the recently opened Mayfair Battlefield.

This was also the year in which the ABC circuit absorbed in

Dominion Harrow (architect: Frederick E. Bromige): opened in 1936 and quickly taken over by ABC. Exterior view dates from opening, auditorium shot from Sixties. The cinema survives in 1993 as the Cannon Station Road, its auditorium split for films and bingo and its stupendous facade hidden behind metal cladding.

the London area the Elite Wimbledon, Hippodromes at Putney and Woolwich, and Majestic Woodford (the last of a group of five Majestics and the second after Mitcham to enter the ABC fold). Elsewhere were added the Playhouse Dewsbury, Picture House Old Trafford (Manchester), Plaza Plymouth, Kidderminster's Central and Empire, Palladium Oldham, Capitol Bolton, and the Haymarket Newcastle. ABC soon enlarged the Haymarket to provide a suitable first-run outlet in this key city centre.

Over the year's end, ABC started to acquire the interests of London-area showmen Abe Goide and A. Glassman, beginning with two George Coles-designed theatres, the Savoys at Acton and Enfield, the latter taken over less than four months after its opening. Glassman was also a partner with Cohen and Rafer in the Mile End Empire which was sold to ABC along with the Savoy Teddington and Regent King's Cross, these two owned by Cohen and Rafer alone. The Mile End and Teddington theatres were soon replaced with modern cinemas keeping the old names. With the proceeds of their disposals, Goide and Glassman quickly erected a new Savoy at Burnt Oak, again designed by Coles, but this one never became an ABC house.

In 1936, ABC bought the Dominions at Southall and Harrow from W. C Dawes and Albert Bacal almost before the paint had dried. Its interests in the Harrow area were further augmented by the Embassy North Harrow and the very recently launched Langham at Pinner. ABC seemed to be taking a leaf from Union's book in blanket-buying properties in certain towns, not so much in the Harrow area (where Odeon were also firmly entrenched) but at Walsall (four cinemas) and Grimsby (three). In the latter two instances, it is obvious that ABC were compelled to take all the theatres to obtain any, and in each town one of the properties was soon demolished to make way for a brand-new cinema.

ABC's undiminished enthusiasm for Birmingham led it to take over the large Piccadilly Sparkbrook along with the less imposing Hockley Palladium while nearby at West Bromwich the Tower, less than a year old, was acquired from C. O. Brettel (it looked just like an Odeon externally, having been designed by that circuit's chief architect when Odeon was likely to have been involved). With the Tower came the County Warwick. ABC's Liverpool area strength now embraced the substantial Reo Fazakerley and the most modern cinema in St. Helens, the Savoy, to supplement the Capitol. In Manchester, the Forum Wythenshawe and Palace Ashton-in-Makerfield became part of ABC, as in Leeds did the Gaiety Harehills. On the south coast, the circuit added the large Plaza Worthing (another Lou Morris enterprise). The Electra Cheadle was one of the year's less striking newcomers.

Now under Scottish control were the Playhouse Galashiels and the Rhul Burnside (Glasgow), while in Wales ABC took over its third centrally located cinema in Cardiff, the Olympia – the first one large enough (with over 2,000 seats) to function as a proper first-run outlet.

In January 1937, a huge, year-old variety theatre, the Globe at Stockton-on-Tees, became part of the chain (ABC's second outlet in the town), as did the Savoy on the outskirts of Reading, which was only ten months old. Then the circuit seems to have ceased buying any cinemas for several months, perhaps because the chief had his eyes set on bigger game...

Maxwell and Gaumont-British
John Maxwell had always nursed bigger ambitions than just the piecemeal expansion of his circuit. He made several efforts to remove portions of the exhibition empire cobbled together by the Ostrer brothers at Gaumont-British so that he might increase his strength and at the same time weaken his principal rival. Then he went the whole hog and made an uncharacteristically ill-thought-out bid for control of Gaumont-British itself.

ABC and Gaumont had often competed to gobble up smaller chains: sometimes they were such bad buys that it can only have been for the numbers or else the result of such haste that the financial implications were not properly considered.

There was the case of United Picture Theatres, formed in January 1928 with an initial chain of nine London halls, augmented by seven more later in the year. Most of these were former theatres and music halls which had required expensive and not entirely satisfactory installation of sound equipment; many were being badly hit by newly-built cinemas nearby. In 1929, the circuit showed a net loss of £19,371 and early in 1930 it was struggling to complete the purchase of a recently opened cinema for which it had offered an excessive price.

Despite these drawbacks, both Gaumont and ABC sought to take over UPT. Gaumont won by taking a small financial interest and entering into a five-year management agreement. The UPT circuit came under Gaumont control in July and gave the company over 300 cinemas compared to ABC's 150.

After UPT went into receivership in 1934 and its six worst situations were sold off, Maxwell approached the Receiver about taking over management of the circuit when Gaumont's contract expired in July 1935. UPT was allowed by the Receiver to regain control of its activities and the management agreement with Gaumont was extended. Maxwell had to be satisfied with gaining, sooner or later, four of the discarded properties. These were the Palaseum Stepney (which was, as previously mentioned, put into the Regent circuit), the Hippodromes Putney and Woolwich, and (via Cohen and Rafer) the Empire Mile End. The Woolwich and Mile End properties provided useful sites for new cinemas while Putney acted as a stop-gap until ABC could build elsewhere on a more prominent site.

In February 1935, Maxwell had put in a bid to take over a much bigger part of the Gaumont empire, the General Theatre Corporation, which included the London Palladium and many other music halls, the Capitol Haymarket and Astoria Charing Cross Road, the Alhambra in Paris, and a large number of mostly antiquated cinemas. GTC's dividend fell in arrears and Maxwell offered cash or shares to preferential shareholders as a prelude to a full bid. GTC, however, remained with Gaumont.

Maxwell had even made soundings in 1934 about taking over the Gaumont-British Picture Corporation itself. Two years later, in August 1936, he opened serious discussions with Isidore Ostrer and his brothers Mark and Maurice, who were as always desperate to raise finance. On 8 October 1936, Maxwell signed a contract under which ABPC agreed to pay more than £600,000 for a large shareholding (250,000 non-voting 'B' shares) in the Metropolis and Bradford Trust Ltd., which controlled GBPC, and – more importantly – for a five-year option to buy (at a cost of around £900,000) a further block of M&BT shares (5,100 out of 10,000 'A' voting shares) which would give Maxwell and ABPC control of the Trust and hence control of Gaumont-British. Under the agreement, Maxwell became a director of GBPC.

What Maxwell had failed to fully consider was that the transfer of the majority of M&BT voting shares required the consent of the owner of the other 4,900 shares – the American company, 20th Century-Fox. Ironically, William Fox had acquired these shares at high cost in 1929, when Gaumont-British had needed extra finance then, under the misapprehension that he would gain control of Gaumont-British from the Ostrers. Now it was Maxwell's turn to find himself frustrated and outwitted by the Ostrers, who must have known or guessed that Fox would block the deal. Maxwell's attempts to buy Fox's voting shares were unsuccessful, apparently because the American company wanted to keep him from totally dominating British film exhibition and dictating terms to Hollywood through control of both major circuits.

Maxwell had spent £600,000 in his attempt to acquire Gaumont-British and all that ABPC had to show for it, given the shaky financial state of GBPC, were shares of dubious value. It was one of the Scotsman's rare financial mistakes. At least his option prevented anyone else buying control until it expired and he did have his seat on the board of GBPC from which to probe the company's affairs. Indeed, he is even quoted (in Alan Wood's *Mr. Rank*) as telling ABPC's company secretary Eric Lightfoot, "Isidore doesn't know it but I'm going to blast him out of Gaumont-British. By the time I've finished with him he'll be only too glad to quit." He claimed that the Ostrers had misrepresented the profits of GBPC in their negotiations with him and that the profits of £700,000 on the balance sheet for 31 March 1936 were overstated. The Ostrers stood by the figures and Maxwell initiated a lawsuit in March 1937, demanding £600,000 in compensation. Maxwell retained his seat on the GBPC board until 7 July 1938 when the case finally came to court and was adjourned after the first day's hearing. The action was withdrawn in October 1938. Judgment was entered in favour of the Ostrers, who were also awarded costs.

The Union take-over
By the time Maxwell's defeat at the hands of the Ostrers had been finalised, he had found another prize with which to console himself. He had taken over the Union cinema circuit and leapfrogged ahead of Gaumont in terms of circuit size, giving ABC a total of around 460 halls compared to Gaumont's 345. The official statement of ABC's acquisition of Union, issued on 14 October 1937 and boasting that the circuit was now second only in size to Fox West Coast in the United States, considerably inflated the figures, combining 325 ABC cinemas with 185 Union halls for a total of 510, with 180 more being built. But even so, and even with the problems of bad management and debt that came with Union, it was a huge expansion that must have given Maxwell much satisfaction.

The Union circuit had expanded at breakneck speed and its properties ranged from a considerable number of lavishly designed modern cinemas built for the circuit to a substantial quantity of very old and dilapidated halls. The American Paramount company had been contemplating an association with or take-over of Union since the previous year but Maxwell's opportunity came when the company over-expanded and its monetary problems reached crisis point on the sudden death of David Bernhard, the 77-year-old chairman and financial director. Maxwell bought a controlling interest for ABC within weeks, rightly confident that he could run Union more sensibly and profitably. According to W. 'Bill' Cartledge, then working for Union, Maxwell was not greeted as a saviour by the executives at the company's head office: "Depression set in; for whilst most people had been looking forward to the Paramount take-over, ABC at that time in their history were looked upon as being somewhat mean in their financial outlook, particularly as regards to the payment of salaries." Fears were justified as a great many department heads were promptly given a month's notice.

The 136 Union cinemas in operation that came under ABC management and control were: Abingdon Pavilion and Regal; Aldershot Ritz; Altrincham Regal; Ammanford Palace; Ancoats (Manchester) Tower; Ashton-under-Lyne Empire; Banbury Palace; Barnsley Ritz; Barrow-in-Furness Coliseum, Gaiety, Palace, Pavilion, Regal, Ritz and Walney; Basingstoke Grand, Plaza and Waldorf; Beckenham Regal; Belfast Majestic, Ritz and Strand; Benwell (Newcastle) Adelaide and Majestic; Beswick (Great Ancoats) Don; Bexhill Ritz; Bexleyheath Regal; Bicester Regal; Bracknell Regal; Botley (Oxford) Majestic; Brighouse Ritz; Cambridge Central, Playhouse, Theatre Cinema, Tivoli and Victoria; Carlisle City, Lonsdale and Public Hall; Catford Plaza; Chatham Ritz; Crayford

Princesses; Denton (Manchester) Rota; Dewsbury Regal; Didsbury Capitol; Dunstable Palace and Union; Eastbourne Luxor; Eccles Broadway; Eltham (Southeast London) Palace; Erith Ritz; Falmouth Grand and St. Georges; Farnworth Ritz; Felixstowe Ritz; Folkestone Central and Playhouse; Gorton (Manchester) Cosmo; Gravesend Majestic, Regal and Super; Great Yarmouth Regal; Grimsby Ritz; Haywards Heath Broadway and Perrymount; Hereford Garrick and Kemble; Herne Bay Casino; Highate (North London) Empire and Palace; Horsham Capitol and Ritz; Huddersfield Grand and Ritz; Hythe Ritz; Ipswich Ritz; Kings Lynn Electric and Majestic; Kingston-on-Thames Union; Lancaster County, Grand, Kingsway and Palace; Levenshulme (Manchester) Kingsway; Leyland Palace and Regent; Londonderry Palace and Rialto; Luton Alma, Empire and Union; Maidenhead Plaza, Rialto and Ritz; Maidstone Central, Palace and Ritz; Neath Gnoll and New Windsor; Newbury Carlton and Regal; Newcastle Olympia; Newtonards Ritz; Nuneaton Ritz; Oxford Electra, Palace, Regal, Ritz and Super; Penzance Ritz; Portsmouth Victoria Hall; Rotherham Whitehall; St. Leonards Regal; Sale Savoy; Scunthorpe Ritz; Sidcup Regal; Slough Adelphi; Southend Rivoli; Swansea Albert Hall, Carlton and Picture House; Tonbridge Ritz; Urmston (Manchester) Empress; Uxbridge Regal and Savoy; Warrington Ritz; Wallingford Regal; Windsor Playhouse, Regal and Royalty; Woking Ritz; Wokingham Ritz and Savoy; Wolverton Empire; and Yiewsley Marlborough.

The jewels in the Union crown were the outstanding new cinemas that had been built to lavish standards by the circuit, including the Ritzes at Huddersfield, Oxford, Belfast, Ipswich, Barnsley, Chatham, Woking, Aldershot, Nuneaton, Cleethorpes and Warrington, the Regal at Cowley (Oxford) and the Union Luton, opened just days before ABC took over. Several other cinemas under construction or in the planning stage opened under ABC control and management: the Ritzes at Armagh, Stockport, Hereford, Hyde (Manchester), Keighley, Wigan, Hastings, Richmond, Market Harborough and Winchester, as well as the new Theatre Royal King's Lynn and (as late as December 1940) the Rex Bedminster (Bristol). But nothing more was heard of many other sites which Union claimed to have acquired.

Union had taken over important and well-appointed cine-

Ritz Barnsley (architects: Verity and Beverley), one of the lavishly designed Union cinemas taken over by ABC. The facade was particularly spectacular when lit up by neon at night.

mas in such places as Altrincham, Beckenham, Bexleyheath, Eastbourne, Kingston-on-Thames and Southend that would become valuable additions to the ABC circuit. The geographical match was generally excellent, although in Chatham and Luton ABC gained modern Union houses where its own plans for new cinemas were well advanced. Construction went ahead giving the circuit two large properties (in Chatham, they almost faced each other). In both cases the Union house was larger but played off-circuit, yet such was the density of population, attractiveness of the cinemas and availability of product that both were able to survive until the early 1970s.

Audiences preferred modern cinemas and the old-fashioned halls on the Union circuit were more of a problem. Many of these resulted from Union's belief in the saturation technique of controlling most or all the cinemas in particular towns to force down film rentals and hopefully deter rivals from erecting new buildings in competition. In Barrow-in-Furness, Cambridge, Horsham, King's Lynn, Lancaster and Oxford, it had taken over several cinemas. Some were "dumps" that had been recently closed by fire or by the licensing authorities for failing to meet safety standards. ABC made no attempt to re-open them, or the Red Lantern at Herne Bay which Union had operated in the summer season only. At King's Lynn, both the Theatre Royal and St. James had been destroyed in fires, leaving Union with the Majestic and Electric. Union had embarked on building a new Theatre Royal and, when it opened under ABC's control, the old Electric was immediately shuttered while prices were reduced at the Majestic to help it compete. It would seem to have been a mistake on ABC's part to dispose of the Electric: now that there were only two cinemas in the town, an independent was encouraged to build a third, the Pilot, which must have divided up attendances to ABC's disadvantage.

Regarding the financial management of Union, ABC inherited what Maxwell called a "truly deplorable state of affairs", referring to some "highly improper" transactions. He made some savage criticisms of the way the company had been run and warned shareholders that it would take a long time to sort out the company's affairs. There was a £1.5 million overdraft and Maxwell thought the assets had been over-valued by £2.2 million. Many Union cinemas were running at a loss or making minute profits, even some of those recently built. The company's 1938 trading profit was £203,000 compared to ABC's £1,347,001. The following year, with the declaration of war temporarily hurting attendances, Union's trading profits were £195,000 compared to ABC's £1,206,856.

Maxwell cut costs in the running of Union properties, seeking to reduce its total liabilities of over £2 million. All the cinemas that were under construction were inaugurated quietly without fuss in the ABC fashion rather than with the pomp and ceremony that the previous management had favoured until the final days of attempting to stave off disaster.

Maxwell abolished the kine-variety policy of many Union halls, dropping it as well at the end of January 1938 from ten London ABCs where it had been featured occasionally, taking the view (shared by Odeon's Oscar Deutsch) that it did not help the box-office: a good film drew good audiences, and a live show would not help a bad picture, so it was either ineffective or unnecessary.

Maxwell was scathing about the way Union had been building cinemas. Many, he said, had been been built at ridiculous expense in small towns of 8-16,000 people that even had competing cinemas, making profits negligible. He referred in particular to a town which he did not identify but which can only have been Horsham. Union had acquired a monopoly with three cinemas. Odeon had decided to build there, so Union put up a new cinema of its own. Thus the town – with a population of 13,579 – had five cinemas. The two poorest Union halls had failed to meet licensing requirements and were forced to close but that still left three – with a total of 2,976 seats – doing badly. (Although they may not have justified their original investment, the two new cinemas did at least adequately in the long term as it wasn't until 1976 that the first of them closed.)

Union's name, which had been on prominent display on the frontages of all its theatres, was replaced by the ABC triangle with the heading "Managed by". In time, the Union cinemas became indistinguishable from the main ABC circuit.

Other take-overs

With its huge intake of Union properties, ABC had plenty to keep it occupied, but in November 1937, the month following the Union take-over, Maxwell gave a nasty shock to the

County Cinemas circuit and its head C. J. Donada by gaining control of Hull City and Suburban Cinemas. This company had built and opened the huge Regal Hull and three identical, smaller suburban cinemas plus the Regal at Beverley, all in association with County Cinemas which had arranged the architect (Robert Cromie) and which managed the group. However, the local directors sold their majority holding to ABC, Maxwell and colleagues replaced them on the board, and County were soon ejected.

ABC concluded the year by leasing two substantial cinemas in the Portsmouth area, the Carlton Cosham and Apollo Southsea, from Boxing Day.

In 1938, the company was clearly pre-occupied with its own theatre-building programme and with further digesting the Union take-over, including the opening of many of its new cinemas. ABC's only acquisitions were the Lyceum Edinburgh and Trocadero Humberstone (Leicester). It disposed of a substantial number of lesser cinemas like the Troc Tankerton and Rialto Wednesbury to independents.

In 1939, South Wales Cinemas took back five cinemas at Neath and Swansea when Union's lease expired. Around this time, ABC gained the Shaftesbury Leeds, a second but significant theatre in the centre of town.

4 | W. R. Glen and New ABCs

Ritz Edinburgh (architects: Gardner and Glen) in 1930: a cinema built for talkies.

The atmospheric interior devised by W. E. Greenwood for the Savoy Dublin (1929). (Courtesy of Kenneth McNally and Ulster Television.)

ABC not only increased its strength by acquiring existing picture houses but by building new cinemas and reconstructing older ones. In all, over one hundred cinemas were opened in the Thirties and in 1940 before the Second World War brought construction to a halt.

The first new cinema opened by ABC was the large Ritz Edinburgh in September 1929. Its architects were Albert V. Gardner and William R. Glen. This was followed in November by the 2,359 seat Regal Glasgow, designed by Charles J. McNair, and by the Savoy Dublin, a 2,792 seater opened by the President of the Irish Free State, William Cosgrave, and the largest ever built by ABC in terms of seating capacity. In contrast to his later reclusive manner, John Maxwell was conspicuous at the opening. As the architect of Savoy Cinemas, F. C. Mitchell had designed the Savoy but the auditorium, in a Venetian atmospheric style with a miniature Bridge of Sighs above the screen, was the work of interior designer W. E. Greenwood (with the assistance of Val Prince). (Greenwood had carried out similar atmospheric designs at the Majestics High Wycombe, Staines and Wembley.) In the case of the Savoy (and the later Savoy at Cork), the owning company was a separate subsidiary, Associated Irish Cinemas. (At some point during the Thirties, the company was taken over by local interests and ABC later started afresh in Eire with the Adelphi Dublin.)

Also in 1929, the Greenock Picture House was reconstructed and re-opened as the Regal. The name "Regal" became the one most frequently given to new ABC cinemas, although "Ritz" and "Savoy" were often used as well (it was not until 1936 that the first "Rex" made its appearance).

William R. Glen accepted an offer to become the staff architect for ABC and moved to London, dissolving his partnership with Albert V. Gardner which had begun in 1919.* He displaced F. C. Mitchell who, following the Savoy Dublin, was working on the Savoy Cinemas' Brighton scheme and another cinema to be built in Liverpool. Arthur G. Yuile became Glen's right-hand man as the quantity surveyor. Although Glen had designed many of the existing SCVT houses, he left future work north of the border to others, principally McNair, until he drew up the first plans for the Regal Aberdeen in early 1938 and handled the reconstruction of the Palace Arbroath, completed in 1940.

His first work for ABC in England included preliminary plans for two ABC cinemas in Surrey – in Claremont Road, Surbiton (to seat 2,500, announced in July 1929) and on the site of the Lodge in Bridge Road, East Molesey (acquired in January 1929). Neither were built, although it is probable that the 1934 Odeon occupied the Surbiton site and that the East Molesey scheme, postponed indefinitely in January 1932, was later the location of a proposed Granada that never happened. Despite these two instances, it was to prove relatively rare for ABC schemes, once announced, to fall through, even if some – like the Savoy Wolverhampton – took several years to happen.

W. R. Glen: a poor quality photograph published at the time of his death in 1950.

* William Riddell Glen MC, FRIAS, LRIBA, had been born in 1884. He won an open competition to study at the Glasgow School of Art and trained with architects Frank Burnett, Bowson & Carruthers before commencing in private practice in 1904, joining up with J. A. Campbell and A. D. Hislop. Glen was associated with the building of the Queen Victoria Memorial School at Dunblane, Central Scotland, presenting the special trowel to King Edward VII for the laying of the foundation stone. He served in the First World War in the Glasgow Highlanders, reaching the rank of Major and winning the Military Cross. His partnership with A. V. Gardner followed. Gardner was already a cinema architect, having designed the Elder Picture House at Govan, Glasgow (opened 11 December 1916). The team's work included the design of such cinemas as the Grosvenor at Hillhead, Glasgow (opened 3 May 1921) and the Strathclyde at Dalmarnock, Glasgow (opened 15 August 1929). After Glen ended the partnership, Gardner continued in practice on his own, working on several cinemas (none of them for ABC). These included the Kelvin Finnieston, Glasgow (in Moorish atmospheric style, opened 12 May 1930); the enlargement of the New Star Cinema, Maryhill (re-opened 22 December 1930); the almost total reconstruction of the Picture House Partick (re-opened 26 January 1931); the Astoria Round Toll (opened 2 February 1931, with 3000 seats the largest suburban cinema in Glasgow); the Orient Gallowgate (another Glasgow super-cinema, 2578 seats in Spanish atmospheric style, opened 2 May 1932); the New Alexandra Paisley (reconstruction, circa 1933); and the enlargement of the Picture House Campbeltown in 1934.

The original auditorium design of the Forum Birmingham (architect: W. R Glen) in 1930.

Glen's work on the Savoy Brighton and the interior rebuilding of the Regent Birmingham went ahead without delays. The Brighton cinema was the second largest ever built by ABC, seating 2,630 at its postwar maximum, and it had the unusual feature of an underground car park beneath the auditorium plus two proper entrances, the main one on a narrow shopping street, the other on the seafront to attract holidaymakers, each having its own restaurant or tea room and ballroom. While it was not a true "atmospheric", the decorative scheme of the auditorium (designed and executed by H. H. Martyn & Co.) introduced Japanese scenes between the pilasters on the side walls with Chinese motifs lower down, and had a light blue ceiling to represent the sky with a "sunburst" central light fitting. The main curtains were decorated with butterflies which become a standard feature in later ABCs although differently arranged here.

The Birmingham cinema, renamed the Forum, had to be reconstructed in a tall and narrow space. It also boasted atmospheric touches in the paintings on the side wall bays but the design was dominated by the semi-dome proscenium surround with a perforated pattern of plaster curls and grilles for the Compton organ. Because of the restricted space, seating was on three levels and projection was from the stalls floor.

In 1930 the Ritz Cambuslang was opened in Scotland by SCVT to the designs of W. Beresford Inglis – as miserable-looking externally as most of the new ABC houses to follow north of the border, without even a canopy (all a little surprising, as Inglis was later architect of the superb Toledo at Muirend which in time became an ABC house).

In 1931, improvements were made to recently acquired theatres: Satchwell and Roberts designed the reconstruction of the Rialto Wednesbury and Glen provided schemes for redecorating the Regent Chatham and Hippodrome Sheffield, introducing a projection box at the latter (an old variety theatre), while in Scotland an unidentified architect arranged substantial alterations that raised the capacity of the Coliseum Glasgow to 3,094, the highest on the circuit (including 1,000 in the gallery).

During this year there were three openings of new ABC houses in SCVT territory – the Regal Hamilton, the especially large Rex Riddrie (2,336 seats), and the Regal Dumfries – against only one in England, the Forum Liverpool. But the Forum was a notable cinema indeed, now a listed building. Glen takes credit in the opening programme as the architect and it is his only work to be listed. Some confusion surrounds the contribution of Alfred E. Shennan, who had been appointed the local resident architect when F. C. Mitchell was planning the scheme. He is described as such in pre-opening publicity and in the opening programme, all suggesting he was primarily responsible for on-the-spot supervision. But Shennan was a prolific cinema architect in his own right (and the architect of many department stores near the Forum).

On a corner site, the tall, curving frontage of the Forum in Portland stone is dignified and commanding. The auditorium is a successful mixture of themes, including art deco relief panels depicting skyscrapers and (among classical features) now-absent urns on top of ante-proscenium towers which retain their inset fountain patterns. The vast ceiling is plain except for a central light fitting with a star-shaped surround creating a sun-burst effect similar to that in the ceiling of the Savoy Brighton. The canopy over the proscenium arch with its line of organ grilles, almost like a bridge, was flood-lit. The location of exits to each side of the balcony front would become a characteristic feature of ABC design. These provide a justification for narrowing the auditorium towards the screen end as the staircases use some of the space behind the splay walls; but exits in this position were not common in other circuits' designs (almost never found in purpose-built Odeons, for example).

None of Shennan's other work is reminiscent of the Liverpool Forum (it includes two cinemas opened in 1932 that were later acquired by ABC: the Carlton Tuebrook and Granada Dovecot); but the auditorium of Glen's next cinema, the Savoy Wandsworth, opened in 1932, bears a noticeable similarity to the Forum, especially in the canopy over the proscenium arch, the boxes or "balconettes", and the side exits from the circle. Externally, the Savoy had a ponderous brick facade stretching 186 feet along York Road, as the shape of the site dictated that the auditorium had to run parallel to the main road instead of extending back behind the entrance. Located in a very poor area, it prompted much scepticism about the wisdom of building a cinema of "West End calibre" while charging as little as fivepence for entry. It was typical of Thirties cinemas constructed in poor, densely

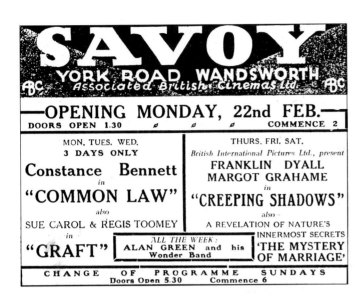

SAVOY
YORK ROAD WANDSWORTH
Associated British Cinemas Ltd

— OPENING MONDAY, 22nd FEB. —

DOORS OPEN 1.30   COMMENCE 2

MON. TUES. WED. 3 DAYS ONLY	THURS. FRI. SAT.
	British International Pictures Ltd., present
Constance Bennett	FRANKLIN DYALL
	MARGOT GRAHAME
in	*in*
"COMMON LAW"	"CREEPING SHADOWS"
also	*also*
SUE CAROL & REGIS TOOMEY	A REVELATION OF NATURE'S
in	INNERMOST SECRETS
"GRAFT"	ALL THE WEEK: ALAN GREEN and his Wonder Band	'THE MYSTERY OF MARRIAGE'

CHANGE   OF   PROGRAMME   SUNDAYS

Doors Open 5.30   Commence 6

Savoy Wandsworth (architect: W. R. Glen): opening advertisement and the auditorium in 1932. The organ was not ready on the first day but live entertainment was provided. Note the primitive ABC logos in the advertisement and the prominent identification of Associated British Cinemas as the owners. Is there a hint of the ABC triangle in the background design of the title block? Parent company BIP receive special credit for having made one of the attractions, Creeping Shadows.

populated inner districts in having a high seating capacity (2,166 seats). There was limited scope for live shows as the Savoy had only two dressing rooms. Although the Forum boasted a gala Saturday opening, the Savoy opened without ceremony like most subsequent new ABC theatres.

Glen's other completed work in 1932 was the interior reconstruction of the Elephant and Castle Theatre. The old Theatre seated only 600 and a virtually new building was created by extending the site. As in the case of the Forum Birmingham, the tall, narrow shape of the auditorium space resulted in the projection room being sited lower down than usual: in this case, under the balcony, providing a direct throw onto the screen. In order to compete with the huge Trocadero immediately opposite, the Elephant and Castle Theatre had a fully equipped, 13ft.-deep stage and full orchestra pit which were regularly used for some years.

Like other expanding circuits, ABC was always interested in taking over schemes that had been prepared by other promoters who were quite often, as in the case of Major W. J. King, the architect as well. ABC's first association with King was at Edgware where the Major had designed a cinema with a fortress-like exterior which he had planned to call the Citadel. ABC opened it as the Ritz Edgware. The entrance hall, tea-lounge and auditorium were in a somewhat superficial atmospheric scheme of stone walls and woodland, created by F. C. Philie. (King had designed an earlier cinema decorated in a similar vein, the Lido Golders Green, which had become part of the ABC circuit circa 1929.)

In Scotland during 1932 there was another huge (2,208 seat) addition to the circuit with the opening of the Regal Stirling. While size tended to be the major distinction of the new Scottish buildings, which were dreary inside and out, there was a further difference, noted by Gordon Coombes ("With ABC in Scotland", *Picture House* no. 12, Autumn 1988): "Cinemas built in Scotland by ABC from about 1929 onwards...had a central division in the stalls which completely separated the front and rear sections, entry to the front being by means of a separate paybox and entrance at the side of the building... The object of this system was, presumably, to prevent patrons of the ninepenny seats bunking back into the one-and-threes and one-and-nines and in this respect it fulfilled its purpose admirably. But when admissions slumped

and cinemas became too large for the patronage they attracted, the cost of an additional cashier and usherette made their
use uneconomic." Coombes also relates that new Scottish
cinemas started a practice, thought up by John Maxwell himself, of including lock-up shops alongside their entrances to
produce extra income. This eventually proved counter-productive when many of these shops sold sweets, cigarettes and
ice-cream, taking away revenue from the cinema's own sales
kiosk and ladies with the tray.

In 1933 and 1934, only two Glen-designed cinemas opened,
the Regal Torquay and the Ritz Leeds, although he was also
responsible for the reconstruction of the Empire Coventry.
The Regal Torquay was built on a site already acquired for a
cinema and may have been an adaptation by Glen of plans
submitted by the previous owner in June 1929. The site was
on a steep slope and the entrance was placed on the lower
corner, to be closer to the town centre. To take advantage
of the site's descent for the rake of the stalls, the screen was
at the same end as the main entrance, the only occasion in
which a Glen ABC was built this way round. This meant a
particularly long walk for patrons using the balcony. The
Regal had a cramped foyer very unlike a Glen scheme. The
decorative treatment was "semi-atmospheric" with scenes of
two popular local beauty spots on the side walls. Like many
early ABCs, it had a full stage and several dressing rooms.
The Ritz Leeds was decorated in a similar style, offering circle
patrons painted vistas of cypress trees and temples on the
side walls.

ABC extended the relationship with Major W. J. King by
taking his sites and schemes for Bowes Road (Southgate) and
Potters Bar and opening them as Ritzes (although the latter
soon reverted to King). The auditoria of these two cinemas
were much simpler in style than at Edgware – already rather
old-fashioned with a central dome and largely plain walls,
interest being centred on the illuminated grille work of splay
walls and the decoration of the main tabs.

While there were no new Scottish cinemas in 1933 or
most of 1934, the last quarter of the latter year saw the
opening of the Regal Falkirk, the most agreeable contribution
to ABC by architect Charles J. McNair, as well as his Regal
Paisley and his reconstruction of the King's Kilmarnock,
renamed the Regal.

Ritz Edgware in 1935: one of several ABC cinemas designed by Major
W. J. King. (Courtesy of Peter Loftus.)

Ritz Leeds (1934): this Glen design shows atmospheric touches in the
landscapes painted on the side walls. Glen's enthusiasm for decorated
grille work is evident around the proscenium arch and on the splay walls.
(Courtesy of Tony Moss collection.)

The ABC (ex-Forum) Liverpool (architect: W. R. Glen with A. Ernest Shennan) in 1982. The area beneath the balcony is now occupied by two small cinemas. The building is listed but a new screen has since been erected in front of the proscenium arch. (Photograph by Allen Eyles.)

In 1935, there was a dramatic expansion in both acquiring and building cinemas, although nothing new appeared in Scotland. Major W. J. King provided the Ritzes Neasden and Harringay, markedly similar in design to those at Bowes Road and Potters Bar. The Roxy Blackheath was essentially a takeover of an unopened building (one of a few cinemas involving the theatre architect Bertie Crewe) while the Cabot Filton was a development which ABC agreed to lease during construction – a modest-sized suburban Bristol hall designed by an accomplished local architect, W. H. Watkins.

W. R. Glen began warming up for the prodigious output of later years by designing the Forum Southampton, Regal Walham Green and Regal Wakefield. At Southampton and Wakefield, full stage facilities were provided. The Forum's auditorium was relatively plain by later Glen standards but showed the architect's penchant for prominent grille work and for decorative plaques (by the front side exits, picked out by concealed illumination). It also had an early example of the scalloped edges that Glen used in stepping down his ceilings, here breaking up the recess in front of the proscenium arch. The Wakefield theatre was also rather plain. The main decorative feature of the auditorium was three lines of circular shapes around the proscenium arch, like beads on a thread. There was concealed upward lighting of the side walls under the balcony and further concealed lighting in a trough at the rear of the main ceiling, reinforced by pendant fittings in the centre with bowls casting light upwards. The foyer was rather cramped by later ABC standards and sharply stepped to stalls and balcony.

The Glen style

The full-fledged Glen style was emerging. Glen became particularly good in handling main foyers, giving them plenty of height and space. These were immediately inviting – impressive without being overwhelming. Glen was fortunate that ABC always sought a strong street presence, rarely accepting sites that allowed only narrow entrances, and usually acquired sufficient ground area to set the actual auditorium some distance back. This gave the space to create such tall entrance areas whereas in many other cinemas the main foyer was more compressed with lower ceilings in order to use the

Forum Southampton (1935): a somewhat tame Glen design, but note the organ with illuminated console and the standard curtains - side-opening festoons with leaves and (lower down, barely visible) butterflies. The scalloped edging across the canopy in front of the proscenium arch became a characteristic Glen feature. (Courtesy of Tony Moss collection.)

space above for part of the rear circle, a circle lounge, café, ballroom, or offices.

Access to a Glen foyer was usually through one set of doors from the street rather than two, letting more daylight into the foyer and creating less of a barrier (but causing draughts and raising heating bills in winter). Main foyers were lit by glass pendant light fittings (usually replaced by the Fifties with "spray" or "cluster" fittings). The walls were sometimes decorated with medallions, freizes and simplified traditional devices like swags and urn shapes, promoting an atmosphere of dignity and good taste. This was somewhat contradicted by the displays of film stars and announcements of forthcoming programmes that would not always be positioned in harmony with the decor.

There were generally twin payboxes set well back in the foyer with stairs to either side. Usually, the stairs in the centre, between the two payboxes, led downwards to an inner foyer through which the stalls were reached. Sometimes there would be a flat passage through to the stalls rather than steps downward, but more often the sites seem to have been excavated to set the stalls lower down or else took advantage of a natural slope downwards of the land. (In busy periods, there was usually a separate paybox down one side of the building at the screen end, providing a no-frills entrance for patrons buying the cheapest seats in the front stalls.)

On the outer side of the twin payboxes, there were usually flights of stairs leading upwards and meeting in an open landing or bridge fitted with a decorative metal balustrade, looking out over the whole main foyer with the stalls entrance immediately below. Behind this landing lay another inner foyer leading to the balcony. This would often have a sloping ceiling reflecting the descent of the rear balcony overhead. Both inner foyers were typically very generous in space compared to other cinemas, maintaining the welcoming atmosphere, and often had concealed (cove) lighting. In ABCs, patrons generally made a forward progress to their seats instead of being deflected sideways to reach the circle, graduating from a light outer foyer to a less bright inner foyer to the often dark auditorium without having to pass through the tunnel-like passages and winding, enclosed staircases of many big cinemas.

A characteristic Glen auditorium would be tall with conspicuous grille work and a highly decorated ceiling. The regular feature of exits on each side of the circle has been mentioned earlier: this helped break up the wall surface besides narrowing the auditorium. Glen favoured a combination of direct illumination from pendant fittings and concealed trough lighting. The soft concealed illumination was changeable in colour and could be harmonised with the combination of colours obtainable from the illuminated console of an organ. As indicated before, Glen was fond of stepping down his ceilings, using scalloped edges emphasised in gold. There was nothing of the streamlined look identified with Odeons.

The main set of curtains were usually silver or maize-coloured satin appliqué – side-opening but hung in festoons with butterflies, tree branches and falling leaves sown on.

From his long managerial career with ABC, Gordon Coombes could comment: "Glen-designed cinemas were planned to utilise every square foot of space – not for him the labyrynthine passages, voids and seemingly interminable flights of stairs all too often found in Robert Cromie's cinemas of the period.* John Maxwell was a canny taskmaster and even when Glen had submitted a plan to his exact specification and costing, Maxwell would demand that a thousand pounds or so be lopped off the final estimate and this was generally achieved."

Though no two Glen cinemas were the same, they had in common superb planning and a skilful manipulation of space.

Grand openings of 1936 onwards
In 1936, the Glen-designed ABC cinemas that opened in the London area were the Regal Hackney, Regal Hammersmith, Rex Leytonstone (the first to use the "Rex" name), Savoy Stoke Newington and Ritz Muswell Hill, while in the regions the Savoys at Exeter, Lincoln and Northampton made their debut. Seating capacities tended to be almost 2,000 – even in a detached London suburb like Muswell Hill where the Ritz seated 1,992. The Regal Hackney represented a particularly ingenious solution to a particularly awkward, roughly triangu-

* Calling Cromie an "otherwise admirable architect", Gordon Coombes based these remarks on his experience of working in Cromie-designed cinemas on the circuit when the manager's office was usually situated to the rear of the back circle – the Capitol Winchmore Hill, Regal Kingston, Regal Bexleyheath, Regal Beckenham and Ritz Ipswich. See "ABC in North London", Picture House no. 8, Spring 1986, page 27.

Glen exteriors. Above top, Regal Old Kent Road (1937). Above, Regal Ilford (1937). Top right, Savoy Portsmouth (1937). Centre right, Regent Knotty Ash (1938). Right, Regal Southport (1938).

Savoy/ABC Stoke Newington, North London (W. R. Glen, 1936):
black-and-white photograph from 1936, colour image (by Allen Eyles) from 1983.

lar site with one side on the main road. Glen inserted the entrance hall into one corner and created an auditorium exceptionally wide at the rear but rapidly narrowing towards the screen end. The Regal Hammersmith had a distinctive decorative feature of galleons on the splay walls of the auditorium while the Rex Leytonstone was the first of several to feature a panel of forest animals in bas relief, here two gazelles in a leafy setting.

The Regal Chesterfield was designed by J. Owen Bond for entrepreneur Lou Morris who, following his practice of rarely holding onto cinemas for long, sold this one to ABC before completion. Although Glen is credited with amendments, the Regal looked nothing like an ABC with an exceptionally bold and simple handling of foyer and auditorium, the circle stairs lacking their usual prominence in the former and the latter dominated by concealed lighting in a long central feature dipping down dramatically towards the screen tabs and echoed by smaller illuminated bands along the side walls. (The auditorium of Lou Morris's later Ritz Bridlington was very similar but with a different architect: this eventually became an ABC house.)

In Scotland in 1936, three McNair-designed ABCs opened: the Regal Coatbridge, Rex Motherwell and the exceptionally large Plaza Govan with 2,280 seats. While north of the border in 1937 there was only the reconstruction of the Opera House Kirkcaldy into the Regal, in England no less than seventeen new ABCs opened with designs by the Glen office. To handle the increasing volume of work, Glen had built up a team of assistants but regrettably their names (other than that of Glen's eventual successor, C. J. Foster) have remained obscure and any individual touches they may have made to ABC schemes have yet to be identified.

It became evident, as at Kirkcaldy, that the name "Regal" was most favoured for new cinemas: those by Glen at Old Kent Road, Wembley, Salisbury, Ilford, Harrogate, York, Chester, Putney, Hounslow and Grimsby all carried the Regal name. There were also the Harrogate and York Regals on which Glen shared credit with local architects. Undoubtedly, the Regal name would have used in other instances but for the fact that an earlier cinema had already taken the name or because the new ABC house was a replacement for an older one when the name of the original theatre would usually be

Savoy Northampton: this Glen design from 1936 is unusual in that all the principal lighting is concealed. As the Cannon, the cinema is one of the least altered and most worth visiting of the surviving ABCs. It is still lit in the same way and has an organ in 1993.

Galleons on the side walls of the Regal Hammersmith (1936)
Woodland tableau on the side wall of the Rex Leytonstone (1936).

The foyer and auditorium of the Regal Chesterfield (1936, principal architect: J. Owen Bond).

W. R. Glen's Regal/ABC Ilford: 1937 black-and-white photograph and January 1984 colour image (by Allen Eyles) taken just prior to closure.

Regal/ABC Harrogate (W. R. Glen, 1937): 1974 photograph by John Fernée. When the building was demolished, the figurines in the niches on the splay walls were saved and moved to another cinema where similar figures had been lost.

retained to please local audiences. The name "Savoy" was now the second choice: this, of course, had been used by the Savoy circuit and applied to many of the early purpose-built ABCs. It was now given to Glen's new ABCs at Swindon, Leicester, Portsmouth, Northampton, Teddington and Wolverhampton. Then there was the Ritz at Sunderland and the Westover at Bournemouth.

Existing Regals at Lincoln and Northampton prompted ABC's selection of the Savoy name there while it was retained at Teddington, having belonged to the earlier ABC theatre on the site. In Sunderland there was not only a vast Regal – Black's Regal – but a small suburban Savoy which restricted ABC's choice of name even further. In Bournemouth, the name Westover was used for continuity as it had been applied to ABC's previous cinema almost adjacent (the name actually derives from Westover Road, on which both cinemas were located).

The new Westover was the largest of the mid-Thirties ABCs designed for the circuit with 2,515 seats, while the Regal Old Kent Road was the biggest of the London suburban halls with 2,485 seats and the Regal Putney was not far behind (2,340 seats). The Old Kent Road, Wembley and Hounslow Regals all featured decorative panels of deer and antelope grazing on the splay walls, similar to Leytonstone earlier.

Yet more 1937 ABCs came from outside architects. There was the Rex Norbury, with a very simple but striking one-off auditorium design by a young architect named Douglas Harrington, son of the original promoter. It is a mystery quite why ABC wanted the Rex, as it had existing cinemas to either side in Streatham and Croydon (although the Streatham hall was an old one, not yet replaced by a modern purpose-built Regal). Usually, new ABC cinemas were located in major centres rather than in the kind of smaller suburban situation that Norbury (or the previously mentioned Cabot at Filton) represented.

Then there was the Regal Cambridge, for which John S. Quilter and Son were the architects; and the Forum West Hartlepool, designed by local architects Percy L. Browne and Son (the previous cinema to open there had taken the Regal name). The Forum was the first of several cinemas delivered to ABC by a businessman in the area, Thomas H. Pailor. Apparently, Pailor contracted with ABC to build a cinema in a

Three Glen foyers. Top, Savoy Exeter (1936). Above, Savoy Portsmouth (1937). Below, Royal Plymouth (1938).

particular town; the site was decided on; Pailor bought up and then demolished property as necessary, obtained planning permission and employed a building firm (usually Pearson's) to put up the cinema (the joinery work was usually by Bottomley's); the completed building was then sold for a fixed contract price to ABC which owned it by the time of opening.

A start should have been made in October on Glen's scheme for a new ABC to replace the Hippodrome Blackpool but this was owned by a subsidiary company with local partners. In *Picture House* no. 6 (Spring 1985, page 12) Gordon Coombes, then an assistant manager at the other ABC house in the town, the Princess, recalls the situation in January 1938: "Work upon the conversion had not commenced...due, I was told, to an injunction being served upon ABC by the local debenture holders, who had fears for their securities in the period between demolition and re-opening. For some reason, ABC did not appear to challenge this ploy even though the structural steel was even then on its way to Blackpool."

Following the take-over of Union Cinemas, ABC opened the Ritz Armagh in 1937 and seven further theatres in 1938 which had been under construction: the Ritzes at Hastings, Hereford, Hyde, Keighley, Richmond, Stockport and Wigan. Most were designed by Verity and Beverley but the Ritz Wigan was the work of John Fairweather, having been initially conceived as an English outpost of Green's Playhouses in Scotland, hence its huge seating capacity of 2,560 and opera house trimmings inside. In many cases, ABC changed fittings to conform with its own house style: thus the Hastings theatre had the ABC style of curtain with leaves and butterflies.

Percy L. Browne, Son and Harding were the architects for ABC's new Regal Darlington, Ritz Gateshead and Savoy South Shields in 1938. The Gateshead theatre was certainly another from the arrangement with Thomas Pailor and the other two probably were as well. (More Black's Regals at Gateshead and South Shields prevented ABC considering the Regal name.)

There was only one new ABC in Scotland, but it was a major theatre: the Regal Edinburgh, designed by Stewart Kaye and Walls as an extension of Lothian House that placed offices over the cinema. However, with its grey stone frontage, it look more like a department store or an office

block than a cinema, the Regal name being restricted to canopy level.

As usual, W. R. Glen's office had designed most of the year's additions: these included the new Regent Knotty Ash, Regal Rochdale (in association with Leslie C. Norton), Ritz Leyton (particularly large, with 2,370 seats, despite a relatively narrow entrance), Regent Chatham (named after a previous Regent), Royal Plymouth (on the site of the Theatre Royal), Regal Harrow Road (Edgware Road), Regal Halifax, Savoy Birkenhead, Savoy Walsall (in association with Hickton and Madeley), Savoy Luton, Ritz Romford, Regal Streatham and Regal Southport. They represent much of Glen's best work. At Harrow Road, Leyton and Halifax were to be found examples of the slim Oscar-like statues or ornaments found in several theatres of this period, placed in niches on the splay walls and lit from above or behind. At Streatham, figurines were mounted on the side walls of the circle and back lit.

The worsening political situation, steel shortages and market saturation combined to slow-down the number of openings in 1939, as it did for other circuits. Before war was declared in September, seven new ABCs had been completed. Leslie C. Norton designed the Regal Cheltenham; Browne and Harding handled the Ritz Wallsend (presumably another arrangement with Pailor); the Ritz Market Harborough from architect William T. Benslyn was the completion of another Union project; and W. R. Glen's office delivered the other four. The Adelphi Dublin gave ABC a major first-run cinema in the Irish capital to replace the Savoy, over which it had lost control. The Regal Staines, Ritz Bradford and Empire Mile End were heavyweight additions to the circuit, the last named after the old Empire music hall which it replaced. Mile End showed Glen at his most confident, with a dramatically stepped-down ceiling. The foyer had a double staircase even though it was off-centre from the auditorium and one side was out on a limb.

"Surfeit"

The expansion of the major chains was frequently greeted by concerted opposition from the existing cinemas in an area. But only one ABC scheme seems to have been thwarted by the common ploy of exhibitors banding together to oppose planning permission. Unlike store chains whose spread was

Royal/ABC Plymouth: W. R. Glen in top form as seen in this 1938 black-and-white photography (courtesy of the Tony Moss collection) and in this colour image (by John Fernée) circa 1975. The auditorium has since been split up for smaller cinemas and bingo.

The Cannon (former Regal/ABC) Halifax (1938): one of the few surviving Glen auditoria as photographed in 1990 (by Barry Chandler) with close-up of one of the figures from the splay wall niches.

unrestricted, Parliament required licensing committees to "have regard to the public interest" in considering whether they should grant a licence. The usual objection was based on the argument of "saturation" or "surfeit" – that a district was already well catered for and it was not in the public's interest that a big combine, able by its booking strength to collar the best films, should be allowed to imperil the existence of smaller, often locally owned cinemas. This argument rarely carried any weight but it was deemed worth a try. (Similar objections have been raised against new multiplexes in more recent years.)

In Stoke Newington, North London, ABC had even started work on a huge new cinema to cost £65,000 in February 1936 when the plans by W. R. Glen were brought before the Entertainment Committee of the London County Council. Sir George Jones, representing the owners of the Plaza, Ambassador, Empress Hall, Empire and the Alexandra Theatre, declared that within half a mile of the proposed ABC house there were nine cinemas which could hold 9,456 people – one seat for every three-and-a-half people in that area. A radius of one-and-a-half miles would bring in twenty-six places of entertainment seating 36,500 – one seat for every seven-and-a-half persons. As the present cinemas had been modernised to meet current standards, he disputed ABC's opinion that its proposed building was needed in the district. The Committee then withdrew to deliberate and soon announced that the licence would be granted. ABC opened their Savoy in October.

However, it was not so simple a matter in Harlesden, Northwest London, after ABC obtained a site next to the Library in Craven Park Road, at the corner with Nicol Road, and announced its plans to build a cinema there. In this instance, the Odeon circuit joined the opposition, keen to protect its recently opened cinema on the same main road, and the owner of the Picardy testified that five local cinemas had each lost a third of their business since the Odeon's arrival.

The Middlesex County Council Entertainments Committee turned down ABC's scheme in July 1937, then approved it in November. The full council became involved and in December 1938 refused to give provisional approval to the plans by 37 votes to 18. ABC had been operating the nearby

The Savoy Stoke Newington was built despite the protests of existing exhibitors in this part of North London.

Hippodrome Willesden until October 1938. The company declared that the lease had run out and the terms for renewal had been unacceptable. But relinquishing the Hippodrome removed another argument that ABC was already represented in the area and may have been a gamble on the company's part. ABC seems to have won its case in the end: a trade press report (*Kine Weekly*, 28 March 1940) stated that work on clearing the Harlesden site for a new ABC had begun...but then the War prevented the new cinema being built.

When plans for new cinemas threatened the prosperity of ABC's properties, the company had no hesitation in raising objections. Back in 1932, for example, it had opposed a licence being granted for the proposed Embassy at Clifton, Bristol, claiming that it was not needed as its own cinemas in the area, the Whiteladies and Triangle, had seen a net drop in attendances of over 3,000 during the year as a result of the Depression. The licence was granted, the rival built, and all three cinemas co-existed until the Triangle was bombed during the War. It was the Embassy that ultimately succumbed to declining business while the Whiteladies has survived comfortably to the present day.

In another instance at Neasden, close by Harlesden, ABC had a Ritz and strongly opposed an application filed in August 1939 to build a new cinema there.

When the building had to stop

The declaration of war on Sunday 3 September 1939 had an immediate effect on ABC's building programme. The completion of Glen's Regal Twickenham was delayed and it opened two weeks later than planned in October, further reducing the operational life of what would be the shortest-lived of all the purpose-built ABCs (it lasted until 1960). Three more Glen-designed properties – the Carlton Nottingham, Ritz Clapton and Gaiety Aston, Birmingham – made their debut later in the year under black-out conditions that prevented any neon signs or exterior illumination.

In 1940 ABC were able to open the new Savoy Holloway, Palace Arbroath, and two Union projects: the Ritz Winchester and the Rex Bedminster. Originally planned back in 1936 by Verity and Beverley, the Rex had been completely re-designed by Glen but had to open incomplete, without a balcony for the time being.

The War halted a number of ABC schemes in progress. W. R. Glen had designed replacements for the Olympia Shoreditch and Hippodrome Woolwich in London. Both had been demolished in preparation and some construction work begun. In Aberdeen, the steel framework was erected for a new Glen ABC and work dragged on until November 1941. Early in 1940, ABC acquired the Prince's Theatre in Manchester – the oldest live entertainment venue in the city – and initially considered converting it (with a new facade) to become the circuit's much-needed city centre outlet, then decided on demolition which began in April 1940. Glen's plans for a new 1,600-seat cinema were passed and a contract even placed with a builder, but construction was not permitted. Glen had also drawn up plans for an ABC house in Gloucester on which some work may have started.

In Cambridge, after the Central was closed by a serious fire in April 1939, Glen succeeded in having plans for repairs passed in March 1940 and it was back in business eight months later. Also in March 1940, an application was made to build a Regal in Clapham, South London (at the junction of Wandsworth Road and Cedars Road) to Glen's designs. It is not clear whether ABC remained interested in a cinema by Glen in Chelsea (417/9 Kings Road and 1/11 Riley Street) which had first been proposed in 1931, then revived in June 1938 without getting underway. ABC had definitely lost interest in a site at 6/8 Rock Street, Finsbury Park, which had been acquired in August 1936: this was on the point of being sold to Odeon in October 1939 when the latter circuit withdrew, having arranged to take over the nearby Astoria instead. (ABC continued to receive the rent from the two houses on the site until it was finally sold at auction, with the houses still occupied, in 1987 by ABC's successors, Cannon.)

Other schemes put forward in mid-1939 almost certainly would have gone ahead but for World War Two. There were plans for new ABCs by Browne and Harding at Macclesfield and Preston. Glen had drawn up designs for sites in Bath (Kingsmead Square); Blackhall, Edinburgh (to seat 1,752); Deptford, Southeast London (High Street and Albury Street); and Newcastle-under-Lyme (London Road and Pickhull Street). No architect was named in connection with two Manchester schemes at Northern Etchells (Hollyhedge Road and Bromley Road) and Wythenshawe (this one presumably

Regal/ABC Streatham: this Glen interior is seen in a 1938 black-and-white photograph and in a 1975 colour image (by John Fernée).

far removed from ABC's existing theatre there, the Forum at Northenden). In addition, ABC had purchased at least one site for which no plans were submitted because of the War: this was in Old Market Street, Bristol, opposite the elderly King's, where the company proposed to build the city's largest cinema.

As a result of the hostilities, it would be nearly fourteen years before another new ABC opened in Britain, and by that time most of the above projects had bitten the dust.

5 | Cinema Operation: Pre-War

Openings

Most new ABCs were opened with a minimum of ceremony, in contrast to the more high profile debuts by other circuits when at least one film star would be in attendance. Typically, an ABC would be opened on a Monday around 1.30pm by the Mayor with the circuit's general manager, Arthur S. Moss, making a brief speech for the owners. The cinema would usually be packed with a mostly paying audience which would then enjoy the first regular programme of the day on the usual continuous performance basis. In the London area, new ABCs would start by playing the week's fixed release for the area in tandem with the circuit's other cinemas.

Clearly the company (or, rather, John Maxwell) felt that as a general rule it was a waste of money to promote an opening when there was enough interest and enthusiasm to fill the cinema without special attractions. Only occasionally would the opening become a gala Saturday evening affair before an invited audience with a reception following the film show. While it is not difficult to understand why a special launch would be deemed advisable in a town of such pomp and ceremony as Cambridge, why it should have been sanctioned at the Forum Southampton or Regal Hounslow is less readily explained.

In some localities, ABC would have a new theatre under construction at the same time as one of its rivals. This occurred in Muswell Hill (London) where ABC and Odeon both started building work at the end of October 1935. Odeon was a clear winner. Crowds blocked the streets for the gala evening opening in September 1936, filmed by British Paramount News for showing at the theatre later, attended by no less than six stars (Basil Rathbone, Robert Woolsey of Wheeler and Woolsey, Richard Barthelmess, Derrick de

Marney, Joan Gardner and Hazel Terry), featuring the Band of the Scots Guards, attended by Odeon head Oscar Deutsch, and capped by a reception in the auditorium after the evening's performance with dancing on the stage (when band-leader Jack Payne made a belated addition to the star guests). Contrast this with the opening of ABC's Ritz a little over three months later (ABC trailed Odeon by three months at Halifax as well). The Ritz opened on the Monday before Christmas at 2pm with a fanfare of trumpets (from a recording) and the National Anthem, after which the silk curtains parted and the show commenced. No speeches, no opening ceremony, on with the show. The programme, headed by Joe E. Brown on *Sons of Guns*, was also playing at the Ritz Harringay and the Astoria Finsbury Park that week. Yet there was a large turnout at Muswell Hill and the Ritz went on to steal a lead on its rival by opening on Christmas Day, and to enjoy many prosperous years.

Programming

Opening or acquiring cinemas was only the first step. Obtaining a regular supply of popular films was the next. ABC had no difficulties in this respect. Like the Gaumont-British chain, ABC was part of a combine that produced and distributed films that were shown in its cinemas (where a rising quota of British pictures had been imposed to stimulate production) while its numerical strength enabled it to strike circuit deals with major American distributors.

ABC was on hand to benefit from the enormous public enthusiasm for the first talking pictures, when attendances at many cinemas probably reached their all-time high. After a special visit to America, John Maxwell had come back enthused by the new sound equipment. Besides ordering

Regal Putney about to open in November 1935.

Ritz Muswell Hill in December 1936.

Alfred Hitchcock's *Blackmail* to be largely re-shot as a talkie, he rushed to equip ABC theatres with sound apparatus, installing both the Vitaphone sound-on-disc and an alternative sound-on-film system at some locations. The legendary *The Jazz Singer* was fully released as a silent in this country and it was the later Al Jolson vehicle *The Singing Fool* that was the big sensation.

A race developed between Green's Playhouse and ABC's Coliseum to be the first cinema in Glasgow with sound. The Playhouse won by two days in showing off a British Photo-tone installation. Boasting both Vitaphone and Movietone, the Coliseum began with talking shorts in the week of 31 January 1928 and showed *The Singing Fool* at a special press and trade show on the Friday, gaining huge newspaper coverage. It opened to the public on Monday 7 January 1929 with four performances advertised for 1pm, 3.30pm, 6.15pm and 8.15pm. There were spontaneous outbursts of applause from packed houses at every screening. The next day, the cinema announced: "Public Apology: The Management beg to tender their sincere apology to the hundreds who were unable to gain admission last night despite the fact that *The Singing Fool* was given an additional run. Please note: Continuous from 1 o'clock. Alteration in times of showing: *The Singing Fool* – 1-3-5-7-9. Prices of admission all day: 2s, 1s 6d, 1s, 6d. No booking. Come early and avoid disappointment." The film was given a second week, and then extended again and again, running five weeks. Its drawing power here and in London (at the Regal) convinced exhibitors of the appeal of talking pictures and there was a general stampede to install sound equipment.

In Liverpool, the circuit's huge Olympia was the first to show talkies and *The Singing Fool* had another phenomenal run, beginning 11 February 1929. In *The Dream Palaces of Liverpool*, Harold Ackroyd (who quotes a total seating of 3,400) noted: "For the first time in many years the enormous seating capacity was insufficient to accommodate the vast crowds, despite four separate performances daily, and queues stretched so far that those towards the back were out of sight of the theatre."

Besides sound, another innovation imported from the United States was the news theatre, which was enthusiastically adopted by Gaumont-British as a way of using small capacity city-centre cinemas that were difficult to programme. ABC only operated one news theatre. This was the Savoy Leeds which was converted from 24 November 1930 for a period of approximately three years.

In 1931, ABC had forged strong links with First National and Metro-Goldwyn-Mayer for its American features. BIP productions were released to the circuit through Wardour and First National Pathe. But in October Warner Bros., which had taken over First National in 1928, decided to handle FN films directly in this country (creating a new, separately managed FN distribution company) and the First National Pathe partnership was dissolved. It would seem that Warner and FN films then favoured the Gaumont chain for some years. Pathe continued as a separate Maxwell distribution company alongside Wardour. The American Pathe had been taken over by RKO Radio which had its own distribution set-up in Britain, and the British Pathe became the distributor for a minor Hollywood studio, Monogram, resulting in a supply of serviceable supporting features for the ABC circuit.

Sometimes ABC went after special attractions from distributors that customarily supplied Gaumont cinemas. Maxwell had rapidly found the Regal Marble Arch a problem to operate and, even after dropping the supporting stage shows and an orchestra in favour of double bills, the place barely paid. In 1931, a new wide screen was specially installed to show a 65mm print of the United Artists release *The Bat Whispers*, and Maxwell tried booking "supers" like *Street Scene* which, as part of the deal with the same distributor, went on to play the ABC circuit. ABC also showed UA's Eddie Cantor musical *Palmy Days* after Gaumont took umbrage at its debut at the Dominion instead of one of its own West End outlets. And, in September 1933, Gaumont was infuriated to lose Radio's sensational attraction *King Kong* to ABC which agreed to pay stiff forty per cent terms. (*King Kong* finally played most Gaumonts in a 1947 reissue.)

The ABC circuit had its own newsreel when the Pathe Super Sound Gazette (later abbreviated to Pathe Gazette) started on 31 March 1930 to compete with British Movietone News, Gaumont Sound News and some surviving silent newsreels. While Pathe Gazette was the newsreel, Pathetone Weekly and Pathe Pictorial featured radio and variety stars. The Pathe Gazette was third in terms of bookings, after

Universal News and Gaumont-British News. When, in 1937, ABC gained the Union cinemas which mostly showed Gaumont-British News, the Pathe Gazette was substituted as soon as possible and became the top British newsreel.

In 1937, ABC took sixteen top features from MGM, eleven from Fox, five each from Paramount, RKO Radio and Columbia, an odd one or two from First National, General Film Distributors and United Artists, plus six British productions from Associated British Picture Corporation (the name of the parent company had been used since December 1936 to replace the names of British International Pictures and Wardour Films. The change must have created confusion with the existing Associated British Film Distributors, or ABFD.)

Main features seem to have been rigidly booked to the whole circuit regardless of appeal, although ABC had to relinquish Paramount attractions to the American company's own cinemas in Brixton and Streatham, while some flexibility was evident in the choice of second features. (The actual titles of the main features or double-bills that played the circuit from this year to the end of 1979, are listed further on in this book.) By the end of the decade Warner Bros. and First National pictures were more in evidence (First National was merged with Warner Bros. in 1939), leading towards an era when Warner Bros. was become the dominant American supplier along with MGM.

Among late Thirties releases, First National's *The Adventures of Robin Hood* had to be booked on exceptionally high "fifty-fifty" terms and was used as the circuit's answer to *Pygmalion* on competing Odeon screens and *The Lady Vanishes* at Gaumonts in the same heady week of release.

On opening its newly constructed cinemas, ABC was usually able to book its circuit release, taking the films away from older cinemas in the same area. Although ABC had several cinemas in Edinburgh already, it was only with the opening of the Regal Edinburgh in October 1938 with its huge capacity and central location that the circuit was able to play films first-run there. In Cambridge, ABC pushed in with a new Regal in 1937 and upset the monopoly on first-run exercised by Union Cinemas with its five properties, all of them less appealing than the newcomer. (Of course, with its take-over of Union four months after the Regal opened, ABC inherited

 **EDGWARE**

Opposite Edgware Tube Station

Telephone : EDGWARE 2164

 AN ABC THEATRE

ADMINISTRATION

Proprietors	Associated British Cinemas Ltd.
Manager	F. J. Drury.
Organist	Arthur Kearsey

Continuous Performance Daily 1.45 to 11
(Saturdays and Holidays excepted). Sundays 5.30 to 11.

PRICES OF ADMISSION :

(Including Tax)

STALLS 9d. 1/-
(Saturdays, Sundays & Holidays 9d., 1/-, 1/6)

CIRCLE 1/3, 1/6, 2/-
(Saturdays, Sundays & Holidays 1/6, 2/-)

Reduced prices for children under twelve if accompanied by an adult, excepting to 9d. seats. No reduced prices for children after 2.30 on Saturdays, or at any time on Sundays or Holidays.

REDUCED MATINEE PRICES DAILY TILL 3.30

(Holidays Excepted) **Saturdays 2.30.**

STALLS - 6d. and 9d. CIRCLE - 1/-

Doctors and Professional Men who are likely to be called by telephone urgently, are requested to leave their names at the Theatre Box Office, and with the usherette who seats them. They will then be notified immediately should such a call be received.

A Public Telephone for the use of Patrons is installed on the right hand staircase leading to the Circle. The number is EDGWARE 0563.

A Car Park is provided for the use of Patrons Cars, etc., it must be understood however, that Patrons use this Park entirely at their own risk. The management cannot be held responsible for loss or damage.

Friday Night is Surprise Night !

In addition to the usual programme added West End attractions. Last performance commences at approx. 7.15 p.m.

Organ recital daily from 1.30 until the commencement of the programme by ARTHUR KEARSEY

Kindly hand in your requests for any particular Music at the Box Office.

This programme is subject to alteration at the discretion of the Manager without further notice.

THE CASTLE SUPER CINEMA
High Street   Merthyr Tydfil

Telephone 76.

CONTINUOUS DAILY from 2 till 10.30.

FRONT STALLS	4d.
BACK STALLS	6d.
FRONT BALCONY	1/-
TOP BALCONY	9d.
CIRCLE	1/3

BARGAIN MATINEES up to 3.30

FRONT STALLS 3d., BACK STALLS 5d,
ALL BALCONY 6d., CIRCLE 1/-.

Children at reduced prices if accompanied by adult

No Bargain Matinees at Holiday Periods

Resident Manager:
HENRY P. HAGGAR.

No Half Price Saturdays or Holidays.
This Programme is subject to alteration.

FROM THE MANAGER'S CHAIR

Dear Patrons.

June—and most of you will be thinking of your holidays and your coach trips to the seaside.

Unfortunately, I will be away during the showing of two of the biggest picture programmes we have yet shown, so big that I recommend them to you now: Week Commencing June 13th we have RONALD COLMAN, with a tremendous cast, in " THE PRISONER OF ZENDA " (this is a Castle Special and was shown for four weeks at Cardiff), and, Week Commencing June 20th, SHIRLEY TEMPLE in " HEIDI," acknowledged by all, including my dear friend at the opposition cinema, to be the best Shirley Temple film made to date, so you must not miss these.

The remainder of the programmes this month are all very strong attractions, and may I again remind patrons that the prices are considerably reduced during the matinees each day, so why not take advantage of the Bargain Matinees ?

Always at your service,

HENRY P. HAGGAR,

Manager.

Pages from the May 1938 programme of the Ritz Edgware and the June 1938 programme of the Castle Super Cinema Merthyr Tydfil. (Courtesy of Peter Loftus.)

OLYMPIA

CINEMA ——————— CARDIFF
Telephone — 4115.

Controlled by ——————— Associated British Cinema Ltd.
Chairman and Managing Director — Mr. JOHN MAXWELL.
Manager — W. J. KEY.

• FOR YOUR INFORMATION •

PERFORMANCES :

> Continuous Daily from 1-30 to 10-30 p.m.
> Doors open 1-15 p.m.

PRICES OF ADMISSION :

MATINEES up to 3 p.m. (Bank Holidays Excepted) :

> Front Circle 1/-
> Back Circle .... 9d.
> Stalls .... 6d.

EVENINGS (after 3 p.m.) :

> Front Circle 2/-
> Back Circle 1/6
> Back Stalls 1/-
> Front Stalls .... 9d.
> Children Half-Price to all parts, except Saturday evening and Bank Holidays. (All prices including tax).

CHOCOLATES, CIGARETTES and ICES :

> Well known brands are on sale in this Theatre.

LOST PROPERTY :

> Should be notified to the Manager immediately the loss is discovered.

Pages from the July 1938 programme of the Olympia Cardiff and October 1938 programme of the Ritz Muswell Hill. (Courtesy of Peter Loftus.)

Ritz Cinema
MUSWELL HILL
—— The landmark of perfection in film entertainment ——

● Controlled by Associated British Cinemas Ltd. ●

Resident Manager - - A. HIGHAM COWEN

General Information

HOURS OF OPENING

Continuous daily from 2 p.m. unless otherwise advertised.
Sundays—Continuous from 5.30 p.m. Doors open 5 p.m.

PRICES OF ADMISSION

Matinees to 3.0 p.m. Saturdays 2.30 p.m.

Stalls	... ...	6d.
Circle	... ...	1/-

No Matinee Prices Bank Holidays

Evenings after 3.0 p.m.

Front Stalls	... ...	6d.
Back Stalls	... ...	1/-
Back Circle	... ...	1/3
Front Circle	... ...	1/6

Sats., Suns. and Bank Holidays

Front Stalls	... ...	6d.
Back Stalls	... ...	1/-
Back Circle	... ...	1/6
Front Circle	... ...	2/-

ENQUIRIES

SERVICE

The Ritz staff are trained to give patrons every courtesy and efficient service. The Manager will be pleased to give his personal attention on request and welcomes criticisms and suggestions.

MESSAGES

Doctors or professional people expecting messages should leave their names at the Pay Office and with the Attendant before taking their Seats.

—— CAR PARK FREE TO RITZ PATRONS ——

DEAF AIDS

Earphones are provided for Front Circle seats and Back Stalls. Please enquire at the Pay Desk.

This Programme is Subject to Alteration

the problem of how to programme so many situations.)

Gradually the company spread its net until there were only a few major town centres where it was unrepresented. Central Manchester was probably the most glaring once ABC had lost the Theatre Royal in 1935. In Dundee, ABC had enjoyed first-run through operating the town's largest cinema, the Plaza, until the even larger Green's Playhouse opened in 1936 and took it away. ABC kept the Plaza going but sold its other house there, the Palace. In Aberdeen, ABC was unrepresented but not for want of trying: John Maxwell had been rebuffed in an attempt to take over the town's Poole circuit cinemas in the mid-Thirties. Swansea became another blank spot on the ABC map at the very end of the decade after the company lost the Union halls that came with the take-over. And in the West End of London, ABC lacked a major central outlet: the Regal Marble Arch was fringe West End and suffering because of its location. As previously mentioned, Maxwell leased the Alhambra in Leicester Square for a short period. He later leased the nearby Rialto, but this could not obtain major first runs because of its small capacity. One notable West End success shared by both Regal and Rialto was Columbia's *Mr. Deeds Goes to Town*, which opened at the Regal and stayed six weeks before being transferred to the Rialto when it ran more than ten weeks.

Maxwell never seems to have contemplated building a flag-ship theatre like the Odeon Leicester Square for either commercial or prestige reasons. In fact, ABC had little practical need for such a theatre, especially after the Warner Leicester Square had opened, because the Empire and Warner not only premiered most of the Hollywood films that played the circuit but were also receptive to ABPC's British productions, if only to fulfill their quota obligations.

Both filmgoers and distributors welcomed the opening of a new ABC cinema. From the distributor's point of view, the ABC houses usually had a bigger seating capacity than their rivals, could charge higher prices of admission, and would be better attended that older, less fashionable cinemas. Patrons found that new ABCs were usually better run, with an exclusive selection of appealing films, attractively up-to-date design, comfortable seating and full carpeting, better sightlines, efficient ventilation and heating, plus the latest projection and sound equipment making them less prone to technical break-

WHILST ON HOLIDAY VISIT A.B.C. CINEMAS

You can always recognise an A.B.C. Cinema by the Red, White and Blue Triangle on the Theatre front.

SEASIDE A.B.C. HOUSES

Blackpool	Hippodrome	Lowestoft	Marina
Blackpool	Princess	Plymouth	Plaza
Boscombe	Carlton	Southampton	Atherley
Bournemouth	Grand	Southampton	Broadway
Bournemouth	Westover	Southampton	Forum
Brighton	Astoria	Southsea	Commodore
Brighton	Savoy	Southsea	Gaiety
Cliftonville	Astoria	Torquay	Burlington
Dover	Granada	Torquay	Regal
Dover	Plaza	Whitley Bay	New Coliseum
Great Yarmouth	Regent	Worthing	Plaza
Hove	Granada		

Advertisement from the September 1938 programme of the Plaza Worthing. (Courtesy of Peter Loftus.)

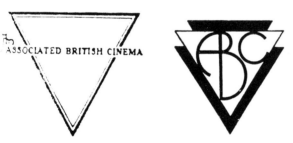

This black-and-white reproduction of the colour cover of the opening programme of the Forum Liverpool incorporates an ABC triangle on the front and repeats it on the back (above left). The design of ABC triangle used from 1935 to 1949 is shown above right.

downs. Some measure of the impact of a new ABC theatre in a drab London suburb is provided by these recollections of a local resident, A. R. Green, featured in a Walthamstow exhibition in 1992: "The Rex Leytonstone was a big advance on other cinemas around. You entered down a few steps and it had a very pleasant, perfumed smell. The curtains had a cream, silky, brocaded appearance... Live acts were shown as well as films. Some time before the War, there was a Japanese high-wire act. A man walked down backwards from the projector room to the stage."

The real competition was provided by the appearance of further new cinemas of comparable standard being erected by Odeon, Gaumont, Granada and others.

Logo

ABC seems to have set about seriously promoting the circuit image with its triangle symbol in 1935. As early as 1931, a triangle device is featured on the front cover of the opening brochure for the Forum Liverpool (and again, in a different way, on the back cover) but this seems to have been experimental or accidental as it is absent from the same cinema's first birthday brochure and from other opening brochures before 1935 available for examination. Certainly, in the later Thirties, the triangle trademark was prominently displayed on the outside of the circuit's cinemas and in the foyers, as well as on the lead-in to trailers on the screen. (Exceptionally, a triangle was even incorporated into the design on the tiles above the entrance canopy at the Regal Harrogate, but this decorative feature was hardly prominent.)

ABC was typical of any large chain in trying to develop customer loyalty and benefit from it particularly in holiday locations – but it was at an obvious disadvantage compared to Odeon, Granada and Gaumont, all circuits using their name for their cinemas. It seems that ABC were particularly spurred to get across a corporate image by Odeon's success in marketing its name.

Although it was not until the Fifties that ABC began renaming cinemas with the company initials, regular film fans of the Thirties can have been left in no doubt from all the advertising that their local Ritz, Regal, Savoy (or whatever) was part of a large circuit called ABC.

Equipment

In the projection box, Ross projectors were always installed, the DC model giving way to the FC one in 1934. These were supplied through an ABC sister company, Pathe Equipment Ltd., the sole selling agents for the Ross projector and its accessories. The screens were masked to provide sharp right-angle corners rather than the rounded ones often found elsewhere. Pathe Equipment also supplied the seating for many new ABCs. The seating at the Ritz Hyde (a Union project opened under ABC control) seems to have been unique, including some larger seats for stouter patrons. The sound system at ABCs was either Western Electric (its new Mirrophonic system from summer 1937) or RCA Photophone.

Most new ABCs had some provision for stage presentations with orchestra pits and some dressing room accommodation, even if few were fully equipped with fly towers. Many had organs.

Variety, Orchestras and Organs

Even before the Union take-over, ABC had acquired several cinemas operating a "kine-variety" policy of including music hall acts with films. In the early Thirties in the London area, ABC continued live shows at the Commodore Hammersmith, Carlton Islington, Dominion Harrow, Royalty Ladbroke Grove (Fridays only: five acts of variety with a twelve-piece pit orchestra led by Alfred Fried) and Forum Ealing (for the first few months, then only once a week with the Commodore Hammersmith orchestra rushing over by coach). The most notable of these was the Commodore. Peter Loftus, who joined ABC at the age of twenty-three as stage manager there, recalls: "When I went to the Commodore in 1934, it had just been taken over by ABC. When it had first opened, the stage shows had been very lavish, similar to the Plaza in the West End. The ABC policy was much lower grade. Every week we had three acts of variety, mostly speciality acts, similiar to what one sees on the Paul Daniels *Magic Show* on TV. They were cheap acts to book. The management did not spend a penny on stage sets. It was left to me as stage manager to provide three specially designed sets each week from stage draperies and stock backcloths.

"The stage of the Commodore was very well equipped. It

1937 advertisement from The Ideal Kinema.

was 25 feet deep with a height of 62 feet to the grid. It had thirty-five sets of counterweight lines for flying scenery and a giant magnoscopic screen which could be flown by one man in thirty seconds. There were two sets of screen tabs; four complete sets of draperies (tabs, legs, borders in gold, silver, plum velvet, light green velvet, black); and, strangely for a modern cinema, quite a number of full-size backcloths – Grand Palace, Thames Embankment, Woodland Glade, Lake by Moonlight, Oriental, etc. – which were used for the variety acts.

"One of the biggest stage presentations at the Commodore was the Eight Piano Rhapsody: eight grand pianos mounted on a staircase of rostrums with eight chandeliers, swagged and festooned drapes. No big stars appeared. Typical acts were: Irwin, Nan and Felix, comedy acrobats; Ivor Vintor and co., comedy playlet; Kay and Edna, tap dancers; the Tom Katz Saxophone Six; Eddie Sharpe, whistler; Ralph Sylvester, songs at the piano; Archie's Juvenile Band; Les Trois Matas, acrobats; Duncan's Collies, performing dogs; Ted Ray, comedian; Izzy Bon, comedian; The Act Superb, living statues; Avon and Vale, trapeze artists; the Andos Family, Japanese acrobats; the Damora Ballet and Can-Can Dancers; the Rodney-Hudson Dance Troupe, sixteen girls; Ganjou Bros. and Juanita, adagio dancers; and tap dancers, jugglers, ballroom dancers, novelty acts... No big salaries to pay. As stage manager, I received £5 a week for three shows a day, and was well satisfied – in those days, it was good money.

"What really made the Commodore famous throughout England was the Commodore Grand Orchestra under Harry Davidson who broadcast a popular programme of light orchestral music from the large theatre restaurant every Saturday from 1pm to 2pm. The signature tune was 'Sons of the Sea' and this went on for several years. The orchestra would then rush down to play in the huge orchestra pit for the stage show.

"A typical weekly programme would be the supporting feature, Walt Disney cartoon, Pathe Gazette, trailers (no adverts in those days), overture by pit orchestra, three acts of variety or a stage presentation, interval and organ solo, then main feature. The shows lasted three-and-a-half hours non-stop, from noon to eleven. The theatre did enormous business in those days as it gave such good value. Audiences came from

The Commodore Hammersmith, West London, in the Thirties. (Tony Moss collection.)

THE

WAY

A smile, a polite word, and you will invariably overcome any ill-humour, but in the day's work you may happen to strike someone who just can't be pleased. When this happens, it's up to you to do your best, and if you fail, call your Chief of Staff or the Manager. You have tried; perhaps your method was wrong—now give someone else a chance to make good. NEVER ARGUE WITH PATRONS.

Occasionally you may not feel quite up to the mark. Do not let this affect your service. Make a brave show and hide your feelings.

Your duty at all times is to render the kind of service you yourself would like to receive.

LOST : A Temper, A Patron, A Job.
FOUND : A Seat, A Smile, A Pleasure.

GENERAL APPEARANCE

A neat and clean appearance is essential at all times. Shoes shined, hair combed and tidy, uniforms put on carefully and well brushed. Good deportment, too, is necessary. Do not lean against walls or barriers.

WE ARE BANKING ON YOUR ABILITY to make good our judgment in selecting you to render the type of Service we require.

Therefore, always be Courteous, Efficient and thoroughly " on the job."

DO NOT . . .

. . . talk loudly, nor indulge in extended conversation with patrons, staff or friends ;

. . . rush up and down gangways—nor loiter in front of seats ;

. . . become so interested in the performance as to divert your attention from your work ;

. . . say " Yes " and " No "—but " Yes, Sir " and " No, Madam," as the case may be ;

. . . deprecate our programmes—nor be swayed by the judgment of others. If you are asked " Is the show good ? " you can honestly answer by saying : " I understand it is ; we always try to have a good show " ;

. . . Finally, do not fail to give the same service to patrons of cheaper seats as you would to those who have paid for higher priced seats ; no discrimination should be shown except in the matter of actual seating location.

THE

WAY

RECEPTION

Greet the patron with a smile. Inform incoming patrons the prices of seats available, politely requesting those not purchasing tickets to pass on, and those going to the Box Office to have correct money ready.

See that people who have not been standing in the queue do not " gate-crash."

Always make it quite clear to patrons what parts are " standing " and in what parts seats are available. Open doors for incoming and outgoing patrons.

ADMISSION

See that you receive a *whole* ticket for every person entering the theatre. This is most important. No person except our Company's officials, etc., of whom you have been notified should be passed under any circumstances without a complimentary or purchased ticket.

Never be persuaded to pass any person who tries to assure you that " It is all right," or that " Mr. So-and-So said they could go through." Always remember—" *If in doubt, keep them out* "—but do so very *tactfully ; politely* refer them to the management.

Keep a strict check on serial numbers, so that a wrong ticket can be discovered at a glance.

Should a *half* ticket only be presented, request production of the other half, make doubly sure that the numbers correspond, and politely inform the patron that it is a rule of the theatre for YOU to tear the ticket in half.

Do not leave your post without permission, nor wander around the foyer.

On tearing tickets in half, inform patrons audibly, but without shouting, which direction they are to take for their seating location, always terminating with the word " please."

DIRECTION

If you are on auditorium direction duty, your work consists of acting as a " go-between " the Check-takers and Usherettes—receiving patrons from the former and " feeding " to the latter. Absolute co-operation is therefore necessary in this case.

Remain at your station and be ready with your flashlight at all times.

Always glance at patrons' half tickets to make sure of directing them to correct seating location.

See that Usherettes keep you acquainted at all times with the number of vacant seats (doubles and singles) on their respective stations.

When the total number of vacant seats at each price is reduced to ten doubles, Cashier must be notified immediately.

Extracts from the ABC Staff Manual given to employees in the Thirties. (CTA Archive.)

THE

WAY

SEATING

You are expected to seat every patron when House Lights are out. Patrons must not go down gangways alone.

If you have a choice of seats find out where the patron prefers to sit.

Always know where your vacant seats are located. Singles, doubles, threes and fours, etc.

Talk to patrons in a low voice and do not hold up the progress of other incoming patrons.

Do not walk too fast down the gangway ; the patron may not be able to keep up with you.

When asking seated patrons to rise, use the words " May I trouble you ? " and " Thank you ! " afterwards.

FLASHLIGHTS

The bulb end of your torch must NEVER be raised higher than the BACK-REST of a seat.

Torch should always be held downwards at *full arm's length*, close to your side.

Light must always be shown on the ground AHEAD of patrons' feet.

Signalling with flashlights is strictly forbidden.

Always remember that patrons experience great difficulty in getting accustomed to a sudden change from natural daylight in the street to the dimmed lights of the auditorium;

Do not wave your torch ; a flashing light is most irritating to patrons.

Flashing a light in patrons' eyes will be regarded as gross inefficiency and thoughtlessness.

Light must not be flashed across seats to ascertain if there are vacant seats in a row ; there is ample Theatre Pilot Lighting for that purpose.

See that your battery is renewed often enough to give a constantly good light.

GENERAL INSTRUCTIONS

You are expected to make yourself thoroughly acquainted with *Fire Drill* and *General* rules posted in Staff Rooms. Ignorance of any rule will not be accepted as an excuse for non-performance of same.

INFORMATION

Several facts concerning the theatre are essential for a really competent and interested staff.

Get to know a few general facts concerning such things as the Air Conditioning Plant, the Sound Apparatus, and the general construction of the theatre. Patrons very often ask questions about such matters. *Know your theatre !*

PROGRAMMES

Make a careful study of various items in current programmes, also the times of commencement of showing.

all over London as it was well served by Underground (Stamford Brook one minute walk), trolley-bus and buses.

"There was a staff of about sixty, all very well disciplined. We all stayed in our own departments: Front of House: Projectionists; Stage Staff; Restaurant; and Orchestra and Artists. Discipline was very strict and one had a sense of pride in working there.

"I was at the Commodore until 1938 when the stage shows and variety came to an end. In 1940, stage shows returned to the Commodore when I doubled as assistant manager and stage director."

With regard to its own, purpose-built cinemas, ABC only engaged a full orchestra and presented variety acts with the films as a matter of regular policy where it was felt necessary to compete with other cinemas already on a cine-variety policy or to win audiences away from nearby music halls. This applied to some inner-London cinemas such as the Regal Hackney (with the Empire down the road) and Regal Old Kent Road (with the Astoria nearby) and was a particular help in the launching phase. Hackney boasted "The Regal Orchestra" while Old Kent Road had "André and His Band". But even this policy was inconsistent, as the Savoy Croydon did not offer stage shows or an organ to compete with the town's huge Davis Theatre. As previously mentioned, John Maxwell became convinced that live entertainment never brought patrons to an unpopular film programme. By August 1937, the company were considering dropping it to save money. In contrast, the Granada circuit remained committed to live acts.

Where the cinema organ was concerned, ABC fell midway between Odeon (which very rarely installed them) and Granada (which made a point of having them). Organs were often but not always included in new ABCs. I am grateful to Tony Moss for this summary of the position:

"The policy of the ABC circuit toward organ installations is hard to fathom as it was inconsistent and, to say the least, fluctuated. Out of approximately eighty theatres built by ABC between 1930 and 1939, thirty-two were equipped with organs, while two were also installed in the acquired Coronation Manor Park and Majestic Mitcham and two had been installed in theatres acquired before 1930: the Savoy Bradford was equipped in 1927 with an eight-rank pipe organ by Jardine of Manchester (the only one of that make ever installed by ABC) and in 1928 the original Regent Chatham gained an eight-rank Christie, one of only two of that make favoured by the circuit.

"Up to 1935, the policy seems to have been to install organs in all newly-built theatres, but then the enthusiasm appears to have waned – unless it was cost-cutting – as the size of the new instruments was drastically cut from 1936 onwards. Nor does the policy seem to have been governed by competitors as other circuits had operative organs where ABC installed none – at Holloway, Leytonstone, Streatham, Birkenhead, Cheltenham, Croydon, Darlington, Gateshead, Hounslow, Nottingham, Romford, Salisbury, Southport, Sunderland, Twickenham, Wolverhampton and Edinburgh. In the case of Croydon, organ chambers were provided by the architect in the left-hand splay wall but never used.

"The acquisition of Union cinemas brought in another forty-five theatre organs, mostly of Compton manufacture but including Wurtlitzers at the Ritzes at Aldershot, Barnsley, Chatham, Hastings, Huddersfield, Ipswich, Luton, Richmond and Stockport; at the Regals at Kingston and Beckenham; and at the Plaza Maidenhead. A fine team of organists was acquired from Union, who were great showmen, but the ex-Controller of Entertainment, Harold Ramsay, left after a few weeks to tour the music halls, Sidney Torch went to the State Kilburn, and Robinson Cleaver to the Granada Welling. A large (16-rank) Wurlitzer destined for the new Union 'flag-ship', the Ritz Richmond, was cancelled and replaced by the 8-rank instrument intended for the Ritz Wigan. It still had the beautifully elaborate Union design of illuminated console but a 'phantom' grand piano was cut from the specification.

"At first ABC or their precursors favoured 8-rank organs with two manuals (keyboards) as at the Savoy Bradford and Regent Chatham, but the first real ABC-built 'super', the Savoy Brighton, had a 3-manual, 12-rank Compton, and this was repeated at the Regal Glasgow and Forum Liverpool in 1931. The Forum Birmingham reverted to a 2/8 but of Compton manufacture, and the Savoy Wandsworth and Ritz Edgware in 1932 both had small 3/6 Comptons. Surprisingly, the Elephant and Castle Theatre, opened in 1932, was equipped with a Christie of 11 ranks, but all installations from 1933 onwards were by Compton. The Elephant and Castle

ABC organs and organists: Reginald Porter-Brown (top) at the console of the Regal Torquay and Edward Farley at the Regal York. (Tony Moss collection.)

instrument was the first Christie, and the first ABC organ, with an illuminated console.

"A new design of illuminated surround first appeared at the Regal Torquay and the rebuilt Empire Coventry in 1933, and this became the standard for all future installations within the circuit. It consisted of three glass 'tiers' on either side, graduating in size from the console outwards, curving towards the audience and linked with a curved glass 'box' across the top. Known as 'ABC-style', it was almost exclusive to the circuit. The Torquay and Coventry Comptons were of 11 ranks, but the Ritz Bowes Road was one rank smaller, i.e. a 3/10.

"In 1934, ABC installed small 3/6 Comptons in the acquired Majestic Mitcham and in the Regal Paisley, while the prestigious Ritz Leeds had a 3/10 Compton. In 1935, only two Comptons were supplied. a 3/10 for the Forum Southampton and a 3/6 for the Regal Walham Green. The Southampton instrument had one of the first three 'Melotone' units supplied: an electronic device that produced the most beautiful sounds, especially when used with a mellow flue pipe rank like the 'tibia' (stopped flute). All future ABC Comptons would have this unit, apart from the Regal Chesterfield.

"A further twenty Compton organs were installed in ABC cinemas between 1936 and 1939, all 3-manual, 6-rank instruments with Melotone, except for: the Savoy Northampton, which had a 7-rank transferred from the Princess Dagenham; Regal Hammersmith, a 5-rank from the Granada Hove; Regal Chesterfield, a 3/7 probably ordered by Lou Morris when it was his project; Savoy Stoke Newington, a 3/5 transferred from the Astoria Cliftonville; and the Royal Plymouth, a 3/8 and Melotone, one of the finest organs installed by ABC. Comptons were ordered for the Regal Harrow Road, Regal Halifax, Ritz Leyton, the rebuilt Regent Chatham and the Regal Salisbury – but not installed.

"Glen, the architect, seemed to favour two organ chambers at one side of the proscenium, usually on the right. One or two of the earlier installations were above the stage but none underneath – which was the location preferred by Harold Ramsay for the Union circuit. All the consoles were placed on lifts in the centre of the pit, except at Bradford where the console was at the left-hand end.

"The policy generally was that each organ-equipped theatre had its own resident organist, as with the other circuits – except Granada, who toured theirs – but occasionally ABC organists would be required to tour. In one way, this was easier for the organist as he/she did not have to present a new show each week."

Cafés and Ballrooms

The earlier purpose-built ABCs in big city centres (Glasgow, Liverpool) and seaside resorts (Brighton, Torquay) usually included a café (the Birmingham Forum did not have one, probably only because space was lacking). Such cafés were almost invariably provided upstairs, usually over the entrance, and had separate entrances so that they could attract non-patrons. Opening hours at the Regal Torquay in June 1938 were 10.30am to 10.30pm excluding Sundays.

Cafés were also included at Stirling and at Bowes Road (an acquired scheme). No catering facilities seem to have been offered at the Wandsworth Savoy, Edgware Ritz or Elephant and Castle Theatre.

From 1934, cafés seem to have been the exception in new ABCs. They were included at the Forum Southampton, Westover Bournemouth, Regal Cambridge, Regent Chatham and Adelphi Dublin. In the case of the Forum Southampton, Tony Moss surmises: "The café may have been an afterthought. The café at the nearby Regal was extremely popular (you had to queue for a table during the War) and I think this may have prompted ABC to provide one at the Forum. It was a makeshift affair – in the circle foyer, with no real separation from the circle-going public."

However, ABC did keep existing cafés going at most of the cinemas it took over, including the Astoria Brighton, Princess Blackpool, Regal Bridlington, Whiteladies Bristol, Princess Dagenham, Forum Ealing, Lido Golders Green, Commodore Hammersmith, Regal Hull, Trocadero Humberstone (Leicester), Picture House Lincoln, Embassy North Harrow, Regent Norwich, Regal Purley, Broadway Southampton, Capitol Wallasey, Regal Walton-on-Thames, Savoy Whitley (Reading) and, far from least, the Regal Marble Arch. The latter had the Chinese-style Orient Lounge in the basement, the Blue Tea Lounge and Soda Fountain on the first floor, and an enormous restaurant overlooking Marble Arch higher up.

In addition, cafés were retained at many Union houses, including the Ritz Aldershot, Ritz Belfast, Regal Beckenham,

Ritz Chatham (competing with ABC's Regent opposite), Union Dunstable, Broadway Eccles, Regal Great Yarmouth, Ritz Hastings, Perrymount Haywards Heath, Ritz Hereford, Ritz Huddersfield, Ritz Ipswich, Ritz and Super Oxford, Ritz Warrington, Ritz Wigan and Ritz Woking. (Unusually, the café at the Regal Beckenham was located on the ground floor next to the entrance and its increased accessibility made it one of the two ABC cafés to survive longest, into the Seventies, although ultimately leased by an outside company. The other long-lasting café was at the Super Oxford. There is still a restaurant, independently operated, attached to the former Ritz, now Cannon, Hereford; but this has not been a cinema continuously.)

Besides cafés, some acquired theatres like the Regal Marble Arch, Perrymount Haywards Heath, Ritz Huddersfield, Trocadero Humberstone and Capitol Wallasey also possessed ballrooms. They were a rarity in buildings designed for the circuit, but the Savoy Brighton apparently had two (just as it had two cafés) – one above the East Street entrance and one on the seafront. All these ballrooms were, of course, hired out for private parties, including wedding receptions.

The café at the Westover Bournemouth circa 1937. The Regal Torquay boasts its café is open daily in this 1946 photograph (taken by H. J. Stull).

6 | War and the Death of John Maxwell

When war was declared on Sunday 3 September 1939, all cinemas were forced to shut from that day onwards as a safety precaution. Peter Loftus remembers: "I had just taken over as holiday relief manager at the splendid Regal Halifax and my first job was to close the cinema and dismiss the staff, with no payment – it was an Act of War! – keeping on just the chief projectionist and chief of staff to act (with myself) as caretakers and watchmen. However, after five days' closure we were allowed to re-open but, having no feature films to show, we made up a scratch programme of old newsreels, cartoons, the organist and sing-alongs and odds and ends. And the 2,000 seater was packed out."

It had soon been realised that the public needed entertainment to keep up its spirits. Most cinemas were back in business from Saturday 9 September or soon after. ABC staff were recalled – with the exception of many organists – and, according to Gordon Coombes, "Alarmed at the prospect of losing managers to the services, ABC instructed those of military age to apply for deferment which they would back on the grounds that the entertainment industry was of national importance in boosting morale. Many of these applications were successful..."

John Maxwell remained, as always, in personal control of ABPC and ABC as chairman and managing director. There had never been any challenge to his authority because the company had prospered: in the eleven financial years to the end of March 1939, ABPC's profits had steadily increased and the original shareholders had more than doubled their investment in dividends. Trading profits of £1,206,856 for the year 1939/40 were only slightly down because of the war situation. The dividend had risen from five per cent in 1933 to twenty per cent in 1938. These were the profits of the ABPC group

(excluding Union Cinemas, which continued as a separate company controlled and managed by ABC):

Year ended 31 March 1933:	£279,692
Year ended 31 March 1934:	£573,198
Year ended 31 March 1935:	£656,725
Year ended 31 March 1936:	£926,483
Year ended 31 March 1937:	£1,265,830
Year ended 31 March 1938:	£1,302,778
Year ended 31 March 1939:	£1,347,001

Maxwell's activities were restricted in the summer of 1940 by illness. He had suffered for some years from diabetes. However, it was a great shock to the British film industry when, primarily as a result of his diabetic condition, he died on the Wednesday evening of 2 October 1940 at Witley, Surrey. Aged 63, he was survived by his widow Catherine, their six daughters and one son, Erik. Mrs. Maxwell inherited 4,050,000 shares, the key to control of the £50 million organisation that her husband had built up. She was forced to sell some of them to meet death duties.

The *Kinematograph Year Book 1941* commented on Maxwell's career: "One may fairly say that after he took an active interest in a big way in [the film industry's] progress its status as a finance-worthy branch of enterprise developed enormously. Before his day, the City had many reasons for regarding it with deep suspicion; his systematic and shrewd conduct of a powerful group of companies made an historic change in the way the film business was regarded, and it was the way he controlled his own enterprises that led to the satisfactory repute the Trade now enjoys."

By 1940, the Odeon circuit had become a full rival of ABC

The late John Maxwell.

Some of the female staff in uniform
at the Hippodrome Blackpool circa 1941.

and Gaumont through its busy programme of theatre construction and through its take-overs, especially of the small but powerful chain of Paramount theatres in the London suburbs and key provincial cities. This meant that films were now being divided between three circuits rather than two and certain distributors, notably Paramount, were now supplying Odeon more than ABC. The ABC circuit had to depend more strongly on the output of MGM, Warner Bros. and Columbia, but in 1940, besides Paramount, it was still taking pictures from United Artists and (for one main feature) 20th Century-Fox. With a sole exception, there was no room for surplus MGM and Warner films on the Odeon or Gaumont circuits and they were forced to play independent and off-circuit halls. In order to fully mine the hugely lucrative British market, these two Hollywood companies needed ABC just as much as it needed them.

The running of two distribution companies was an unacceptable luxury with war raging and, from the first day of 1941, Associated British Picture Corporation ceased its distribution activities and all films were channelled through Pathe. After handling the low-grade Monogram and PRC output from Hollywood that yielded only an occasional supporting feature for main circuit release, Pathe with its cockerel trademark now had "Something to Crow About", although British production was curbed by the requisitioning of Elstree studios and the limited shooting space at Welwyn Garden City. (Maxwell had been negotiating to acquire the new Amalgamated Studios at Borehamwood but was outsmarted by some quick cheque-signing from J. Arthur Rank, who then sold it to the government for non-film use. After the War, it became MGM's British studios.) Another change at this time was modernising the name of the Pathe Gazette newsreel to Pathe News.

After Maxwell's death, Eric Lightfoot, a close ally of the late chief since 1927, was appointed managing director. At least ten offers were received for Mrs. Maxwell's shares over the next few months, but none of them emanated from British financial circles. Warner Bros. made the best bid and there was considerable alarm in film circles that ABPC would be taken over by Hollywood, although the Treasury welcomed the influx of American money. In fact, Mrs. Maxwell sold only two million shares to Warner Bros. at a cost of £900,000, but

A notable acquisition: the Bristol Birmingham, showing an off-circuit programme circa 1946.

Warners were allowed to appoint Max Milder, the American who headed its British production and distribution companies, as joint managing director of ABPC with Eric Lightfoot. Max Milder was an aggressive extrovert whose manner and ideas upset Arthur Moss, chief supervisor of the ABC cinemas and long one of Maxwell's trusted lieutenants, who soon left the company. Various British businessmen were recruited to the board but quickly left while Milder remained. As W. 'Bill' Cartlidge comments in his book *Golden Hill to Golden Square*, "How ironical it all was when you come to think that John Maxwell had spent almost his entire working life in devising ways and means of precluding any American domination of the British film industry, and yet in a short period following his death Associated British should really have read 'Associated American'."

Take-overs

During the War, many smaller circuits and individual cinemas were taken over by the majors, who were making big profits and could not spend the money on construction.

In June 1940, ABC opened the Regal Camberwell. Despite the Glen-like arrangement of the entrance hall, it seems to have been acquired in the final stages of building from entrepreneur D. J. James who had engaged one of his regular architects, Leslie Kemp, on the project (which had been first announced as far back as June 1937 when the cinema was to be called the Florida). Although within weeks the Regal was temporarily closed by bomb damage (which killed some patrons), it was quickly re-opened and went on to be a very successful theatre for many years. However, ABC came unstuck when it acquired the Coronet Hartlepool in February 1942 which had nearly been completed. The company began work to finish its construction, and started booking the first films it would show in a few weeks' time. Existing cinema owners who were being deprived of these films protested to the Northern Branch of the Cinematograph Exhibitors Association that, unlike West Hartlepool (where ABC had its Forum), Hartlepool was badly depressed by the War and had enough cinemas already. Work was halted (it is not clear whether this was done voluntarily by ABC) and the building was requisitioned by the Ministry of Food for the duration of hostilities and named the Comet.

ABPC completed its acquisition of the Union circuit. In the summer of 1942, it bid for the twelve per cent of ordinary shares it did not already own, and at the end of the year it was compulsorily acquiring those it had been unable to purchase.

A few functioning theatres were acquired in single deals during the war years. The most important were the enormous Apollo Ardwick (Manchester), which more than replaced ABC's much smaller adjacent theatre that had been bombed, and the Bristol Birmingham, a modern city centre house. However, both these cinemas played second run and did nothing to solve the circuit's first-run difficulties with its lack of a central Manchester outlet and its low capacity Forum in the heart of Birmingham.

Other newcomers to the circuit were the Savoy Stourbridge, Rex Consett, Rembrandt Ewell and Metropole Nottingham. At some point (possibly after the War), ABC acquired two picture houses closed by severe bomb damage, the Alcazar Edmonton and the Regent Hayes, with a view to building new cinemas on their sites in the future.

ABC's biggest expansion of this period came in a £700,000 deal for most of the Mayfair circuit, announced on 17 August 1943 and completed at the end of the month. Mayfair Circuit (Control) Ltd. had been established by financier George Elcock, former right-hand man of Oscar Deutsch, after Deutsch died and he had been forced out of Odeon. Arthur Cohen was another director of what had been a rapidly expanding company.

ABC acquired nineteen Mayfair halls outright: Regal Atherstone; Grand Banbury; Majestic Bridgnorth; Regal Bridlington; Regal Caversham (Reading); Regal Cirencester; Regal Dursley; Picturedrome Gloucester; Rex Hanworth; Regal Lichfield; Forum Newbury; Granby Reading; Beacon Smethwick; Empress Sutton Coldfield; Rex Tilehurst (Reading); Regal Tring; Regal Trowbridge; Regal Walton-on-Thames; and Lyric Wellingborough. There were few real gems in the batch, which included several small-town Regals designed to a pattern by Harold S. Scott in 1937 and later that would in many cases prove a real headache to operate profitably. Three of the better theatres – at Bridgnorth, Bridlington and Walton-on-Thames – were Lou Morris ventures recently acquired by Mayfair. The deal gave ABC three theatres in the Reading area to add to the two it already possessed, with the Granby an important second house close to the city centre. The Mayfair circuit retained a dozen or so properties, and suggestions that ABC would be managing these as well were misplaced.

Disposals

During the war years, ABC continued to dispose of many cinemas that were of little value or a liability, often by not renewing leases. The most significant problem it had was the Regal Marble Arch, which John Maxwell had been so eager to acquire in 1929. The Regal had lost access to the parent company's British productions when ABPC's Elstree Studios were requisitioned. Attendances had been very severely hit by the Blitz and opening hours had been curtailed for long periods. ABC were paying Abrahams, the landlord, £650 a week for the Regal and losing around £1,000 per week. Abrahams was approached when ABC's occupancy had six more years to go but he wanted too high a sum of £30,000 in January 1942 to abrogate the lease.

ABC decided to persevere with the Regal and tried reviving cine-variety from 19 January 1942, when Jack Payne and Orchestra and singer Inga Andersen supported Columbia's *You'll Never Get Rich*, starring Fred Astaire and Ginger Rogers, which ran three weeks (Billy Cotton and His Band replaced Jack Payne in the last week). Peter Loftus was transferred from the Commodore Hammersmith, where he had been stage director, to take the same position ("actually stage manager") at the Regal. He recalls: "The stage show policy at the Regal was done on the cheap as far as settings were concerned. It was an oddly-shaped stage, like a triangle, but fully equipped. Remembering that this was during the war years, it was remarkable that for one whole year the Regal was able to put on a different band show each week. In 1942, the cinema was well patronised by the American G.I.s who were pouring into London. All the big bands of the period appeared on the stage: Jack Payne's Band, Henry Hall and His Orchestra, Ambrose Orchestra, Nat Gonella, Edmundo Ros, swing bands, military bands, gypsy orchestras, Hungarian bands, all plus the famous Christie organ. The orchestra pit was disused except for the organ, so it was transformed into an ornamental garden with artificial flowers, grass and a fountain!

The most famous act to appear there was Max Miller, who was quite out of place and not very popular in those ornate and palatial surroundings and with a cinema audience. Incidentally, British films were held in such low esteem that, to fulfill quota regulations, they were shown in the mornings when the cleaners were cleaning the cinema and the organist was rehearsing! A very small admission charge was made. One was very proud to be working at the Regal. We all felt very 'superior' to the suburban cinemas. There was a staff (in wartime) of sixty. When the stage shows finished, the Regal went over to double features and organ."

Stage shows lasted until the end of 1942. Most feature films ran one or two weeks, although Columbia's *The Talk of the Town* ran three. In 1943, the Regal opened *Casablanca* simultaneously with the Warner and held it for two weeks. There was a five-week run of Fox's *Tales of Manhattan*.

The Regal remained such a problem to run that ABC gave it up early in January 1945, following the run of Warner Bros.' *Janie*. It then became an Odeon and was a success for many years before once again becoming a problem house.

J. Arthur Rank

After ABC's option on the key voting shares in Gaumont-British lapsed in October 1941, J. Arthur Rank's General Film Finance Corp. had purchased them from the Ostrer brothers and taken control of GBPC. Rank also purchased ABPC's non-voting Gaumont shares for £450,000 – £150,000 less than Maxwell had paid for them, but slightly above their market value.

Rank's control of both Odeon and Gaumont caused considerable alarm in government circles, and he agreed in July 1943 that he would not acquire any further cinemas or theatres without the consent of the Board of Trade. At this point, Rank's cinema empire totalled 607 properties. In February 1944, Mrs. Maxwell and Warner Bros., as the shareholders jointly controlling ABC, gave an undertaking to the Board of Trade that ABC would not acquire more cinemas than Rank and that ABC would not exceed the booking strength of Rank's largest circuit (Odeon or Gaumont) in either the London area or the country as a whole. This imposed a restriction on the number of ABC cinemas that could take the weekly circuit release first run, but it is not clear whether this necessitated a change in programmming at some theatres or whether the circuit was under the limit.

The continuation of the War forced a change in the release of films in suburban London. Since 1935 they had played first in North London and then south of the Thames but a wartime economy measure in 1943 limited to forty-one the number of prints of a new film that could be circulated. The ABC circuit agreed with its rivals to split North London into two regions so that films took a week longer to arrive on the other side of the river. This accelerated a habit whereby keen South Londoners would cross the Thames to catch new films ahead of time (this was particularly true after the War and most damaged Putney cinemas as local film fans could easily reach Hammersmith).

In December 1944 it was reported that Sidney Bernstein (of Granada) and David Mountain were bidding for Mrs. Maxwell's two million shares, but nothing came of it.* This would not be the last time Granada showed an interest in buying the Warner Bros. holding.

Yet another of Maxwell's old colleagues left the company. Eric Lightfoot resigned from his post as joint managing director in April 1945, apparently after a row with Max Milder, leaving the American in sole charge. A few months later, Sir Philip Warter, the husband of John Maxwell's daughter Kitty and senior trustee of the John Maxwell estate, became the new chairman and principal custodian of British interests in the running of the company.

* After her husband's death, Mrs. Maxwell continued to take an interest in the film business, donating £2,000 to the Royal Film Performance of *A Matter of Life and Death* in November 1946 to increase the proceeds which went to the Cinematograph Trade Benevolent Fund. (Mrs. Maxwell died on 22 October 1951. Her son Erik became a director of ABPC in November 1964.)

7 | Postwar ABC

ABC emerged from the war with 415 cinemas in operation. At least three had been bombed beyond repair: the Astoria Cliftonville, Queens Forest Gate (London) (where the Christie organ was salvaged and installed at the Regal Halifax), and the Ardwick Manchester (where the site was cleared to provide a car park for the newly acquired, adjacent Apollo, a more than satisfactory replacement). Another theatre, the Palace Kirkcaldy, was lost in a fire at the very end of 1945, while further blazes would claim the St. George's Falmouth, Regent Leyland and Carlton Newbury over the next five years.

In London, the Roxy Blackheath, which had been closed by war damage, was re-opened early in 1947 (but the Carlton Upton Park, which had lost its striking Egyptian frontage, had much longer to wait). Two requisitioned properties were returned: the Theatre Cinema Cambridge, which re-opened in 1947 under its old name of the New Theatre on a foreign film policy (but was soon being operated by ABC as a live theatre); and the Coronet Hartlepool, retrieved in the spring of 1949 but still in need of work before it could ever open. The Regal St. Leonards was back in business from 1946, having been dark for six years after the evacuation of the area decimated attendances.

Two London-area cinemas were purchased by the circuit, the State Barkingside (from Kay Bros.) and the Super Stamford Hill. The very large State (with a restaurant and ballroom) had been requisitioned during the War for non-cinema use, shared by the War Office (which occupied the ground floor) and local authorities (the balcony). Now it was refitted out on "an austerity basis" with new projection and sound equipment to provide ABC with a second house in the Ilford area from February 1948.

The Super and the State were curious acquisitions for the Super took the Odeon release while the State fluctuated between the ABC release and "alternative programmes".

The Warner controversy

In August 1945 Warner Bros., at the instigation of Max Milder, had quietly bought a further million ordinary shares from the Maxwell estate for £1,125,000, giving the American company thirty-seven-and-a-half per cent of the issued capital. When this became public knowledge in February 1946, it was suggested that Warner Bros. as the largest shareholder effectively controlled ABPC. Sir Philip Warter responded that the trustees of the John Maxwell estate had retained the voting rights in the million shares sold to Warners but, with Max Milder remaining managing director of both ABPC and the Warner Bros. British organisation, there can be little doubt that Warners' interests were well protected. Britain was the most lucrative market anywhere in the world for Warner Bros.: it had a much bigger market share here than even in the United States. Every Warner feature trade-shown in 1946 obtained an ABC circuit release (although *The Two Mrs. Carrolls* waited more than a year). However, Warners also made an agreement to lend some of its stars to ABPC and to distribute three of ABPC's British productions annually to American cinemas (this pact resulted in such films as *The Hasty Heart*, pairing Richard Todd with Warner stars Patricia Neal and Ronald Reagan; though it was short-lived, the basic rapport between the two companies continued unabated.)

MGM were worried enough to obtain a guarantee (which remained in force for several years) that its films would have as much showing time on the ABC circuit as those of Warner Bros. In 1946, Warner Bros. and MGM films seemed to be taking it in turns to play the ABC circuit, interspersed with occasional British films from Pathe, Anglo-American and other British distributors. As far as main features were concerned, no other Hollywood company got a look in.

As noted in the introduction, it was the regularity with which Warner and MGM films played ABC cinemas that became one of the circuit's defining features in the boom years of going to the pictures. For the fan, the pictures made by Warner Bros. and MGM had their own particular stamp. It was not just that stars like Spencer Tracy, Clark Gable, Errol Flynn, Bette Davis and Joan Crawford appeared in their films as contract artists but also that they had a distinctive (if hard to define) look and sound (in the Warner films, for example, there was the unmistakable, full-bodied and melodious scores of Max Steiner and the particularly pungent echo of gunfire in films like *The Big Sleep* and *Mildred Pierce*).

New homes come first

ABC was keen to resume its building programme immediately the War ended but it was case of "homes come first" and no major licences were forthcoming for what turned out to be a period of nine years. The schemes at Aberdeen, Woolwich, Gloucester, Shoreditch, Manchester and Bristol had to wait. In Manchester the vacant lot was used as a car park while a poster promised passers-by that a modern ABC theatre would be erected. At Bristol, in August 1949, ABC had the plans for its Old Market Street site rejected because this was now earmarked to become an intersection on a new ring road; the company appealed in vain. In the following month, ABC had no difficulty gaining approval of its latest plans for reconstructing the Hippodrome Blackpool but could not obtain the building licence.

The company was so irritated at not being allowed to complete the Coronet Hartlepool that it put the building up for sale in January 1951. By 1950, at least three applications for a licence to rebuild the fire-damaged Regent Leyland had been rejected. W. R. Glen would have been in a state of total frustration had not ABPC been allowed to reconstruct Elstree Studios after it was de-requisitioned. (This work kept Glen and his team busy for two years and would be the Scotsman's last major undertaking. He then semi-retired, remaining a consultant to the company, and was ill for more than a year

This thank you for wartime victory appeared in ABC local newspaper advertisements in May 1945. It features both the standard ABC triangle (top) and a prototype of the new slimmer version (at bottom left). The Regal Dursley was a small-town cinema that generally played split weeks, combining the ABC circuit release with off-circuit and some Gaumont programmes (the town also had an Odeon theatre). (Courtesy of Bob Wood.)

before his death on 19 February 1950, aged 65. He left a widow, two daughters and a dog called Ritz.)

ABC had purchased some new sites for cinemas – in Sheffield, in Dundee (in the Overgate development near City Square), and in Lewisham, Southeast London (taking a 99-year lease on an island site comprising 1-9 Lewis Grove, 33-45 Mercia Grove and 1-23 Albion Way). Then there were the sites, mentioned earlier, of the war-destroyed Alcazar Edmonton (North London) and Regent Hayes (Middlesex), which may have been acquired at this time.

Building restrictions did not apply in Eire and ABC's local subsidiary opened the Adelphi Dun Laoghaire. In Britain the company had to be content with redecorating theatres like the Carlton Boscombe and Victoria Hall Portsmouth, re-equipping some like the Savoy Brighton, and putting in new seats at others including the Ritz Edgware.

Boom years

If ABC was unable to invest in its future, it had the consolation of enjoying an unrivalled period of box-office prosperity. There were few alternative sources of amusement and, despite the run-down condition of many of the cinemas, people flocked to them as never before or since. A severe shortage of fuel and regular electricity cuts in the appallingly cold winter of 1946/47 forced many cinemas, including those of ABC, to reduce their hours of operation, opening at 4pm for several weeks in some areas (ABC estimated that it lost £200,000 as a direct result). Restrictions were placed on the use of lighting and tabs.

Then, of course, when Britons had the relief of an exceptionally fine summer in 1947, they didn't want to spend as much time in the cinema and attendances suffered. In more general terms, the slow return to normality had a detrimental effect on admissions, especially in the afternoons as there were fewer servicemen and workers at a loose end following demobilisation and a return to more normal hours in the factories. This also helped cinemas return to full staffing, which meant a twenty-five-per-cent increase in wage bills.

The ABC circuit reported 246,288,711 admissions in the ten months from April 1946 to the end of January 1947, which (extended at the same rate for a full year) adds up to just under 300 million admissions. The all-time record national total of 1635 million was reached in 1946, and ABC therefore had approximately an eighteen per cent share of all cinema admissions.

In the spring of 1947, the circuit's Scottish branch lost its independence. Although its original name, Scottish Cinema and Variety Theatres, had been retired in the spring of 1938, it had continued to operate very successfully as an autonomous part of ABC under the general management of David A. Stewart who had, of course, been one of John Maxwell's earliest film business associates, going back to 1913. Stewart's retirement on 31 March 1947 provided an opportunity to integrate Scottish administration and general operating procedures with the rest of the circuit – a move that was unpopular with the Scots even without the extra paperwork that ensued.

Saturday morning pictures

ABC had decided in October 1945 to start children's clubs of "ABC Minors" at their cinemas on Saturday mornings, to compete with the clubs at Odeons, Gaumonts and other rival establishments. Given wide publicity, these clubs generally started with huge audiences and then tailed off at least a little. There were eighty-three clubs running by the summer of 1947 and most of the circuit had them by the end of the decade. In some instances, clubs failed – the Ritz Newtonards and Ritz Oatlands gave up in 1950/51; the Rhul Burnside, Empire Clydebank and Palladium Oldham abandoned them in the mid-1950s but not until the current serial had ended.

ABC's shows provided a wonderful time for thousands of children and many will identify with CTA member J. A. Smallwood's recollections: "I have happy memories of the Albion Castleford in the early Fifties, being a member of the ABC. We would queue up on a Saturday morning to see Flash Gordon, Batman, etc., and sing the ABC members' song (to the tune of 'Blaze Away'):

We are the boys and girls well known of:
Members of the ABC
And every Saturday we line up
To see films we love and
Shout aloud with glee.

We love to laugh and have a sing-song
Just a happy crowd are we.

We're all pals together.
We're members of the ABC."

Catering

In the early postwar years ABC operated approximately seventy-five cafés (some with associated ballrooms). The wartime acquisitions had added several to the circuit: the Apollo Ardwick (144 places, with a ballroom for 300), Regal Bridlington (148 places, with ballroom for 100), Rembrandt Ewell (75 places), Regal Lichfield (60 places), Granby Reading (46 places), Regal Walton-on-Thames, and Savoy Whitley (Reading) (16 places). The biggest catering operation was at the Savoy Brighton with 300 places in two separate cafés. This and ABC's other Brighton house, the Astoria, were among the few cinemas licensed to sell alcohol.

Import duty

When the Labour government attempted to prevent Hollywood taking so much money out of the country by imposing an ad valorem tax on imported films in August 1947, this resulted in a boycott by the Hollywood studios. The major circuits were forced to eke out the remaining supply of new American films with reissues until the tax was withdrawn from 3 May 1948. ABC closed the lesser of two theatres in Haywards Heath, the Broadway, to dramatise the way the tax would hurt admissions, but re-opened it after the tax was lifted. Attendances did drop sharply in 1947 and at the end of the year ABC cut the salaries of some one hundred managers under performance-related agreements. After Rank refused to penalise any of its Odeon and Gaumont managers, recognising that they had been facing abnormal problems, ABC backed down and refunded the deductions it had already made from managers' pay packets. Fortunately, business recovered somewhat in 1948, probably as a result of the flood of top Hollywood attractions late in the year.

American influence

Max Milder became seriously ill in 1946 from the strain of his workload: he typically spent each morning supervising Warner Bros.' distribution affairs in Wardour Street, each afternoon at Golden Square on ABPC business, and each evening at the Warner Theatre in Leicester Square. He was able to resume work on a limited scale in 1947. Warners transferred an American executive, C. J. Latta, from its South American office and had him appointed to the board of ABPC as an heir apparent. After Milder died on 1 August 1948, Latta was duly appointed managing director of ABPC in his place. Having once been a Warner theatres zone manager in the United States, Latta was expected to ensure that the dividends kept flowing in from the profits of the cinema chain (ABPC's film production side was making losses in 1948/9). Booking manager D. J. (Jack) Goodlatte became managing director of Associated British Cinemas but had to work under Latta's close eye.

When cinema attendances started falling, the American's interventions were, according to Gordon Coombes, a mixed blessing as he "started to compare operating costs with those of the cinemas he had supervised in the States and declared the circuit to be grossly over-staffed, ignoring the fact that British licensing regulations were much more stringent than their transatlantic equivalent. He also expressed surprise that close-covered carpet in auditoria, foyers and staircases was the rule and decreed that bare boards between seating in all but the front circle would now be the order of the day, while staffs were pruned ruthlessly. However necessary these extreme measures had become, they brought about a reversal in what had first of all attracted the masses to the movie cathedrals of the Thirties era – the comfort, luxury and standard of service compared with that of the average working class home... On the credit side, C. J. was a great believer in showmanship and public relations as an aid to increased business..."

Another American expatriate from the Warner chain in the United States, J. Andrew Neatrour, was put in charge of publicity and, Coombes relates, "it would be true to say that Andy revitalised the publicity side of ABC... he was able to promote nationwide contests tied up with the national release of an appropriate film and the makers of products whose names were household words." One such was a contest to find the British Esther Williams, sponsored by Four Seasons Fruit Squashes in connection with the release of *Neptune's Daughter*. (See "ABC in North West London", *Picture House* no. 8, Spring 1986, page 28.)

In the latter half of 1950 and early 1951, with 601,051 seats

The Palace Erdington, Birmingham, announces the start of children's matinees in June 1946 and shows off its new ABC triangle sign. Note the entrance to the Palace Ballroom at right. The theatre also had a café and tennis courts.

The Regal Hounslow with its new triangle sign in February 1947.

Charlie James, the manager of the Regal Dursley, stands proudly beneath the canopy as the outside lights come on again at night on 2 April 1949. (Courtesy of Bob Wood and the Gloucestershire Gazette.)

in 408 cinemas, the ABC circuit had average weekly admissions of 4,104,194 (i.e. 213,418,088 in a full year). This represented a weekly average of 10,059 attendances per cinema or 6.83 per seat (i.e. an average total of a full house per day). This was only slightly below ABC's figures for 1930 when seats were occupied on average 7.58 times weekly and cinemas averaged 10,417 admissions (the circuit then had only 120 cinemas seating approximately 165,000 with average weekly attendances of 1,250,000.)

In the annual report for the year ending 31 March 1952, it was stated that the circuit had recorded 207,700,717 admissions, down two per cent on the preceding year. This gave the circuit approximately fifteen per cent of the national total as compared to the eighteen per cent estimated for 1946/7. The fall in patronage at ABC theatres would seem to have been more severe than the national average.

The big switch-on

One ray of light in the gloom of the immediate postwar years was the opportunity to introduce the company's triangle trademark in three colour neon. Previously, the ABC trademark had been only modestly displayed on the frontage of cinemas. The triangle was re-designed to be narrower with more modern lettering and now, on most frontages, it was to be dominant, with the name of the theatre incorporated in a band across the triangle below the letters "ABC". It was a way of strengthening the identity of the circuit in the public eye at the expense of the individual theatre and making it more of a rival to Odeon and Gaumont, both of which were giving many acquired theatres their circuit name. However, the new sign was never installed at some smaller ABCs.

Neon had fallen into disuse through the blackout requirements at the outbreak of war and postwar energy-saving restrictions included a ban on front of house display lighting which was only lifted on 2 April 1949 (and then re-imposed with weekday restrictions from 2 October). Only a quarter of the old neon still in place was in working condition, but ABC had installed many of the new signs in readiness for 2 April (the one on the Regal Hounslow had been put up more than a year earlier). This gave the circuit an advantage over rivals merely lighting up their old, familiar name signs. At numerous cinemas, local dignitaries had been invited to pull the switch as dusk fell. People gathered outside to cheer as the lights came on again.

In some locations, the triangle went up on the side of a cinema rather than over the entrance. This was true of the Forum Newbury, and of the Granby Reading where it was placed in the centre of the long side wall facing the main road. The Regal Kingston-upon-Thames even had two signs, one on the front and one on the side.

There was one aesthetic disadvantage: in the original design of many theatres, spaces and recesses had been included in the facades to display the cinema name, and these were now often left blank, spoiling the look of the buildings. (Further ugly spaces were left at some cinemas when back-lit racks high on the facade, into which letters had been slotted to spell out the films showing, were discontinued. This was particularly harmful at the Regal Streatham, which had one of the most accomplished exteriors among purpose-built ABCs.)

Around this time, the Pathe distribution company was renamed Associated British-Pathe to ensure that audiences recognised it as part of the ABPC group, directly linked to ABC cinemas.

Departures

Several properties went from the circuit when leases expired. Essoldo took over the Apollo Southsea and Carlton Cosham, presumably outbidding ABC for these profitable cinemas, but were probably welcome to three cinemas in Barrow and the Palaseum Stepney. Other sites where leases ran out included the Hippodrome Sheffield, Central Canterbury, Regent King's Cross (soon operated by Granada), Palace Leyland (where ABC had already lost its Regent in a blaze), and the Kemble Hereford, a problem hall which ABC had tried running as a live theatre.

When the licensing authorities demanded approximately £5,000 worth of repairs to the small County Warwick, ABC decided the expense was not warranted and contemplated approaching the Clifton circuit, owner of the town's other cinema, the New, to see if it would either buy the County or sell its cinema to ABC. In the event, the County was closed in 1951 and the New remained a Clifton cinema. Business at several places was causing concern in 1950 and ABC were glad to eventually sell off or lease out the Alma Luton, Grand

Lancaster and Palace Maidstone, the last of which had been run as a live theatre in recent years. ABC tried to terminate the lease on its second house in Dewsbury, the Regal (Essoldo took over in 1954), and kept its second Dover hall, the Plaza, open primarily because the terms of the lease required this. The company looked forward to ending its lease on the Majestic Blackburn in 1953, although business had improved here early in 1950. The Capitol Didsbury was another headache property which a series of cheap live shows had not cured.

Then there was Regal Caversham which was not even on a bus route although one was in the offing. Here, and at the Regal Dursley, ABC hoped that new housing being erected nearby would improve business. Besides these two theatres, others acquired from Mayfair in 1943 were causing serious problems. At the Regal Tring, staff had been cut to an absolute minimum and cheaper films booked. At the Rex Hanworth, six-day bookings had been spreading the audience too thinly and a split-week policy was resulting in a small profit. A different kind of problem was being experienced at the Balham Picture House where an excessive rent of £80 per week left an inadequate profit – this seems to have been resolved by buying the freehold.

There were worse times ahead. The British film industry had seen the harmful effect of television in America and the panic caused in Hollywood, but there was hope: the studios there were responding with more colour films and new screen systems. By 1953, the fight was on in Britain to increase attendances…

8 | The Fighting Fifties

ABC stepped up pressure on the Government to relax building restrictions so that it could restore cinemas still closed by war damage and complete work on new ones interrupted by the War. In 1953, the Carlton Upton Park re-opened with a completely new modern entrance block to replace the Egyptian extravaganza destroyed by a rocket bomb. In Aberdeen, the local Member of Parliament prodded Westminster and a building licence was granted in November 1953. It was not until the summer of 1954 that the £5,000 limit on "luxury" building expenditure was officially lifted and that a steel shortage dating from 1951 ended.

Now that the company could go ahead at Aberdeen, Woolwich and Gloucester, the original Glen designs were revised to give the buildings a more modern look and to accommodate CinemaScope-width screens. C. J. Foster was the company's chief architect, having succeeded W. R. Glen. Appointed deputy architect early in 1949 when Glen was ill, he had been a member of the architect's department since 1929, the year it was formed. (He had come with the best of training, having been articled to W. E. Trent, the architect for PCT and Gaumont-British).

Work on the new ABC at Shoreditch (where the Olympia had been demolished) was never resumed and the site was sold. The big scheme at Lewisham was dropped and ABC settled for the Plaza Catford as its main circuit outlet in the area (the Prince of Wales Lewisham was usually off-circuit; the independent Rex eventually gained access to the ABC release). The Manchester scheme in Oxford Road would have gone ahead but for circumstances to be described later.

The first postwar ABC cinema to open was the Regal Aberdeen in July 1954, followed by the Regal Woolwich in September 1955 and the Regal Gloucester in March 1956. In contrast to the low-key pre-war openings, these were launched with personal appearances by star names from the Associated British contract stable – usually including Richard Todd, accompanied at Aberdeen by Anne Crawford, one of the lesser stars of the opening attraction, *Knights of the Round Table*.

The Aberdeen theatre had a narrow, shop-width entrance on Union Street, as modest as that of the Forum Birmingham. There was no room for a large triangular neon sign as the floors above were let to other companies and ABC had to be content with a vertical "Regal" sign between the windows above the canopy. Small ABC triangles were mounted on the front edge and ends of the canopy which jutted out a mere couple of feet over the pavement. But the auditorium behind was substantial, seating 1,914, and had a proper entrance with canopy above facing the car park.

In his massive history of Aberdeen cinemas, *Silver Screen in the Silver City*, Michael Thomson notes of the Regal: "In the interior, use was made of materials unheard of before the War, the lower parts of the auditorium walls being covered with a type of washable mock-leather and the upper parts finished in a light mushroom-toned satinised paint. The lighting system, made up of dimmable fluorescent tubes, was the largest of its kind since the idea's introduction a few years previously at the Royal Festival Hall, London. In the ceiling above the centre stalls and balcony were set distinctive saucer-style light fittings, and in the side walls were little lamps with star-shaped shades. A star pattern was also used to break up the otherwise plain surfaces of the walls in the proscenium area."

Unfortunately, ABC's first British opening in fourteen years was marred by one of the hitches that haunt such occasions.

The Union Street entrance and the much wider side entrance of the Regal Aberdeen (1954), photographed as the ABC in September 1963. The triangle device has been retained as part of the new style of signage.

The newly-opened Regal Woolwich in 1955 with modern canopy over the entrance but without the triangle sign. The plain interior was typical of the period and of new ABCs.

The postwar Regal Gloucester has become the ABC in April 1963, seen here offering a week's run of a local live production of the musical Annie Get Your Gun instead of films.

The Capitol Dundee was a take-over of a postwar cinema, promptly renamed the ABC and seen here in August 1977. (Photograph by Allen Eyles.)

The curtains opened slightly and then jammed. It took many long minutes to reach the curtain track and wind the curtain open by hand. At least the portable Hammond organ was there to be played by Hubert Selby – the van in which it was being transported had been stolen but was recovered by police early in the morning of the opening day.

The Regal Gloucester opened with an Associated British picture, *Now and Forever*, and with one of its stars, Janette Scott, in attendance This cinema incorporated full stage facilities, which were put to early use for live shows and pantomimes. (After it closed in 1990, superseded by a new MGM multiplex, these facilities have prompted interest in using it as a theatre.)

In 1955, ABC even purchased four cinemas – the Wallaw Blyth, Regal Litherland, Avenue Higher Blackley and George Glasgow – although these were its first acquisitions since early 1948 and the last until 1959. In the latter year ABC made two significant additions to the circuit in Scotland. The company took over the large La Scala Clydebank and, giving up the site it had obtained shortly after the War in Dundee, purchased the recently built Capitol from the J. B. Milne circuit in a deal which gave Milne ABC's now unwanted Plaza in Dundee and some ABC halls elsewhere in Scotland including the Capitol Galashiels and Kings Montrose. The Capitol Dundee had been playing "fourth circuit" 20th Century-Fox pictures but otherwise had no access to a major circuit release: there was an Odeon and Gaumont cinema in Dundee and the huge Green's Playhouse showed the ABC release. When ABC acquired the Capitol, it took half the circuit releases away from the Playhouse and also functioned as a road show house for extended runs of special attractions (see below). Eventually the Playhouse went over to bingo and the Capitol had complete access to the ABC release.

Various cinemas were improved. The old-fashioned frontages of the Picture House Balham and the Palladium Brixton in South London were completely modernised in the mid-Fifties and the cinemas renamed Ritz and Regal respectively, although the equally old-fashioned auditoria were not substantially altered. In Maidstone, ABC lost both the Ritz and Central in separate fires and reconstructed the Central as virtually a new theatre, giving it the Ritz name. The pre-war scheme to replace the Theatre Royal Preston was revived and it was closed and demolished, although it was over three years before the modern replacement opened.

Many closures also took place. Between 1953 and 1955, ABC sold the Ritz Hythe, Kings Glasgow, Plaza Basingstoke, Capitol Horsham and Palace Walsall. None of these were missed but more of a setback must have been the loss of the circuit's large and well-appointed sole outlet in Slough, the Adelphi, presumably on expiry of lease. Part of the former Union group, this was now acquired by Granada as their second big house in the town. ABC leased out three more unwanted cinemas – the Palace Maidstone, Grand Bournemouth and Electra Cheadle – and gladly relinquished, when the leases ran out, the Majestic Blackburn and Regal Dewsbury. It also "gave up" the Queens Cardiff. The highly seasonal, flood-prone Casino Herne Bay and the Olympia Darlaston were closed. Two more difficult theatres became television studios (see below).

In 1956, the New Theatre Cambridge, Marlborough Yiewsley and Regal St. Leonards were closed, while the Regal Altrincham was destroyed by fire and the Plaza Wishaw declared an unsafe building. Then in November/December 1956, at the same time as Rank were dramatically shutting fifty-nine Odeon and Gaumont cinemas, ABC closed thirteen of its own: the Public Hall Carlisle, Ritz Erith, Tivoli and Playhouse Cambridge, Picture House Erdington, County Lancaster, Ritz Crayford, Hippodrome Nuneaton, Regal Barrow, and four in the Liverpool suburbs: Popular Anfield, New Coliseum Paddington, Regent Tranmere and Coliseum Walton. None of these were modern or outstanding buildings, although ABC had invested money in modernising the Crayford cinema in 1951 in an attempt to re-launch it as a cinema after a period as a live theatre. The first London-area closure, of the Empire Highgate, came in February 1957. Later that year, both the circuit's Levenshulme cinemas, the Regal and Kingsway, suffered serious fires and only the Regal was re-opened. The Regal Wallingford and Majestic Stoke-on-Trent were sold and the Albion Castleford leased.

In the first half of 1958, a new round of closures claimed the Don Beswick, Claremont Moss Side, Gem Liverpool, Beacon Smethwick, Regal Tring, Gaiety Leeds, Popular Derby, Regal Caversham and the second Highgate cinema, the Palace, although some would re-open under new owners. The lease

ABC were still promoting their spread of seaside cinemas in August 1952: this poster could be seen at the Ritz Hereford.

on the Shaftesbury Leeds expired and it went to Star. Later in 1958, the Electra Oxford, Rex Tilehurst, Empress Urmston, Super Gravesend and Picture House Old Trafford were sold, and the lease on the Kingsway Hadleigh expired. Most of these were obviously surplus and outmoded theatres. There were more significant temporary closures in the London area around this time of the Capitol Winchmore Hill, Savoy Wandsworth, Dominion Walthamstow and Savoy Teddington: these are discussed later.

The decade ended with the sale of La Scala Motherwell and the Capitol Barking, and the closure of the architecturally distinctive Rota Denton as well as the Pavilion Barrow and two Hull cinemas, the Rex and Regis, which had opened days apart in 1935 with an identical design and which now closed in tandem. The lease ran out and was not renewed on the Prince of Wales Lewisham (it was well-regarded locally and did "fabulous" farewell business in its last few weeks after closure was announced). Fire claimed the Empire Clydebank but ABC took over La Scala two months later. The new ABC at Preston finally opened with *The Reluctant Debutante* and a personal appearance by Richard Todd.

ABC Film Review

ABC launched a monthly film magazine, *ABC Film Review*, at Christmas 1950 with the January 1951 issue, price four (old) pence (it had been started a year earlier as *Film Review* by Associated British-Pathe.) With a vivid colour cover, this promoted the new circuit releases and gave particular emphasis to new players under contract to Associated British and films in production at Elstree studios. It was attractively laid out and had crossword puzzles, competitions, record reviews, horoscopes and other standard magazine features.

Vigorously pushed by staff, *ABC Film Review* went on to achieve a print run of over 400,000 copies with a net sale of over 300,000 a month and a readership of one million per issue, more than any other film journal. (Former editor Norman Taylor recalls that the highest sale of any individual issue was one featuring a colour plate of the Beatles which sold 420,000 copies.) It was hard to enter an ABC cinema without being directly offered a copy. The magazine was not sold anywhere else and its profits went into the ABC Benevolent Fund, which had been instituted in 1945 to provide assistance for employees, past employees and their dependents in need. The fund had originally been supported by the one penny charge for a monthly programme listing the attractions at each ABC house (smaller cinemas had smaller programmes). More basic free programmes were now issued, giving films and starting times.*

Screen advertising

In February 1952, faced with declining attendances and ice-cream sales (after sweet rationing ended), ABC reversed its long-standing opposition to screen advertising which had become a useful source of revenue to most other cinemas (including the Rank circuits), and appointed Pearl and Dean as contractors for the circuit. The first adverts were screened three months later and these became a feature of each ABC programme, shown after the supporting feature but before the Pathe newsreel, trailers and main feature. Early advertising included slides for local businesses and was mostly in black-and-white but this was soon all on film and usually in colour.

Booking changes

ABC began the decade following the standard industry policy of showing old films on Sundays (when a percentage was levied for charity) and opening the week's circuit release on the Monday for a six day run. A few London theatres had been holding the programme for an extra day, the following Sunday, but now others were beginning to open the week's programme a day earlier, on the preceding Sunday.

There were still some cinemas not permitted to open on Sunday. In Scotland, most opened only one Sunday in four, as was the custom, although the Regal Coatbridge opened every Sunday. For England and Wales, it was ABC's goal to have every cinema operating on the Sabbath and the company's head of public relations, Sydney Lewis, had been given this as one of his primary tasks in 1946. After some 151 campaigns, which usually required organising and winning a local referendum, Lewis finally achieved his goal in January 1959 when a

*ABC Film Review became simply *Film Review* with its May 1972 issue and covered all the new releases so that it could be sold in shops and at other cinemas. The magazine was sold after Cannon acquired ABC and is still being published in 1993.

large majority voted in favour of the Ritz Penzance opening on Sundays. This merely left Lewis with the task of gaining reductions in the Sunday charity contribution, in which he was often successful as the industry's financial problems were widely known.

The 1952 re-release of *Gone with the Wind* was booked into cinemas on Sunday where possible and in 1954 *The High and the Mighty*, a John Wayne flying drama in CinemaScope, was shown throughout the circuit from Sunday for seven days where allowed. This gradually became the standard policy, as it did at cinemas generally.

ABC remained generally resistant to extended runs or increased prices at its suburban houses, refusing to make an exception for special attractions like *Guys and Dolls* on London release.

In response to dwindling attendances in the United States, Hollywood began making more films in colour. For the ABC circuit, this meant fewer films in Technicolor as Warner Bros. introduced its WarnerColor process and MGM came up with shortlived AnscoColor and then Metrocolor. The range of subject matter also broadened and the X certificate was introduced in 1951 so that films unsuitable for children could be shown to audiences of over-16s only.

In the London area at least, the main ABC circuit was very inflexible compared to Odeons and Gaumonts where programmes sometimes switched between circuits and supporting features often varied. A week of French films (changed daily) at the Rex Norbury and of the Associated British-Pathe release, *The House on Haunted Hill* (with "Emergo", a gimmick involving a skeleton on a wire), at the Regal Brixton were very exceptional deviations for those theatres. Only on two occasions did ABC's bookers fully address the problem that many films were too sophisticated to do well in what were known as "poor class localities". *The Tales of Hoffman* and *Julius Caesar* played in most situations but were excused some rougher neighbourhoods where audiences were presented with *Highway 301* and *The Moon Is Blue* (a notorious X-certificate sex comedy) instead. In the case of the big-budget Marlon Brando version of *Julius Caesar*, the distributors, MGM, fought tooth and nail to keep as many ABC cinemas as possible, insisting that it play in such places as the Edgware Road, Kensal Rise and Kentish Town in North London, leav-

ing head office hoping that it could renegotiate terms if the picture did as badly as expected. One film performed so disastrously everywhere that it had to be almost totally withdrawn – this was the Laurence Olivier version of *The Beggar's Opera*. A later opera film, *Oh, Rosalinda!!*, was double-billed with an X-certificate gangster picture, *The Big Combo*, in an attempt to improve attendances.

CTA member John Gibson has usefully examined the way in which ABC releases (and those of Odeon and Gaumont) reached his area circa 1952: "ABC would often show films for two weeks at their Haymarket cinema in Newcastle, and sometimes for three weeks, although none of 1952's films played for more than two weeks. By contrast, Rank had a somewhat rigid booking policy. Films would first be shown in Newcastle where they would be screened strictly for one week only and then three weeks later would go into local Odeon and Gaumont cinemas. Programmes took much longer to reach local ABC cinemas, typically a couple of months rather than the three weeks of Rank. Also, instead of playing all cinemas in the same week, ABC would show films at different cinemas, apparently on a random basis, so that several more weeks would elapse while a film worked its way round the circuit. Presumably this had the effect of reducing the number of prints required. Rank soon abandoned their policy of showing every film for one week only, no matter how popular, but otherwise the differences between Rank and ABC persisted well into the Sixties."

The same B feature was booked to all ABC theatres showing a particular main feature: especially favoured were series of half-hour crime featurettes made by Anglo-Amalgamated and introduced for a while by Edgar Lustgarten (these were useful for British quota and for pairing with the longer features then being produced, but were equally designed for sale as television series abroad). Programmes also included, of course, Pathe News and the print was sometimes shared by two theatres as it had been (as an economy measure) in wartime. (It was bicycled between the Ritz Richmond and Regal Twickenham, not without incident as on one occasion the film came out of the can while the member of staff was crossing Richmond Bridge and had to be shown much the worse for wear. Another was taken from the Mayfair Tooting to the Ritz Balham for showing at the end of the pro-

The concluding titles of trailers at ABC cinemas circa 1952.
(Courtesy of Carl Chesworth.)

gramme there, causing some confusion among patrons on their way out from the last house when the News came on rather than the National Anthem. Some stood but hardly anyone bothered sitting down again to watch it.)

When 20th Century-Fox broke its ties with Rank's Odeon and Gaumont circuits after their refusal to install full stereophonic sound for Fox's new CinemaScope system, the American company established its own circuit based on Granada and Essoldo cinemas, hoping to add many ABC theatres. But ABC did not generally open its key theatres to Fox films in London, even when they were big hits, and booked them selectively into B circuit halls, others that had regularly taken independent releases, and to some extent at such main-circuit situations as the Luxor Eastbourne. In the London area, Fox CinemaScope films were to be found at such B circuit cinemas as the Ritz Balham, State Barkingside, Regal Hammersmith, Empire Islington, Langham Pinner and Super Stamford Hill, and were useful for slotting in at the Rex Tilehurst and others of its large Reading group as well as at the off-circuit Regal Norris Green, Liverpool. But ABC's support of Fox's breakaway was lukewarm, and never included the full stereophonic sound installations that were part of the original CinemaScope package and the cause of its rupture with Rank.

When in 1958 Rank re-organised its Odeon and Gaumont circuits to create two new groupings, the Rank circuit of top cinemas from both the old circuits and the National circuit of the remainder, Rank hoped that fifty-three ABC houses could be included among the latter. ABC refused to commit itself to supporting the National circuit. Most of its theatres that couldn't play the ABC circuit release were being closed and by the autumn of 1962 it had only ten that could not obtain the ABC or Rank release.

The X certificate

The heads of Rank were very reluctant to show X films on the Odeon and Gaumont circuits because they barred the family audience and could disrupt a weekly habit of visiting a particular cinema. ABC initially shared these fears. But in 1952, the company gave a full main circuit release to two X films from one of its regular suppliers, Warner Bros.: the Humphrey Bogart drama *Murder Inc.* and the sensational *A*

CENTRAL
READING 3931

Monday, March 17th, for six days
Doors Open 1.40   Last Perf. 7.10

Anna NEAGLE - Anthony QUAYLE
Zsa Zsa GABOR

THE MAN WHO WOULDN'T TALK
2.10 5.25 8.45   (U)

Robert Armstrong
THE CROOKED CIRCLE
(Naturama) 3.50 7.10

Circle 7.10

Sun., March 16th. Doors Open 4 p.m.
Rod Cameron - Faith Domergue:
Santa Fe Passage (Trucolor) (U) 5.35
8.25. Dennis O'Keefe - Coleen Gray:
Las Vegas Shakedown (A) 4.20 7.05

REX · READING 67293

Monday, March 17th, for six days
Doors Open 1.15   Last Perf. 6.55

PAT BOONE - SHIRLEY JONES

APRIL LOVE
(CinemaScope)   (Eastman Colour)
1.35 5.05 8.35   (U)

James Craig - Audrey Totter
GHOST DIVER
(RegalScope)   3.30 7.00   (U)

An All-"U" Programme

Stalls 2/-, 3/-. Circle 3/9

Sun., March 16th. Last Perf. 7.00.
Scott Brady - Rita Gam: **Mohawk**
(U) (Eastman Colour)   5.35 8.25.
Rod Cameron - Julie London: **The
Fighting Chance** (U) 4.15 7.05

GRANBY READING 61465

Sun., March 16th. Doors Open 4.00.
Mohawk (U) (Eastman Colour) Scott
Brady - Rita Gam. 5.35 8.25. **The
Fighting Chance** (U) Rod Cameron -
Julie London. 4.10 7.00.

Monday, March 17th, for six days
Doors Open 1.05   Last Perf. 6.50

PAT BOONE - SHIRLEY JONES

APRIL LOVE

(Eastman Colour)   (CinemaScope)
1.40 5.10 8.40   (U)

James Craig - Audrey Totter
GHOST DIVER
(RegalScope)   3.30 7.00   (U)

REGAL
CAVERSHAM Tel. 72150

Monday, March 17th, for three days
Open Mon. 1.00.   Last Prog. 6.45
Open Tues., Wed. 4.40.   L.P. 6.40
Peter Finch - Mary Ure
WINDOM'S WAY
(Eastman Colour)
Mon. 1.25 4.55 8.25 (U)
Tues., Wed. 4.55 8.25
Griffith Jones - Honor Blackman
ACCOUNT RENDERED
Mon. 3.15 6.45 (A) Tues., Wed. 6.45

Thurs., March 20th, for three days
Open Thurs., Sat. 12.50.   L.P. 6.30
Open Fri. 4.15.   Last Prog. 6.25
Jane Powell - Cliff Robertson
THE GIRL MOST LIKELY
(RadioScope)   (Technicolor)
Thurs., Sat. 1.05 4.50 8.40 (U)
Friday 4.50 8.35
Anton Walbrook - Sally Gray
DANGEROUS MOONLIGHT
Thurs., Sat. 2.45 6.30 (U) Fri. 6.30

Sun., March 16th.—**The Eternal Sea**
(U).   **Cats Claw Mystery** (A).

SAVOY
READING 81381

Sun., Mar. 16th.—**The Eternal Sea**
(U).   **Cats Claw Mystery** (A)

Monday, March 17th, for three days
Open Mon. 1.45.   Last Perf. 7.10
Open Tues., Wed. 5.00.   L.P. 7.15
Barbara Shelley - Robert Ayres
THE CAT GIRL
Mon. 2.40 5.55 9.10   (X)
Tues., Wed. 5.55 9.10
Peter Graves - Beverly Garland
IT CONQUERED THE WORLD
Mon. 4.00 7.15 (X) Tue., Wed. 7.15
No person under sixteen admitted

Thurs., March 20th, for three days
Open Thurs., Sat. 12.45.   L.P. 6.45
Open Friday 4.30.   Last Perf. 6.45
Stewart Granger - Rhonda Fleming
GUN GLORY
(CinemaScope)   (MetroColor)
Thurs., Sat. 1.30 5.15 9.05   (U)
Friday 5.15 9.05
Robert Taylor - Dorothy Malone
TIME FOR ACTION
(CinemaScope)
Thurs., Sat. 3.05 6.50 (A) Fri. 6.50

*In the Reading group of ABC
cinemas in March 1958, the
main circuit house, the Central,
plays the circuit release as
always. The Granby and Rex are
showing a fourth or Fox circuit
attraction. The Savoy and Regal
are second-run cinemas playing
split weeks. Reading had Odeon
and Gaumont cinemas taking the
other two main releases.*

What's On AT YOUR ABC THEATRE

RITZ OXFORD 4607

TODAY:
All "U" Programme

HIGH JINKS IN HIGH SOCIETY!

M-G-M presents
REX HARRISON ·· KAY KENDALL

The Reluctant Debutante
JOHN SAXON
SANDRA DEE
ANGELA LANSBURY
In CinemaScope and METROCOLOR · AN AVON PRODUCTION
An M-G-M Release · Cert. U

DAN DAILEY   CLAIRE KELLY
UNDERWATER WARRIOR

Doors Open 12.55	L.C.P. 6.35	Reluctant Deb. 1.20 : 5.00 : 8.35	Underwater Warrior 3.00 : 6.40

REGAL OXFORD 4234

Tues. and Thurs. Nights are
"LATE SHOW" Nights
Programmes Start Later—
End Later (11 p.m. approx.)

TODAY: Cont. 1.35 (Tues. & Thurs. 2.20)

HOWARD KEEL   ANNE HEYWOOD   CYRIL CUSACK

FLOODS OF FEAR
1.55, 5.15, 8.35 (Tues. & Thurs. 2.40, 6.00, 9.20)   (A)

BRIAN REECE   MARGOT GRAHAME   SIDNEY JAMES
ORDERS ARE ORDERS
3.30, 6.50 (Tues. & Thurs. 4.15, 7.35)   (U)
Last Complete Programme 6.50 (Tues. & Thurs. 7.35)

SUPER OXFORD 3067

TODAY:
Cont. from 1.30
Last House 6.50

LOVE AND LAUGHTER ON A
VIRGIN ISLAND
JOHN CASSAVETES VIRGINIA MASKELL SIDNEY POITIER
In Eastman Colour   (U)   1.35, 5.00, 8.30

JACK HAWKINS   GEORGE COLE
DENNIS PRICE   MICHAEL MEDWIN
THE INTRUDER
3.20, 6.50   (U)

REGAL ABINGDON 322

TODAY:
Cont. from 1.0

Elvis Presley Dean Jagger **KING CREOLE** 1.00, 4.35, 8.20 (A)
Ferlin Husky, Rocky Graziano and Guest Star Zsa Zsa Gabor
2.55, 6.35   **COUNTRY MUSIC HOLIDAY**   (U)

*ABC had a monopoly on circuit releases in
Oxford and so played its choice of all the new
programmes. The major cinema, the Ritz, usually played the ABC release, as in this week of
January 1959. The Regal Abingdon played a
range of programmes weeks after their run in
Oxford. The Regal in Oxford is conducting an
experiment with a later evening performance
on two mid-week nights.*

Streeetcar Named Desire, both of which did much better business in big cities than elsewhere. In 1954, after a British film, *The Heart of the Matter*, drew dismal audiences on its first leg of London release, it was propped up with a tough new X certificate crime drama *The Big Heat*, one of the rare occasions when a Columbia picture was played in this period.

By 1956, partly in response to a shortage of product, ABC was screening a number of sensational, exploitable X films dispensing sex, horror and violence. The very few X certificate pictures Rank allowed onto its circuits were serious productions like *Desire Under the Elms* and *The Bachelor Party* and two anti-drug dramas, *The Man with the Golden Arm* and *Monkey on My Back*. Rank did eventually join the horror band wagon in 1958 by playing the new Hammer version of *Dracula* but many Hammer films distributed by Rank (on behalf of Universal) like *The Mummy* went to ABC, suggesting that it had developed the biggest audience for horror fare. While Columbia's major films were reserved for Rank, the most promising of its sensational or exploitable releases now played the ABC circuit – these included the notorious *The Camp on Blood Island* and other Hammer productions, the prison drama *Cell 2455, Death Row*, and several non-Hammer horror films, including the double-bill of *Night of the Demon* and *20 Million Miles to Earth*.

ABC's production arm delivered the X-certificate prison drama *Yield to the Night* with Diana Dors through Associated British-Pathe, which also distributed an adults-only British big-screen version of George Orwell's *1984* as well as the prison drama *Riot in Cell Block 11* and a stark crime exposé, *The Phenix City Story*, the last two from its link-up with Allied Artists (formerly Monogram) in Hollywood. From the circuit's principal Hollywood sources, MGM and Warner Bros., came many X films: the two juvenile delinquency dramas, *Blackboard Jungle* and *Rebel Without a Cause*, the provocatively-advertised *Baby Doll, New York Confidential* (another crime exposé), *I'll Cry Tomorrow* (a study of show-biz alcoholism) and *Something of Value* (an African terrorist drama).

ABC would have been under considerable pressure to show the MGM and Warner Bros. X films in any case, but the clearest demonstration of its enthusiasm for adults-only fare is shown by its releasing of product from foreign film distributors like Miracle. Highly-praised features like *Rififi* and *The Fiends* and the lurid Brigitte Bardot picture *And Woman...Was Created* were shown in subtitled or dubbed versions, double-billed with British horror films.

3-D and CinemaScope

Hollywood launched first 3-D and then CinemaScope and other wide screen systems to regain audiences. ABC showed considerable enthusiasm for 3-D, which was largely ignored by Rank and Granada. The success of 3-D shorts at the Festival of Britain's Telekinema revealed a keen interest in stereoscopic films, which was confirmed when ABC experimented with programming the same shorts at the Victoria Cambridge and Bristol Birmingham, and with spot bookings of early 3-D features like Columbia's *Fort Ti*. Despite the amazing West End success of Warner Bros.' X-certificate horror film *House of Wax*, it did not have a full ABC circuit release but largely played the 'B' circuit, achieving a four-week run at the Astoria Brighton.

In 1954, it was decided to equip the majority of the circuit's theatres to show films in 3-D, using synchronised projectors with 40-minute spools to show the two images required simultaneously on the screen, necessitating an interval in mid-film to reload the projectors. The Ross D arcs and the later Ross 'Streemlites' in most of the projection boxes were replaced by Peerless Magnarcs which could accommodate larger carbons. In addition, filters were placed in front of each lens with blowers. Staff had to man each machine and leave was often cancelled during weeks of 3-D. It was not possible to equip all theatres (the circular auditorium of the Elite Middlesbrough would not provide a satisfactory picture from the edges).

A full circuit release was given to *The Charge at Feather River, Kiss Me Kate, Phantom of the Rue Morgue* and the John Wayne western *Hondo* with most ABCs showing them in 3-D and the others showing them "flat".

This was also the era of the panoramic wide-screen and CinemaScope. Wide screens were installed faster than the necessary new projection lenses could be obtained. Cinemas trumpeted their panoramic and 'scope installations and ABC were frustrated when, through the shortage of new lens, it had to keep on showing films for several weeks in the old, small 'Academy ratio' in the centre of new 'scope screens at

3-D and CinemaScope films on ABC circuit release in 1954 and 1955 at ABC and other cinemas. 3-D is downplayed in group advertising because of the many cinemas showing the film "flat". In the ad for A Star Is Born, Peterborough has miraculously become part of N. & W. London.

the Ritz Aldershot, Ritz Leyton and elsewhere while rival cinemas were siphoning off audiences with their giant images. At Leyton, ABC eventually installed Dutch Del-rama mirror-type anamorphic lenses for CinemaScope – these were never very satisfactory, giving warped images (bending verticals) at the ends of the screen.

The first CinemaScope films to play the circuit were Warners' *The Command*, *Lucky Me* and *The High and the Mighty* and MGM's British-made *Knights of the Round Table*. ABC generally installed a system whereby the screen had a standard height and the masking simply moved outwards to show CinemaScope pictures, but in many theatres there was insufficient width to fit a suitably sized CinemaScope screen. One solution was to demolish the sides of the proscenium arch to create more room, as happened at the Metropole Sherwood (Nottingham). Another was to erect the screen in front of the old proscenium arch with new curtains. However, in some cinemas, exits right alongside an old screen in a narrow proscenium arch had to be kept and the unsatisfactory solution was to lower the masking on the standard screen so that CinemaScope pictures were smaller than the rest of the programme. In the projection room, recalls Alan Ashton, "When CinemaScope came, the Peerless arcs were more generally installed in order to cope with the increased coverage in screen area." The CinemaScope installation at the Lonsdale Carlisle was regarded as unsatisfactory while a miscalculation at the Globe Stockton resulted in too large a screen being installed so that it couldn't be fully seen from many seats, presumably in the rear stalls area.

It was usually necessary to remove the first few rows of stalls seating as patrons needed to be further back to take in the whole of the wide screen, which was also often set further forward so that the ends could be seen. (A cartoon in *Picturegoer* showed a husband and wife watching different ends of the screen and reporting what they saw to each other.)

Like Rank, ABC rejected full stereophonic sound on cost grounds, but it welcomed the Perspecta "stereophonic" sound system developed by MGM and first heard in this country at its West End showplace, the Empire: this had one optical track with three speakers behind the screen and no auditorium speakers. ABC installed it first at the new Regal Aberdeen and subsequently at more important theatres.

Off-circuit

As previously indicated, ABC had more than one cinema in many localities and the secondary cinemas, unless they were able to programme the Odeon or Gaumont release, had to play off-circuit programmes.

ABC theatres that usually played the Odeon release in the London area included the Regal Walham Green, Regal Hammersmith, Royalty North Kensington and Super Stamford Hill. The Gaumont release normally appeared at the Prince of Wales Harrow Road and Regal Sidcup. (In turn, there were surplus Odeon and Gaumont theatres such as La Bohemia Finchley and the Tower Peckham that took the ABC release.)

These cinemas were useful barometers of the opposition's strength (or weakness: after a bad year of Gaumont releases, the manager of the Regal Sidcup pleaded to be given the ABC programme) and they had an advantage in being able to duck the weakest programmes but, as they were irrelevant to the strength of the main circuit, they were prone to disposal. Other theatres like the Ritz Balham and Regal Purley were in the useful position of taking the ABC release when it was strong and playing off-circuit when its appeal was dubious.

The most awkward theatres were those unable to play any of the three principal circuit releases but this drawback could be overcome to a degree by imaginative booking, especially for cinemas in big towns like Birmingham, Brighton, Chatham and Luton. *House of Wax* was a lucrative opportunity, mentioned earlier. The Bristol Birmingham, which had switched from second-run to off-circuit first run in January 1949, held the European premiere of Columbia's *Rainbow Round My Shoulder* on 23 August 1952 at a time when the film's star, Frankie Laine ("Mr. Rhythm"), was having a huge success live at the London Palladium.

These city-centre cinemas could also be used for extended runs at increased prices, contrary to policy on the main circuit. MGM's epic *Quo Vadis* (which started out with the initial handicap of an X certificate, later reduced to an A) generally opened in independent cinemas but had its first booking outside London at the Astoria Brighton where it ran for four weeks from July 1952, six months after its West End debut. ABC's Elite Nottingham and Bristol Birmingham played it for three weeks and four weeks respectively in January 1953. It

'B' circuit cinemas of the ABC chain are prominent among those playing these off-circuit releases of 1956. Off-circuit Odeon and Gaumont cinemas are conspicuous by their absence.

then had a release on the main ABC circuit at normal prices late in 1953.

ABPC's distribution arm, Associated British-Pathe, handled more films that could be accommodated on the main circuit, especially the output of Monogram/Allied Artists. Most of this Hollywood studio's pictures were B features or tacky A ones but its better offerings, like its Joel McCrea westerns in CinemaScope and colour, played the main circuit. Some of its releases were double-billed and booked to ABC's 'B' circuit cinemas, often enjoying more popularity than the main release. Typical off-circuit programmes were *Flight to Mars* with the Bowery Boys comedy *Ghost Chasers* and *Aladdin and His Lamp* plus the Bowery Boys' *Feudin' Fools*, released to catch children and family audiences in holiday periods in 1952, or the X-certificate *Invasion of the Body Snatchers* in 1956. Towards the end of the decade, AB-Pathe merged with Warner Bros. as a cost-saving measure to trade as Warner-Pathe.

Television

BBC Television dealt the film industry a blow, especially with its live coverage of the Coronation in 1953 which encouraged millions to obtain their own sets. At one time, it had been thought that cinemas could take advantage of the new medium by offering television transmissions on a large screen (and many did present the Coronation). The Commodore Hammersmith installed large-screen television at the end of March 1953 to show the Boat Race which, of course, was happening very close by on the Thames. Various events like major boxing matches would be shown on closed-circuit television as at Holloway's ABC theatre among others but television's occasional benefits were far outweighed by the damage it inflicted on attendances generally.

The arrival of ITV on 1 September 1955 was a major setback to the cinema industry. Not only did it enormously strengthen television as a counter attraction by providing a less stodgy alternative to the BBC but it enabled the major circuit owners to obtain a financial stake in commercial television, which pre-occupied them and eventually made them less dependent on the cinema side. When ABPC won the Midlands and North ITV licence for weekends, it feared heavy losses in the beginning and created a contingency fund by selling the central Manchester site on which it had been intending

at last to build a new cinema in Oxford Road. The money was never needed. On top of that, the Astoria Aston and Capitol Didsbury were closed to become studios for ABC Television Ltd., which began transmitting on 4 May 1956 (although, as previously indicated, neither cinema was of much value to the circuit). The Capitol, where attendances had been causing concern for some years, retained its circle to accommodate studio audiences.

Fighting ET

Many cinemas were losing money after paying Entertainments Tax and the film industry campaigned hard for a reduction or abolition, especially before each Budget time.

ABC went on the attack just before the 1958 Budget. Closing ten cinemas, it pointed out that two of them, the Dominion Walthamstow and Savoy Wandsworth, had become loss-makers in providing the government with £8,052 and £9,627 respectively in Entertainments Tax the previous year and they were now only used for wrestling one night a week, which was classed as a sport and not subject to the tax. Had the tax been reduced, they might still be open and providing the government with revenue. When the Highgate Palace had closed, it was decorated with big posters reading "Taxed out of existence!" In fact, the recent opening of a brand-new Odeon round the corner had made the shabby, ancient Palace unviable.*

A "crisis" message, seemingly prepared by Pathe News (it was narrated by the newsreel's regular commentator, Bob Danvers-Walker), was shown to cinema audiences, describing the plight of the film industry, citing the many cinemas in danger of closure, and declaring "These lights must not go out!" However, it occurred to some that this public anti-tax campaign and dramatisation of closures might be counter-productive, suggesting to the average person that cinemas had had their day and film-going was no longer a fashionable pastime.

The film industry was granted £13 million of tax relief by the Chancellor and ABC announced that it would re-open the

---

* Tony Moss informs me that ABC owned a large piece of the land surrounding the Palace for rebuilding, possibly inherited from Union – but this option was clearly no longer of interest.

Savoy Wandsworth and two other closed cinemas, the Savoy Teddington and Capitol Winchmore Hill, as they could now be "operated economically provided the public supports them". The Dominion Walthamstow also re-opened following petitions and pressure from the local council. At the Savoy Wandsworth a policy of split-week bookings was tried, using only the stalls seating with no weekday matinees: the regular ABC release played half the week and reissue programmes the other half. The old films generally did the better business, while there were near riots when more sophisticated circuit releases like *Tea and Sympathy* played this working class area. The Savoy Teddington started well thanks to a bus strike which kept patrons from going to Kingston or Richmond but, in all these cases, the public did not rally round and the cinemas soon closed permanently, as the Ritz Gloucester would later after being given a similar reprieve.

ABC also embarked on another campaign to improve attendances. This was based on the slogan "Don't Take Your Wife for Granted – Take Her Out to the Pictures." ABC encouraged other cinemas to adopt the line, although the rival circuits declined to take it up and share the costs.

New look/new name

ABC was confident enough about its more profitable theatres to embark on substantial modernisation schemes. It also decided to phase out the triangle trademark in favour of a new emblem and to drop the variety of theatre names by calling them ABC, thereby giving the circuit a stronger identity with the public. Other major circuits generally used a standard name, and it is possible that ABC had been deterred in the past from using its initials by a chain of ABC (Aerated Bread Company) teashops that had often been in the same High Streets as its Regals, Rexs and Savoys.

The first theatre to be renamed "ABC" was the Lido at Golders Green when it re-opened in October 1957 after four months of work costing £100,000, during which time the original faded semi-atmospheric auditorium scheme was discarded in favour of a more modern look. Outside, the classical columns and Egyptian motifs disappeared in favour of bland, plain surfaces. These "improvements" included a new style of canopy later nicknamed an "icebox" and lit from with-

The Lido Golders Green, North London, before modernisation in 1957 and afterwards in 1960. This was the first cinema to become known simply as the ABC

in: this had the programmes mounted twice in lettering on two sides that sloped back in a shallow V shape rather than having a wide straight front. (In later years, staff at some theatres were not always too diligent in putting up the programme information twice.) The ABC triangle motif was retained on the flattened apex of the canopy

ABC had been experimenting in press advertising with the style of lettering seen on the front cover of this book, while also retaining the old triangle sign alongside. However, it decided to have the letters of ABC spaced out in "lozenge" shapes and this was introduced in the press around April 1958. Unlike most companies which completely discard an old trademark in launching a new one, ABC kept both old and new emblems going for some time as a form of transition.

The company decided on the expensive step of slowly installing signs with the new emblem on the front of cinemas, very often at the same time as modernisation was carried out. The colourful triangle signs faced with red and blue neon with the theatre name in green were replaced by the ABC letters in sombre black on white, each encased in a lozenge-shaped fitting lit from within that was much easier to maintain than neon. A fourth, detached fitting carried a small reproduction of the old triangle.

Whereas the ABC triangle sign had usually been fitted centrally, high up on the facade, the new emblem was often fitted vertically to one side, throwing the facade off balance and leaving an ugly blank space where the triangle sign and original name had once been. Only in a few cases – such as the Regal Uxbridge and Beau Nash Bath – did the conditions of a lease prevent the name being altered, although a more modern sign was still introduced.

The introduction of the new name was spread over more than ten years and many cinemas closed without making the change-over. Some highly distinctive appellations like Rembrandt and Toledo were lost in the process – but while the Toledo name had reflected the theme of the interior decoration at Muirend, there was little in the treatment of the Ewell theatre other than a reproduction painting in the foyer to warrant its original Rembrandt name. (Curiously, the Rembrandt did feature a decorative bas-relief panel of two figures that also appeared at the Royal Plymouth, opened three months earlier.)

SAVOY EXETER 75274 MONDAY, APRIL 21st, for 6 days Open 12.20. Last programme 7.05
ELVIS PRESLEY "JAILHOUSE ROCK" (A)
CinemaScope — 2.10, 5.30, 8.50
Edward Binns, Virginia Gregg, "PORTLAND EXPOSE" (A) — 12.35, 3.50, 7.10
SUNDAY, APRIL 20th, for 1 day Doors open 4.30
— ON THE STAGE instead of the usual film show —
WINIFRED ATWELL and THE ERIC DELANEY BAND — 5.15, 7.45

ABC REGAL GLOUCESTER PHONE 22399
ALL THIS WEEK (except Thursday)
CURT JURGENS   DOROTHY DANDRIDGE
TAMANGO
CinemaScope, Technicolor (A) At 2.0 - 5.20 - 8.35
Randolph Scott "COMANCHE STATION" (U) Tech.
CinemaScope. Showing at 3.45 - 7.0

THURSDAY, 11th FEB. — FOR ONE DAY at 6.15 & 8.30
ON THE STAGE
LONNIE DONEGAN
WITH FULL SUPPORTING VARIETY BILL

BOOK NOW   Prices: 7/6, 5/6, 4/6, 3/6. Plenty of Seats for 6.15 Performance.

Live shows are part of the fare for one day of these particular weeks at the Savoy Exeter (in April 1958) and the Regal Gloucester (in February 1960).

Live shows

Another response to the decline in cinema-going was the increasing use of large ABC cinemas for one-day live shows. Before now, distributors would not have permitted their prints to lay idle during the week's run of their films but times were indisputably changing.

Summer shows had long been established at the Hippodrome Blackpool and Regal Great Yarmouth. The Globe Stockton was put to heavy live use as a regular touring date for variety and theatrical presentations, artists that played the theatre in the period 1956-60 including Lonnie Donegan, Benny Hill, Tony Hancock, David Whitfield, Al Read, Max Bygraves, Norman Wisdom, Russ Conway and Bruce Forsyth. Less successful was a season of variety tried out from October 1954 at the Regal Kingston-on-Thames.

Television was occasionally turned to advantage. At the Commodore Hammersmith, a hit TV show *Oh Boy!* was mounted on the stage for two performances on Sunday 25 January 1959 with Cliff Richard as the star. A version of TV's *The Army Game* was the highly successful summer show at the Hippodrome Blackpool in 1960. However, television's greater usefulness was in permitting feature film versions ("spin-offs") of its hit shows.

Todd-AO

Through Pathe Equipment, a number of theatres were equipped with Todd-AO projectors and big screens for showing films in 70mm as well as 35mm. The first to be fitted out in this way was the Astoria Brighton, which was internally reconstructed and gained a new lease of life in 1958 when it re-opened with separate performances at advanced prices of *South Pacific*, concurrent with London's West End, for a run that lasted over a year. For several years the Astoria remained the only cinema in Sussex able to show 70mm films and it had the pick of new attractions released in the format, including films like *Spartacus* and *El Cid* that were distributed by Rank and would normally have gone into that company's Odeon and Gaumont theatres. (Rank was therefore compelled to make substantial alterations to the Regent Brighton in order to have its own 70mm outlet.)

The huge success of *South Pacific* at the Astoria and other non-ABC venues led to various ABC theatres being converted to 70mm presentations. These included the newly acquired Capitol Dundee, the Ritz Belfast, Adelphi Dublin, Forum Southampton, Savoy Leicester, Ritz Oxford, Regal Hull, ABC Bristol Road Birmingham, ABC Nottingham, ABC Leeds, Regal Edinburgh, Whiteladies Bristol, ABC (Regal) Glasgow and Olympia Cardiff. This dented the earnings of many conventional circuit releases that were denied playing time in these key theatres. The Futurist Liverpool and Deansgate Manchester were specifically acquired by ABC in 1960 for 70mm roadshow use.

In the summer of 1959, while the Astoria Brighton was engaged with an extended run of *Gigi* (not in 70mm) along with the Elite Nottingham, *South Pacific* had moved into the Regal Hull, Savoy Leicester, Ritz Oxford and Forum Southampton in place of the regular circuit release, although Rank had by that time outfitted its own theatres to obtain the film in most of the bigger provincial centres. While the roadshow system lasted, it was the salvation of the large off-circuit houses like the Astoria Brighton and Bristol Birmingham, which the shortage of product had made increasingly difficult to programme.

The cinema organ

Tony Moss comments: "During the War most of the organists were called up but in 1946 one hundred organists were on the ABC payroll which meant that virtually every organ had a resident organist. From 1947, drastic cuts were made in the number of organists."

ABC were reported in November 1947 to have discharged forty-four organists, keeping forty on. However, the organ was re-introduced at the Elephant and Castle Theatre on 6 June 1949 with Rae Victor at the console after it had been "recently remodelled at great expense".

Back to Tony Moss: "By 1953, only fifteen of the one hundred were still employed, plus Peter Kilby (based at the Regal Torquay) and Tony Fenton (Regal Walton-on-Thames). Of the original one hundred, Joseph Seal had come over to be the new Musical Director and the other fifteen remaining were Molly Forbes (Putney), Arthur Lord (Woking and Aldershot), Harold Nash (Northampton), Reginald New (Beckenham), Hubert Selby (Ipswich, later Chatham), Rae Victor (Mitcham), Stanley Wyllie (Belfast), Clifford Birchall

(Kingston), Albert Brierley (Ardwick), Gilbert Handy (Edgware), Austin Raynor (Lancaster), Harry Speed (Stockport), Joseph Storer (Chester), Harold Stringer (Exeter) and Trevor Willetts (Barnsley). Wyllie, Stringer and Kilby were virtually resident at their respective theatres but the others toured from their base theatres. When touring, a solo interlude was always performed unless they were accompanying variety (e.g. amateur talent), but when at base they normally played only during the sales intervals.

"In 1953, the first Hammond electronic organ was purchased for touring, ostensibly to theatres without pipe organs, and Hubert Selby was appointed to accompany it. Two more were later purchased. In the early Fifties, some of the organs were thinned out and in 1956 a drastic cut was made, reducing the team of organists to just seven, i.e. Arthur Lord, Hubert Selby, Stanley Wyllie, Clifford Birchall, Peter Kilby, Albert Brierley and Trevor Willetts. New cinemas opening in the Fifties and Sixties always had a Hammond for at least the first week, with Hubert Selby and later Clifford Birchall. Some organists were also allocated to theatres showing 3-D, e.g. Tony Fenton with *House of Wax* on separate performances at the Ritz Luton."

The organ also made a comeback as Entertainments Tax could be avoided if one third of a programme was live and advertised. Tony Moss notes: "Organs were brought back into use from 1959 to 1960 for preludes to long-run films such as *South Pacific, The Nun's Story, Gigi, Oklahoma!* and *Can-Can.* Twenty-five additional organists were taken on between mid-1959 and the end of 1960, including well-known names like John Howlett, Bobby Pagan, Robinson Cleaver, John Mann, Terance Casey, Doreen Chadwick, Florence de Jong, and a return of Joseph Storer, Molly Forbes, Dudley Savage, Hubert Selby and Harold Nash. Todd-AO was installed at the Ritz Belfast for *The Nun's Story* and the prelude was given as a duo by Stanley Wyllie at the Compton and Clifford Birchall at a grand piano. However, the Compton was removed from the Astoria Brighton to make way for Todd-AO."

9 | The Slimmer Sixties

Having been introduced as a temporary war measure in 1916, Entertainments Tax on cinemas was finally abolished on 10 April 1960. It had become obvious even to politicians that the cinema was in a desperate state. Attendances had declined from 1,396 million nationally in 1950 to 515 million in 1960, and they would continue their dramatic plunge to 193 million in 1970 with even worse to follow. During the Sixties, ABC's cinemas dropped in number by one third, from 339 to 229. Among earlier closures were two of the last to be opened during the War, the Ritz Winchester and the Regal Twickenham. Soon demolished, the Regal closed a few weeks short of its twenty-first anniversary. The Ritz has now spent more years as a bingo hall than it did as a picture house. While many cinemas would be demolished for supermarkets and other buildings, most would be converted, at least initially, to other leisure uses.

Tenpin bowling

In the late Fifties, both ABC and Rank had become excited at the prospect of converting under-performing cinemas to more profitable use as ten-pin bowling alleys. ABC allied itself with a leading American company, AMF, while Rank took up with Brunswick. It was AMF that opened the first bowl in Britain on 20 January 1960 at the former Super Stamford Hill, which had a long, single-level auditorium ideal for conversion. Initial results were encouraging and ABC decided to convert another single-floor auditorium at the Princess Dagenham, ending films there in April 1960. It re-opened with bowling on 24 lanes on two levels, using AMF pin re-setting equipment leased on a royalty basis. A new company, ABC Bowling, was formed to run the bowls. Conversions costing in the region of £300,000 totally gutted the interiors of the cinemas, leaving no trace of the original decoration. Various film stars were recruited to lend glamour to the openings: most were under contract to ABPC and compelled to encourage a rival form of entertainment.

Further ABC cinemas lost to this mechanised form of skittles were the Pavilion Wylde Green, Sutton Coldfield; Rex Leytonstone, North London; Regal Levenshulme, Manchester; Regal Litherland, Liverpool (another single-floor cinema); Savoy Acton, Northwest London; and Embassy North Harrow, North London. In the case of the Embassy, the building was completely demolished and a new one built incorporating a supermarket at ground floor level with a bowling alley above. In order to establish bowling in Aberdeen without losing its Regal cinema, ABC acquired the vast City cinema from the Donald circuit on a 35-year lease, closing it in July 1963 to provide two floors of bowling alleys which were inaugurated in May 1964. In Glasgow, ABC originally planned to convert the Toledo Muirend in late 1960 but this charming theatre was happily spared. In Manchester, the Casino Rusholme had been considered after a major fire in October 1960 but the Regal Levenshulme was chosen instead.

At Bexleyheath and Stirchley (Birmingham), adjacent car park space was used to build bowling alleys alongside cinemas. At Hanley, ABC built a new cinema on top of a new bowling alley and opened the pair as the ABC Cine-Bowl in 1963. Schemes for new Cine-Bowls at Blackpool and Coventry were later revised to become cinemas only.

After a few good years, bowling alleys proved to be very largely a passing fad and most had to be closed. The diversification added up to a very expensive miscalculation. While the Hanley bowl closed on 24 June 1972, the cinema is still operating more than twenty years later.

The Rex Leytonstone (seen with wartime grime in 1947) has been smartened up externally after converson to ABC Bowling in 1961.

Bingo

Far more enduring and less expensive to install as an alternative use for cinemas was the craze for bingo that exploded in the early Sixties when it became "eyes down" on the score card rather than eyes up on the screen. While Rank and Granada enthusiastically explored the possibilities, the board of ABPC were somewhat reluctant to become deeply involved in a form of gambling.

The long troublesome Dominion Walthamstow was the first ABC to close specifically for bingo in March 1961, reopening as the Alpha Bingo Club (a name which discreetly kept the ABC initials). It was followed two months later by the Majestic Benwell, Picture House Govanhill and George Kilmarnock. More substantial theatres like the Granada Dovecot, Majestic Mitcham and Ritz Bexhill succumbed before the year's end. Bingo was also introduced on Sunday afternoons at some cinemas but did not last. And not all of ABC's conversions took: the New Royal Openshaw returned to films after five months and carried on happily as a cinema until hit by a Compulsory Purchase Order.

Many more cinemas had gone to full-time bingo operation by ABC or other companies before the somewhat shocking switch of one of the circuit's former flagships, the Commodore Hammersmith, in June 1963. As the largest of the circuit's three cinemas in Hammersmith, it had been the ABC release outlet but its position well out of the main centre and its huge size made it vulnerable and ABC was able to transfer its circuit programme to the more modern and better located Regal. (At one time, ABC had frequently played its weekly circuit programme at both the Commodore and its most central Hammersmith theatre, the Broadway, thereby maximising returns.)

In contrast to the changes wrought by bowling, bingo preserved the interiors of buildings to a large degree, although garish colour schemes were introduced, stalls floors were stepped in level sections for tables, auditoria were flooded with direct light destroying the original schemes of illumination and, as the years have passed, more severe structural alterations have occurred.

Film supply

By the start of the Sixties, ABC was struggling to find enough

GREAT ENTERTAINMENT FROM
UNIVERSAL-INTERNATIONAL

SHOCK... SHOCK... SHOCK!!!

PETER
CUSHING

DAVID
KNIGHT · MOIRA REDMOND
JENNIE LINDEN
AND BRENDA BRUCE

THE EVIL OF FRANKENSTEIN
EASTMAN COLOUR — X

PETER WOODTHORPE · DUNCAN LAMONT
Produced by ANTHONY HINDS
A HAMMER FILM PRODUCTION FOR UNIVERSAL INTERNATIONAL

NIGHTMARE
SCOPE — X

JIMMY SANGSTER
FREDDIE FRANCIS

NOW SOUTH LONDON at ABC & OTHER LEADING THEATRES

BALHAM Ritz	CRYSTAL PALACE	KINGSTON A.B.C.	UXBRIDGE Regal
BECKENHAM A.B.C.	Granada	LEWISHAM Rex	WALTON-on-THAMES A.B.C.
BEXLEYHEATH A.B.C.	DEPTFORD Odeon	OLD KENT ROAD A.B.C.	WOKING A.B.C.
BLACKHEATH A.B.C.	ELEPHANT & CASTLE	PECKHAM Odeon	WOOLWICH A.B.C.
BRIXTON A.B.C.	Theatre	PETTS WOOD Embassy	
BROMLEY Astor	ELSTREE Studio	PUTNEY A.B.C.	ALSO SHOWING AT
CAMBERWELL A.B.C.	ELTHAM A.B.C.	REIGATE Majestic	BEDFORD Plaza
CATFORD A.B.C.	FOREST HILL Capitol	RICHMOND A.B.C.	CHELMSFORD Regent
CLAPHAM JUNCTION	GRAYS Ritz	RUISLIP Rivoli	
Century	HIGH WYCOMBE Rex	STREATHAM A.B.C.	THURSDAY NEXT
CROYDON A.B.C.	HOUNSLOW Regal	TOOTING A.B.C.	SOUTHEND A.B.C.

In 1964, Universal-International horror films, distributed by Rank, were still to be found playing the ABC circuit rather than Rank cinemas. The latter were showing the U certificate drama The Chalk Garden *(another U-I picture handled by Rank) in the same week as this double X bill.*

new films to play the main circuit. Full circuit revivals during 1961 of *East of Eden* with James Dean and Alfred Hitchcock's *Strangers on a Train* were evidence of the famine. (The 'B' circuit no longer existed, its cinemas having closed or gone over to roadshow presentations.)

The problem was not just that Warner Bros. and MGM, ABC's main sources of Hollywood product, were failing to deliver as many pictures as before, but they were also providing fewer sure-fire box-office hits. Furthermore, MGM had contracted to supply Rank's cinemas with some of its films under a "split arrangement" which resulted in such top-flight pictures as Alfred Hitchcock's *North by Northwest*, the Shirley MacLaine comedy *Ask Any Girl* and the Frank Sinatra war film *Never So Few* being played by the competition. ABC's advertising slogan – "The Pick of the Pictures" – could not have been more inappropriate (this had succeeded "This Week's Better Entertainment" in Spring 1958 and was replaced four years later by "The First Name in Entertainment", which was, at the very least, alphabetically accurate).

When MGM and Warner Bros. did make really big attractions like *Ben-Hur* and *My Fair Lady*, these were given long runs in city centre cinemas and had lost much of their drawing power by the time they reached the suburban and small-town cinemas that comprised the bulk of the circuit. It was not just the appeal of television that hurt cinemas – it was the lack of product, together with the reduced appeal on average of what was available, that caused audiences to abandon the big, well-run circuit cinemas. The drought had not only brought about the collapse of the fourth (or Fox) circuit but at the end of 1958 prompted the amalgamation of the best Odeons and Gaumonts into the previously mentioned Rank circuit with the remainder forming the core of an optimistically-named National circuit which rapidly foundered. The Rank circuit took the cream of the pictures available from the regular sources of supply to the former Odeon and Gaumont circuits – this gave it first choice of films not only from its distribution partner, Rank Film Distributors (handling Rank's British productions plus Universal's output), but from Columbia, Disney, Fox, Paramount, and United Artists. The Rank circuit had more good films than it could handle while ABC still depended on Warner Bros., MGM and its own productions. (There were some other smaller companies, as well as the traditionally independent British Lion, with films that could play any circuit, but they were of only limited help to ABC.)

The National circuit relied for its films principally on the distributors supplying the Rank circuit, but it offered nothing like the same earning potential as the Rank or ABC circuits. In Rank's original calculations, a strong National release would have been booked by fifty-three ABC houses but ABC disputed the attachment of any of its cinemas.

The inevitable realignment came in Spring 1961 when Paramount had a Technicolored Dean Martin/Shirley MacLaine comedy *All in a Night's Work* that was refused a booking on the Rank circuit. Paramount in turn declined a National release and decided to link up with ABC, ending a relationship under which its output had been shown on the Odeon and Gaumont circuits for the past fifteen years, with only the rarest of bookings to the main ABC circuit (e.g. *The Naked Jungle* in 1954). *All in a Night's Work* was not a great coup in itself, but access to all subsequent Paramount releases was a major catch that added some much needed sparkle to ABC screens when it brought the Marlon Brando western *One Eyed Jacks* and Audrey Hepburn's *Breakfast at Tiffany's*. Of course, it did oblige ABC to screen some of Paramount's weaker films, such as *Too Late Blues*, for which the distributor might well have agreed to a National release under its old arrangement.

An analysis carried out by Rank in 1961 indicated that an average release on the ABC circuit would play 276 ABC cinemas, twelve Rank ones and 1,500-1,600 other places, bringing in £75-£85,000 to the distributor. In the London area, there would be sixty-five bookings to ABC cinemas, one to Rank and twenty-four to others, amounting to ten per cent of the total playdates but fifteen per cent of the total income to the distributor. An outstanding film would play an additional four ABC cinemas in the London area and thirteen more in the provinces; it would also attract five more Rank houses and nine independents in London, plus eleven more Rank halls and up to 250 more other cinemas in the provinces, raising its total bookings to 2,100 or 2,150 and total revenue to the distributor to £275,000-£300,000. (Rank calculated that an average booking on its own circuit would attract almost as many bookings and be worth £10,000 more, while for an outstanding attraction the total number of playdates would be the same as for ABC or slightly higher but worth £330,000 to £350,000. This would include showings of the average film at one London-area ABC cinema and twenty-five provincial ones, and of an outstanding film at two London-area ABC properties and forty-nine elsewhere.)

Distribution patterns were slowly changing. In the summer of 1960, ABC showed Joseph E. Levine's acquisition, *Hercules Unchained*, released in the UK by Warner-Pathe under Levine's supervision, with an unprecedentedly massive publicity campaign and saturation release that involved a then record number of 100 prints being played at the same time, mainly at ABC cinemas. The film repeated the success it had enjyed with similar ballyhoo in the United States. Towards the end of 1964, ABC gave a two-week circuit release to another sensational production from Joseph E. Levine (this time distributed by Paramount), *The Carpetbaggers*. Films at the main theatres in the largest cities had often played more than a week as in the West End of London, but it was rare at local ABCs – *Dunkirk* had been retained for a second week at many situations and the circuit had experimented with extended pre-general release runs of films like *Ben-Hur*, *Gigi* and *The Nun's Story* at selected suburban outlets – *Ben-Hur*, for instance, played a three-week season at the Regal Camberwell but was exclusive to that area for the period. (Rank had also carried out extended runs of films like *Around the World in 80 Days* and *South Pacific* at some of its local theatres.) But the rigid simultaneous two-week booking of the X-certificated *The Carpetbaggers* in all ABC cinemas playing the film was a real break with tradition.* Local audiences were still conditioned to seeing a film within a week and attendances for *The Carpetbaggers* were huge in the first week but tailed off badly in the second. (One might guess that it suffered from weak word-of-mouth: it was advertised as a sensational attraction, drew in everyone who wanted to see it in the first week, and was not so warmly recommended that

---

Gone with the Wind had played the circuit for two weeks in 1942 as the exception that proves the rule. *The Great Caruso* and *The Dam Busters* were brought back on the full ABC circuit for a second week but after a gap of a few weeks. When Granada, Essoldo and other cinemas on the Fox or "Fourth" circuit tried two-week "pre-release" runs of *The King and I* at local cinemas, no ABCs seem to have participated.

★ AN IMPORTANT LETTER FOR **Ⓐ Ⓑ Ⓒ** PICTUREGOERS

Dear Patron,

A new two-way general release system for London cinemas will come into operation on the 30th December. From this day there will be only two areas of release, North London and South London, replacing the present method of a three-way release, London North West (first week), London North East (second week) and London South (third week). Under the new system the whole release will be played off in two weeks instead of three as heretofore.

This theatre will be included in the South London release area, and its programmes will be advertised in the London Evening News and Evening Standard under "ABC Release Theatres SOUTH LONDON Area."

The new system means that London cinemagoers will in many instances be able to view films at an earlier date, and the Film Industry hopes that the public will welcome this speedier system of release.

Yours sincerely,

The Manager

A full list of theatres in the new NORTH LONDON and SOUTH LONDON release areas is given overleaf.

NORTH LONDON   SOUTH LONDON

NORTH LONDON	SOUTH LONDON
HAMMERSMITH - Commodore	UXBRIDGE - Regal
EALING - A.B.C.	HOUNSLOW - Regal
† FULHAM ROAD - A.B.C.	RICHMOND - Ritz
HARROW - A.B.C.	WALTON-ON-THAMES - Regal
N. HARROW - Embassy	KINGSTON - A.B.C.
NEASDEN - Ritz	ELEPHANT & CASTLE - Theatre
WEMBLEY - A.B.C.	OLD KENT ROAD - Regal
† HARROW ROAD - A.B.C. (Regal)	CAMBERWELL - A.B.C.
KENSAL RISE - Palace	BRIXTON - Regal
GOLDERS GREEN - A.B.C.	TOOTING - Mayfair
EDGWARE - A.B.C.	STREATHAM - A.B.C.
MUSWELL HILL - A.B.C.	CROYDON - A.B.C.
HARRINGAY - A.B.C.	WIMBLEDON - Elite
SOUTHGATE - Ritz	CATFORD - A.B.C.
ENFIELD - A.B.C.	FOREST HILL - Capitol
KENTISH TOWN - Forum	BECKENHAM - A.B.C.
HOLLOWAY - A.B.C.	ELTHAM - Palace
ESSEX ROAD - A.B.C.	BEXLEYHEATH - A.B.C.
MILE END - A.B.C.	BLACKHEATH - Roxy
HACKNEY - A.B.C.	WOOLWICH - Regal
CLAPTON - A.B.C.	* PUTNEY - A.B.C.
STOKE NEWINGTON - A.B.C.	* EWELL - Rembrandt
LEYTON - A.B.C.	* PURLEY - Regal
STRATFORD - Rex	* BALHAM - Ritz
UPTON PARK - A.B.C.	* SIDCUP - Regal
MANOR PARK - Coronation	
ILFORD - A.B.C.	
WOODFORD - Majestic	
ROMFORD - A.B.C.	
* BAYSWATER -- A.B.C.	
* HAMMERSMITH - Broadway	
* BARKINGSIDE - State	

* These Theatres will play either the A.B.C. General Release Film OR an alternative programme. (See Local Press each week for details.)

† London's two NEW Pre-Release Theatres, ABC (Regal), Harrow Road ★ ABC, Fulham Road, will play at least one week prior to North London Release.

This announcement was issued in December 1962.

many others followed in the second.) The next two-week booking on the circuit was *Alfie* in 1966, followed by several more in 1967.

The three-week London suburban release reverted to the pre-war two-week North and South arrangement from 30 December 1962, speeding up the arrival of films in South London and acknowledging that closures had substantially reduced the number of prints needed. There were twenty-seven ABC situations in North London committed to the ABC release and twenty-one in South London. In addition, the ABCs Fulham Road and Edgware Road were promoted to pre-release status, playing the circuit programme a few days ahead of the rest of North London (in much the same way as Rank's Astoria Charing Cross Road and Tivoli in the Strand had regularly screened the ABC release a few years before). Six other London ABC theatres (including the ABC Bayswater) varied their programmes between strong ABC releases and alternative programmes while the Broadway Hammersmith usually played off-circuit.

There was considerable resistance to some of the circuit bookings on Sundays in rougher areas, especially to sophisticated comedies and romances, so the Rosalind Russell/Alec Guinness comedy *A Majority of One* was dropped on the Sunday at many inner London ABCs, as was the religious epic *King of Kings*, while the Debbie Reynolds romantic comedy *Mary Mary* started on Monday throughout South London (and was not shown at all at the Elephant and Castle). Sunday audiences could be so rowdy that police with alsatians routinely patrolled the auditorium of the ABC Essex Road, Islington.

A few features put on circuit release in the mid-Sixties proved so catastrophic on their debut in North London that they were completely or largely withdrawn. One was almost prophetically titled *Stop the World I Want to Get Off!* Its demise was so unexpected that alternative programmes were not chosen in time for press advertising deadlines and in the *South London Press* the ABC group advertisement simply disappeared for the week.

Opportunities were taken to boost some of the large, inner-London ABCs with special premieres of appropriate British pictures. The Old Kent Road Regal/ABC hosted star-studded launches of *Tommy the Toreador* starring the locally born Tommy Steele in 1959, and *Joey Boy* in 1966, plus gala showings of *The Sundowners* and *The Young Ones* (both in 1961) while the East End setting of *Sparrows Can't Sing* made the Mile End ABC the obvious venue for its debut in 1963.

ABC converted two of its properties outside London to the Cinerama process, following the successful introduction of a fiction film, *How the West Was Won*, in the three-camera/three-projector process. These were the Bristol in Bristol Road, Birmingham, and the Coliseum Glasgow which were totally reconstructed at a cost in each case of approximately £140,000, bringing Cinerama to the regions for the first time in 1963. (Rank was not far behind, its installation of Cinerama at the Gaumont Birmingham opening a month later.)

As a knock-on effect, the Todd-AO 70mm equipment and stereo sound taken out of the Bristol were installed at the ABC (ex-Gaiety) Coleshill Street, Aston, which also gained a giant new screen 42ft. wide and was soon given the Midlands premiere run of *My Fair Lady*. As former staff member John Duddy relates, the cinema was often paired with the ABC (ex-Forum) New Street in playing new releases: "Some 70mm films ran concurrent with the ABC New Street which charged higher prices to see the same films in 35mm mono optical sound and, despite this, usually had more admissions. Such films couldn't be billed as Todd-AO for obvious reasons so we got round it by describing them as 'A Mammoth Screen Presentation in Stereo'."

Other cinemas were equipped to show films with 70mm prints for the improved sound but without giant new screens. London-area ABCs taking 70mm included those at Ealing, Kingston, Streatham and Turnpike Lane (Harringay).

Live shows became more prominent on the circuit. A tour by the Beatles in 1963 covered a great many cinemas, including ABC halls in Belfast, Carlisle and Plymouth. In that same year, a completely new ABC Blackpool opened on the site of the Hippodrome and was largely used for live shows with a built-in capacity for television recording and transmission. *Blackpool Night Out* was televised from here on Sundays for the ITV network by ABC TV for many years, with Albert Brierley and one of the touring Hammonds in the orchestra pit.

In 1965, the circuit experimented with abolishing the second feature at some of its local cinemas – in the London area, at Brixton, Catford, Golders Green, Walton-on-Thames and Woodford. This enabled the main film to be shown twice every evening and four times daily. This revived what had been the practice with hit attractions like *Ivanhoe* in the late Forties and early Fifties of four shows daily to maximise audiences, but it was now applied to every film of suitable length. The experiment was soon dropped, leaving one to assume that audiences felt cheated by the shorter programmes.

Another change – this one adopted by the industry as a whole – was to start weekly programmes on Fridays from 1 July 1966. Weekend attendances were much higher than the rest of the week and it was hoped that audiences would flock to films when they opened and then encourage higher patronage in the following weekdays by good word-of-mouth. However, cinemagoers were simply confused and programmes returned to their traditional Sunday start from 12 February 1967 for a while.

New theatres and "luxury lounges"
Despite the decline in audiences, the company still built the occasional new cinema or acquired existing properties like the Embassy Peterborough and Scala Liverpool. Following the openings at Aberdeen, Woolwich and Gloucester in the mid-Fifties, a second wave of new cinemas had begun with the ABC Preston in 1959. This was followed by a near total reconstruction of the ABC cinema at Londonderry in 1960.

Completely new was the ABC Sheffield, which on its opening in 1961 gave the circuit representation in the town for the first time since 1948. This was on the stadium plan, seating 1,327 with one of the largest screens in the country (60ft. wide) and had the kind of cutaway walls to each side of the screen found pre-war in cinemas designed for Holophane like the Apollo Ardwick. This was the dawning of the age of plainness with a vast curtain following the curvature of the screen in place of the usual proscenium arch and sweeping round behind the side walls. There was a suggestion of old "atmospheric" schemes in a floating ceiling that supposedly simulated a night sky with randomly placed lights suggesting stars. Sightlines were excellent and the Phillips projectors could take 35mm and 70mm prints while the sound installation had optical sound for conventional prints and four-track and six-track magnetic heads for CinemaScope and Todd-AO respectively.

In 1963, the prevously mentioned ABC Cine-Bowl at Hanley was the first dual-purpose building of this kind in Britain. The cinema section was very similar to Sheffield in appearance and equipment, with another giant screen that was 60ft. wide at maximum for Todd-AO presentations. Also mentioned earlier, the replacement ABC Blackpool was specially designed for alternating film and live show use.

There was a three-year gap before any further new ABCs opened. The first was at Bristol in late 1966, anticipating a new trend with its location in a shopping centre and seating only 806 in the usual stadium plan. This was followed by the ABC Doncaster, substantially larger with 1277 seats in stadium plan but so hideously plain externally it must be the worst-looking postwar cinema. Somewhat more pleasing (its brick facade at least had windows) was the ABC 2 Glasgow, almost adjacent to the existing ABC. Seating 922 seats in a stadium plan, this was built to take extended runs while the old ABC 1 played the regular release schedule. The last new cinema of the decade opened in 1968 at Newport in South Wales where ABC had lost its previous cinema in 1964: this seated 1322 in a stadium plan and incorporated seven shops.

During the Sixties, many other cinemas were modernised. In *Golden Hill to Golden Square*, W. 'Bill' Cartlidge picks out improvements at the former Elite, now ABC Middlesbrough, in 1964: "I was especially pleased; principally because the old cinema was a difficult shape and caused much difficulty in transforming it into the modern requirements of the day. However, the large sum (at it was then) of £120,000 was not expended in vain – the entrance and auditorium were a joy to behold; our talented team of architects, headed by Jack Foster, had brought about a fantastic transformation; the main curtains instead of taking a concave line gave us the unusual spectacle of a huge convex spread, which, lit from above and below throughout its entire width was simply breathtaking in its beauty. When the curtains opened the scene gave way to a huge concave screen which gave the impression to the audience of an almost circular stage apron – quite a remarkable design for which Jack received many congratulations."

600 seats were lost in this conversion (which was to last

The ABC Sheffield: an exterior view dating from May 1963 and the spectacular auditorium as it looked on opening in 1961 with its vast screen exposed.

The Coliseum Glasgow in 1963 hides most of its ancient exterior from view as a theatre converted to the modern 'miracle' of Cinerama.

less than ten years). Many other cinemas had their capacities reduced to make them more inviting. ABC introduced the "luxury lounge" by which the stalls floor was respaced, reseated and generally modernised. This was first carried out at Lancaster and Pinner in 1966. In some locations, such as Dover and Windsor, the circle was closed and the walls painted black to hide it as much as possible (resulting in a particularly desolate view for the projectionist, now unable to see any part of the audience). At other sites, such as the Elephant and Castle, the circle remained open and unaltered, except that its seats were now cheaper than those in the luxury lounge on the old stalls floor. In the latter instances, it was hoped to attract noisy young cinemagoers upstairs where they would not bother audiences below. However, at least one manager noticed that older patrons were reluctant to throw aside tradition, which said that the best seats were always upstairs. No other circuit took up the luxury lounge idea, although in most cinemas the rows of stalls seating had usually been re-spaced for some years to provide more generous leg-room (stepped circle seating could not be altered in the same way).

Another widespread, regrettable form of modernisation was the updating of frontages, continued from the Fifties. Now this often took the form of curtaining with vertically corrugated blue metal cladding. Thus F. E. Bromige's spectacularly futuristic treatment at the ABC Harrow was covered up along with the crumbling citadel exterior of the ABC Edgware. Some old buildings like the Coliseum Cinerama Glasgow, Grand Mansfield and Elite Wimbledon were similarly refaced, as were the bland and hardly offensive facades of the ABC cinemas at Bayswater, Edgware Road and Leeds. This cladding has not always lasted well (as at Edgware) and hopefully did little damage to the original frontages, perhaps one day enabling some that remain to be reinstated. A more elaborate but no less unattractive modernisation of a perfectly acceptable exterior was the checkerboard pattern imposed on W. R. Glen's well-mannered corner entrance at the ABC Southport. Similarly, the central section of the pleasant faience-covered exterior of the Langham Pinner with its central windows was replaced with a flat rectangular surface of dark blue tiles that clashed with all that could be seen of the old building, including its green roof tiles.

ABC continued to look for ways to increase the profitability of its sites. Besides bowling alleys, car park space was used to construct a pub at Streatham and a squash club at Walton-on-Thames. Cafés were converted into more profitable public houses, beginning at the Whiteladies in Bristol. At the ABC Grimsby, the stalls floor became a supermarket while the old circle upstairs was extended forward to continue as a cinema. At Clydebank, the circle remained a cinema while the stalls area was converted to a completely separate bingo club.

However, attendances were still plunging and seating capacities were far too large. Rank pioneered the subdivision of an existing cinema into two smaller cinemas at the Odeon Nottingham in 1965. ABC delayed taking the plunge until 1969 when it closed the huge ABC Edinburgh for conversion into three auditoria at a planned cost of £170,000. The scheme was designed by ABC's own architects' department and carried out by a main contractor and a number of specialist firms. Shortly after work started, the project became entangled in the biggest boardroom shake-up in the history of the company.

10 | The EMI Years

It was at this time that the music and industrial conglomerate EMI (Electrical and Musical Industries) showed an interest in acquiring ABPC. The company's Achilles heel had always been the substantial shareholding held by Warner Bros., even though this had been reduced to a twenty-five per cent stake when ABPC bought back some of its shares circa 1961. Alarm bells rang in the corridors of ABPC whenever control of Warner Bros. itself changed or threatened to change. There had been considerable relief back in 1951 when Jack, Harry and Albert Warner discontinued negotiations to sell their controlling interest to a San Francisco financier, Louis Lurie. Consternation reigned five years later when the three brothers did sell most of their stock to a group headed by Serge Semenenko, and Granada Theatres reportedly offered $5.6 million for the thirty-seven-and-a-half per cent stake in ABPC. It was followed by relief when Semenenko decided the shares were not for sale. (This was the second time that Granada had been reported eyeing Warners' ABPC holding.)

In 1967, Seven Arts, an independent production company and film library owner, acquired Warner Bros. and renamed it Warner Bros.-Seven Arts. The new owners sold what was now a twenty-five per cent stake in ABPC to EMI, which then wanted to buy up the rest of the company. EMI already owned and operated the Shipman and King circuit, which had come with its acquisition of the Grade Organisation in 1967. Bernard Delfont and John Read were elected onto the board of ABPC to represent EMI's interests and were soon at loggerheads with some of the older directors.

At the end of 1968, EMI declared its intention to make an offer for the other seventy-five per cent of the shares. Over ninety per cent of shareholders accepted the EMI offer and it took over control of ABPC on 27 February 1969 to the shock and anger of the staff in the Golden Square headquarters. ABPC's chairman Sir Philip Warter and chief executive Robert Clark were replaced by Bernard Delfont. ABPC was renamed the EMI Film and Theatre Corporation. The cinemas – now 242 in number – continued to be called ABCs (one wonders if EMI ever contemplated substituting its initials) but the old ABC triangle sign, which had persisted on the front of theatres in a fourth "lozenge" shape after those with the ABC initials and in the middle of canopies and elsewhere in foyers, was replaced with EMI's rectangular logo.

At the end of February 1970, the cock on Pathe News crowed for the last time. This had nothing to do with the change of ownership: unable to compete with the news on television, Pathe News had increasingly leaned towards a "general interest" format and its demise was inevitable.

Under Delfont, the conversion scheme at the Edinburgh ABC was upgraded to a far more luxurious level, doubling expenditure to £350,000 and delaying completion so that it was closed for over nine months. Similarly expensive and time-consuming conversions to twin cinemas were approved and carried out at the ABCs Bournemouth, Leeds and Leicester, as well as at the Adelphi Dublin where the large café area now provided a third screen. In most instances, the frontages were also severely modernised. These schemes were again devised by the company's own architects' department. At Bournemouth and Leeds, the ABCs were clearly responding to the example of rival Rank cinemas, closing two months after they had re-opened as modern twins.

Delfont appointed Bryan Forbes as production head at what were now called EMI Elstree Studios and several productions were soon underway. Delfont decided that ABC

The Westover Bournemouth as it looked on opening in 1937 and after its expensive twinning into ABC 1 and 2 in July 1970. It is now the MGM. The Adelphi Dublin about to re-open as a three-screen cinema in October 1970.

needed a West End showcase to premiere the Elstree productions. Despite an out-of-the way location on the wrong side of Cambridge Circus, the old Saville Theatre in Shaftesbury Avenue was acquired and internally rebuilt to create two cinemas at a cost of £600,000. When these were ready in December 1970, a new Elstree production, *The Railway Children*, was one of the opening attractions.

At the same time as these developments were taking place, marginal cinemas were sold off. Delfont also decided to take EMI out of bingo operations. Star (Associated) Holdings were given a twenty-one year lease on twenty-five ABC properties. This included some cinemas splitting the week between films and bingo, which were taken over by Star on 30 June 1969: the Regal Abingdon, ABC Bicester, Majestic Bridgnorth, ABC Bridlington, ABC Cirencester, ABC Dunstable, Regal Dursley, Regal Lichfield, Ritz Market Harborough and Ritz Wokingham. Star continued to show films at these locations for a while. The other, bingo-only sites were at Balham, Banbury, Beverley, Clydebank (excluding the cinema area above), Gravesend, Hyde, Leigh, Salisbury, Springburn, Stirchley, Stratford, Wellingborough, Windsor, Worthing and West Bromwich. Star also acquired two full-time cinemas, the ABC Miles Platting and the Plaza Plymouth, where films continued for a while. ABC were abandoning towns as substantial as Salisbury and Worthing to the rival Odeon circuit (and also, in the case of Worthing, to the independent Dome).

In other instances during the early Seventies, ABCs were lost to compulsory purchase orders (New Royal Openshaw; ABC Coleshill Street, Aston), leased to others for Asian film shows (ABC High Street, Aston; ABC Charing Cross, Glasgow), leased for continued conventional programming (Coliseum Whitley Bay), closed singly as being uneconomic (ABC Cheetham Hill, Manchester; Mayfair Battlefield, Glasgow); leased to Mecca or Ladbrokes for bingo (ABC Essex Road, Islington; ABC Fishponds, Bristol; ABC Camberwell; Metropole Nottingham; ABC Hove, ABC Boscombe, Bournemouth; ABC Maidstone), or simply sold off for redevelopment (ABC Hastings, replaced by a supermarket; ABC Kentish Town, still standing as a live music venue). But EMI took a positive approach to much of the circuit and, while the number of sites declined gradually, the total number of screens rose sharply.

(Courtesy of David Cheshire.)

Following the conversions at Edinburgh, Leeds, Bournemouth, Dublin and Leicester, ABC's architects prepared and supervised the twinning of the ABC Staines at a cost of £204,000. After this, the in-house architects' department was closed. ABC continued to convert its sites into smaller cinemas in package deals using a number of contractors quoting a firm price for the designing and carrying out of the work. At Romford and Luton, the ABC was converted into three cinemas rather than two, and this became the general rule for subsequent conversions, although some smaller properties like the ABC Sidcup could only be twinned while some larger ones like the ABC Enfield accommodated four screens. Costs were reduced to approximately £180,000 for a triple and £250,000 for a quad. In time, the original twin conversions were converted to triples by often awkward subdivision of one of the large auditoria: this happened at Staines in 1972, less than two years after it had been twinned.

A few brand-new ABCs appeared on the scene in the first half of the Seventies: two-screen cinemas at Basildon and Stevenage and a single-screen one at Coventry. An isolated, more ambitious redevelopment at Putney involved the demolition of both the ABC and the adjacent Odeon to make way for a new three-screen ABC within an office block. According to managers concerned, Rank's agreement to sell its popular Odeon and vacate Putney was tied up with the closure of the ABCs at Richmond and Walton, which left Rank the sole cinema operator in those towns.

At some ABC cinemas, a compromise was favoured to meet the reduced interest in films without closing entirely. First seen at Clydebank, this involved subdivision so that the stalls area was used for bingo while the old circle functioned as a smaller cinema with a new screen set up in front. The ABCs Kidderminster, Carlisle, Harrow, Dumfries, Woking, Lincoln, Newbury, Canterbury, Cleethorpes, Barkingside, Hereford, Warrington and Exeter were all treated in this way in 1972 (although Exeter also had a second cinema, created in the top half of the stage area). The ABC Coatbridge was the last cine-bingo conversion, re-opening in 1973. Other cinemas were divided up to provide a ground-floor pub called the Painted Wagon with western saloon décor in much of the former rear stalls area: the ABCs Tooting and Chesterfield led the way in 1971, followed by such theatres as those at York, Harrogate, Preston, Eastbourne and Huddersfield. These conversions sometimes provided more than one cinema or retained some of the stalls seating.

The Odeon circuit had also given up expensive conversions and generally adopted a "drop wall" treatment of tripling its buildings which closed off the space under the balcony to create two small cinemas, usually seating a little over 100 each. Under this method, the circle and old screen were retained to create the largest of the three cinemas, and the original decor was largely preserved. Not only was this treatment cheaper in itself but the circle could remain open in the evening during the conversion, except perhaps for the final stages, so that the building was still earning some money and maintaining the attendance habit.

ABC followed the drop wall procedure at some locations, including Falkirk, Greenock, Halifax, Ilford, Mile End, Rochdale and Wolverhampton – seemingly places where there was some doubt over a sufficient rate of return to justify a larger investment. But in most instances of tripling, it carried out a more thorough transformation that extended the circle forward, created two larger cinemas beneath, and ruthlessly eliminated most of the old décor. In some places, parts of the ceiling had to be demolished to allow the projection beam to reach the higher screen in front of the extended circle. In many instances, the old proscenium arch and grille work and decorative features on the splay walls survived, but hidden from view behind the screen and new walls (the galleons are still there in Hammersmith). Although cinemas had to be closed for several weeks, ABC could re-launch them more convincingly as entirely new film centres while the smaller cinemas avoided the cramped, "cupboard" look of the 100-seaters at many Odeons.

Not every cinema could be changed. Apparently, the ABC Muswell Hill was surveyed but, as a result of the sharp downward slope of the site, it was not suited to take the strain of sub-division. This left it open for the town's Odeon to become a triple and out-survive the ABC.

Nor did all the changes to British cinemas meet with universal trade approval. In October 1978, when attendances had risen sharply on a wave of box-office hits, the head of 20th Century-Fox in London, Ascanio Branca, told *Variety*: "No country in Europe is so badly served as Britain as to the condition of its theatres. Many of the multi-auditoria put up here are lousy. There are continual complaints about sound and comfort. It is pitiful... [British exhibitors] have no faith in the business. If they don't react now and build new theatres when things are going great, they will eventually be proven right and the business will collapse."

Booking patterns

In the early Seventies more films of specialised appeal were being made and these were ill-suited to a full circuit release. But ABC and Rank still adhered to this concept, causing some strain with their regular suppliers. In ABC's case, the long-standing relationship with Warner Bros. had been weakened by the sale of the Warner interest in ABPC which had been followed by the dissolution of the joint distribution company, Warner-Pathe. EMI formed a new company with MGM, called MGM-EMI while Warners teamed up with Columbia. Warner films still played ABC until the circuit refused to take the controversial British production *Performance*. Subsequent Warner films like *There Was a Crooked Man* and *Woodstock* had to play at a handful of Rank and independent cinemas (including most Granadas) until the rift was healed.

Rank's long-standing arrangement to distribute Universal's films in the UK came under strain in the early Seventies when many rather experimental British-made productions backed by the company, like *Fahrenheit 451, Work Is a Four Letter Word* and *Secret Ceremony*, were denied a substantial release in Rank's cinemas. This prompted Universal to extend Cinema International Corporation (CIC), its distribution partnership with Paramount in other parts of the world, to this country as well and to switch to the ABC circuit. Except for a few horror films, Universal pictures had never been released on the main ABC circuit. The first Universal film to play on ABC screens everywhere was the Clint Eastwood starrer *Play Misty for Me* in January 1972, followed shortly by *The Omega Man, Never Give an Inch* and Hitchcock's *Frenzy*. MGM broke off the distribution tie-up with EMI to join CIC in 1974. (CIC has since been renamed United International Pictures, UIP.) EMI continued to release films on its own.

There were many new (but short-lived) distribution companies in the field, mostly related to the American television networks entering film production. Many of these hooked up

The ABC Streatham becomes the latest cinema to be tripled in 1977.

STEPTOE & SON

Shatters all time Box Office Records

STEPTOE & SON

Shatters all time Box Office Records

ABERDEEN, ABC	£4,954
ACTON GRANADA	£1,743 record
ARDWICK, ABC	£9,106
BARKINGSIDE, ABC	£4,172
BALHAM ODEON	£1,519 record
BAYSWATER, ABC	£2,446
BEDMINSTER, ABC	£5,731 record
BLACKPOOL, ABC	£8,517 record
BRIGHTON, ABC	£7,841 record
BRISTOL, ABC	£8,322 record
CAMBRIDGE, ABC-1	£5,994
CARDIFF, OLYMPIA	£10,057 record
CHELMSFORD, REGENT	£3,582
CLAPTON, ABC	£6,364 record
DUNDEE, ABC	£4,298 record
EALING, ABC	£6,402 record
EDGWARE, ABC	£4,435 record
EDGWARE ROAD, ABC	£5,227
EDINBURGH, ABC-1	£8,381 record
EDINBURGH, RITZ	£4,140 record
ENFIELD, ABC	£3,153
ESSEX ROAD, ABC	£2,654 record
FINCHLEY, GAUMONT	£2,856 record
FULHAM ROAD, ABC	£6,061
GLASGOW, ABC-1	£12,741 record
GLASGOW, COLISEUM	£4,530 record
GOLDERS GREEN, ABC	£2,267
HACKNEY, ABC	£2,393 record
HAMMERSMITH, ABC (Regal)	£3,144
HOLLOWAY, ABC	£5,650 record
HOVE, ABC	£3,820 record
ILFORD, ABC	£5,655 record
IPSWICH, ABC	£8,300 record
JERSEY, FORUM	£2,600
KILBURN, STATE	£3,395 record
LEEDS, ABC-2	£9,802 record
LEYTON, ABC	£5,454 record
LIVERPOOL, ABC	£16,310 record
LONDON, WEST END ABC-1	£13,877
LUTON, ABC-1	£7,008 record

Released by MGM EMI

MANCHESTER, STUDIO	£4,021
MILE END, ABC	£5,140 record
MUSWELL HILL, ABC	£2,324 record
NEWCASTLE, HAYMARKET	£13,296
NEWPORT, ABC	£7,156 record
NORWICH, ABC	£9,756 record
OXFORD, ABC	£6,470
PINNER, ABC	£2,593 record
READING, ABC-1	£7,189 record
ROMFORD, ABC-1	£6,976 record
ST. ALBANS, GAUMONT	£1,925 record
SCARBOROUGH, FUTURIST	£2,883 record
SHEPHERDS BUSH, ODEON	£2,789 record
STOKE NEWINGTON, ABC	£2,709
SUNDERLAND, ABC	£10,435 record
SWANSEA, ALBERT HALL	£6,249 record
TURNPIKE LANE, ABC	£7,052 record
UPTON PARK, ABC	£5,859 record
WALTHAM CROSS, EMBASSY	£3,364
WATFORD, ODEON	£5,763 record
WEMBLEY, ABC	£3,803 record
WOKING, ABC	£2,381 record
WOODFORD, MAJESTIC	£3,280 record

Nat Cohen presents an Anglo-EMI film Associated London Films production of
RAY GALTON and ALAN SIMPSON'S

STEPTOE & SON

starring
WILFRID BRAMBELL as STEPTOE   **HARRY H. CORBETT** as SON

also starring
CAROLYN SEYMOUR   EMI

Screenplay by RAY GALTON and ALAN SIMPSON · Executive Producer BERYL VERTUE · Produced by AIDA YOUNG
Directed by CLIFF OWEN · TECHNICOLOR® · Distributed by MGM EMI

Released by MGM EMI

Steptoe and Son *was the sixth biggest hit of 1972 after* Diamonds Are Forever, The Godfather, Fiddler on the Roof, Bedknobs and Broomsticks *and* The Devils, *but it seems to have created a surprising number of box-office records. This double-page advertisement appeared in the trade press, evidently to raise interest among foreign film buyers. It was extremely rare to see figures published for cinemas outside the West End and the extraordinary variations in takings give some idea of the different pulling power of ABC cinemas, at least for this kind of sit-com feature.*

with the ABC circuit, giving it a substantial number of star attractions in the early Seventies. From Cinema Center (releasing through 20th Century-Fox) came westerns *Monte Walsh*, *Rio Lobo*, *Little Big Man* and *Big Jake*, plus the racing drama *Le Mans*. National General Pictures supplied ABC with *Pocket Money*. Cinerama (now handling conventional format pictures) came up with *The Getaway* and *The Life and Times of Judge Roy Bean*. Scotia-Barber released *Puppet with a Chain*. With parent company EMI producing hit films like *On the Buses* and acquiring useful American pictures as well, shortage of product was no longer a problem and double-bill programmes were normal, usually offering weaker American main features as strong supporting attractions.

Circuit bookings were at last becoming more flexible. Only the very strongest attractions – like *Dirty Harry* or *The Godfather* or an EMI production like *Steptoe and Son* played the full circuit. Up-market offerings like *England Made Me* were confined to a few suitable cinemas like the ABC Streatham; down-market offerings (obscure horror and musical exploitation pictures) would be booked into cinemas mostly on their last legs like the once mighty Old Kent Road ABC. Some American-style "four walling" deals were done, by which specialist distributors hired screens to show their films for a fixed fee and took all the receipts.

Multi-screen cinemas were given priority over remaining single-screen ones, playing hit films earlier. They could be held as long as business warranted, moving from the largest auditorium down to the smallest one to complete a run. Doubtful films could play in one of the smaller cinemas and exit after a week. Foreign films were also tried out in the smaller cinemas, like *The Garden of the Finzi-Continis*, but they were soon crowded out by the extended runs of mainstream films. Phenomenal runs could be achieved: the original *Jaws* played at the ABC Croydon for six months in one or other of the three cinemas there.

Last picture shows

The trading figures of many cinemas did not warrant conversion to three-screen film centres. By Spring 1973, the Metropole at Sherwood was averaging only a thirteen per cent occupancy on just eight performances a week, even though it was the sole Nottingham suburban cinema that had

first-run concurrency with ABC's city centre cinemas. The Metropole was turned over to bingo, which was not much more successful in the long run. Of course, its closure also helped improve business at the ABC and Elite Nottingham as some patrons then attended them instead.

The crunch came for several ABCs when the power cuts of 1974 devastated business. "The End" played for real at the Regal Bracknell, ABC Bowes Road (Southgate), ABC Blackheath, ABC Wythenshawe, ABC Walton (Liverpool), Ritz Armagh, ABC Wallasey, ABC Sparkbrook, ABC Sale and ABC Lancaster (as well as a Shipman and King cinema, the New Coronet Didcot). The "uneconomic" ABCs at Eccles, Bridgeton and Barnsley were also shuttered at this time.

Twenty cinemas said to be "marginally profitable" (plus three Shipman and King properties) were put on a "disposal list" in the autumn of 1975. To the company's credit, it was in no hurry to close any of them and they were for the most part offered "fully equipped" and still operating, for sale or lease. The list was circulated to Cinematograph Exhibitors Association members to encourage offers for their continued use as cinemas. Several were eventually acquired by local independents with mixed results. They included the ABC Barrow-in-Furness and Grosvenor Hillhead, Glasgow, which have prospered as well as the ABCs Nuneaton and Stockport which soon closed. Another, the ABC Horsham, was imaginatively converted to an arts centre including a smaller, full-time cinema. The others, including several closed the year before during the fuel crisis, were the Majestic and Strand Belfast, ABC Dover, ABC Eccles, ABC Falmouth, ABC Keighley (closed, but with seats remaining), ABC Lancaster, ABC Lowestoft (the first to be sold), Rex Motherwell, ABC Sale (with only circle seating intact), ABC Bowes Road (Southgate) (with only seats and carpets in place), ABC Southport, ABC Stourbridge, ABC Wallasey and ABC West Hartlepool.

At the same time EMI went back into bingo by buying for £5.7 million the bingo side of Star (which retained its cinema interests). This included 104 bingo halls operated solely by Star and fifty-four ex-ABCs (some split for both films and bingo) in which it had held a half-interest.

The Eighties

Cinemas continued to be converted into multi-screen centres

at a slower rate into the early Eighties. The ABC Edgware Road was a late conversion to a quad. The Elephant and Castle ABC, which had largely gone off-circuit to play exploitation pictures, was given a new lease of life when conversion to a triple took place in 1981. Peterborough was converted just afterwards and the last cinemas to be tripled were the ABC Muirend (Glasgow) and the ABC Portsmouth early in 1982.

The early Eighties were dismal years for film exhibition as video and cable began to make their presence felt and attendances continued to decline. The two major circuits' primary response was to close more cinemas for bingo or redevelopment, reducing attendances even further. Foolish economies were made in ABC press advertising, so that, for example, the group of cinemas appearing in the *South London Press* had a miserably small amount of space that changed position from week to week and lacked any eye-catching display material. These were the years when the last Saturday morning children's clubs closed down and when sex films, kung fu movies and other exploitation fodder particularly tarnished the image of all the circuits and cinema-going generally. EMI had given up the expensive business of distributing on its own in 1978 and joined a Hollywood tandem to create Columbia-EMI-Warner.

In most large towns, the ABC and Odeon cinemas had both been twinned or tripled and remained in competition. But now many of these places were being reduced to just one mainstream cinema. Odeon closures left towns the size of Croydon, Luton, Watford and Wolverhampton with one EMI house – in the case of Watford, a small two-screen cinema out of the town centre. Not to be outdone, EMI pulled out of towns like Cheltenham, Exeter, Harrogate, Middlesbrough, Preston and Warrington. While favouring its traditional distributor ties, the surviving cinema in these towns also played the best releases that would previously have gone to the opposition house. In its programming, the single Odeon in one town became scarcely distinguishable from the single ABC elsewhere.

Audiences were frustrated that so few films were on offer, but nowhere more than in Derby where both the ABC and Odeon triples closed in favour of a single commercial screen in the latter, operated by EMI. So glaring was the deficiency

that two American multiplex operators were lured into filling the gap. (Preston, left with just two Odeon screens after the single-screen ABC closed, has also attracted two multiplex companies.)

Some attempt to widen audience choice at ABCs came with the introduction of video cinemas. These could be inserted into small areas, like former cafés, where there was not enough room for a conventional projection box. Such cinemas appeared at Woking, in some of the S&K properties, and at one of the three screens at Muirend, Glasgow. However, the poor image quality and problems with the equipment led to the closure of these cinemas or a switch to conventional film projection.

Thorn EMI

In late 1979, EMI merged with Thorn Electrical Industries to become Thorn EMI with a new 'thorn' logo. An American, Gary Dartnall, took charge of the film side from May 1983 at a time when EMI was licking its wounds after some of its big-budget pictures had failed at the international box-office. EMI's income from its video label was the brightest part of its entertainment division. At the end of the year, Dartnall amalgamated the Elstree studio operation, film production, exhibition and video into what was called Thorn EMI Screen Entertainment (TESE). Using market research carried out in 1983, young executives from the video side were delegated to revitalise the cinemas, especially in marketing. The research indicated, somewhat unbelievably, that less than seven per cent of people questioned had quoted cinemas as run down or dirty and less than eighteen per cent said they couldn't afford to go to the cinema. The new policy for the ABC circuit proposed, among other things, surcharges on major blockbusters, guaranteed runs in its main cinemas for films fully promoted in advertising, and participation in an industry-wide scheme of full page advertising in the national press.

But the ABC circuit continued to shrink and attendances plummeted to an all-time low in 1984. (Rank had closed even more of its theatres, now operating on just 75 sites with 194 screens, while TESE had 107 sites and 287 screens.)

A bright note was sounded with the renovation of the ABC Fulham Road, West London, which had always been one of the most profitable cinemas on the circuit. A leading designer, Tessa Kennedy of Kennedy Sumner, was engaged to bring a fresh look to the building with a new style of ABC sign, the reinstatement of many original features and the addition of a modern upstairs bar. Unfortunately, the scheme could not tackle the awkward subdivision of the building that had converted it into five cinemas several years earlier, in particular the wall down the centre of the old circle. Completed at the end of 1984, the Fulham Road scheme remained a one-off rather than becoming the prototype for alterations elsewhere.

In 1985, the industry set about reversing its fortunes by launching British Film Year, to which Thorn EMI (now with an estimated thirty-two per cent of the UK exhibition market) made a substantial financial contribution. This promotion inhibited the company from closing any more loss-making sites even though it regarded as many as a third of surviving ABCs (mostly in blighted inner city areas) as no longer viable and was receiving eighty per cent of its total gross revenues from only one fifth of its cinemas. In a last-ditch attempt to improve attendances at some of the worst cinemas during British Film Year, ABC made drastic price cuts to £1 admission every day at nine cinemas and £1.50 at eight others (Rank reduced prices similarly at seventeen of its sites). This experiment proved to be extremely successful – at Darlington, attendances increased by 115%, while the ABC Hanley also registered a dramatic improvement. Thorn EMI marketing manager Martin Stafford was quoted as saying, "We would simply prefer to get twice as many people going to the cinema at half the price. Once they have started to return, we trust they will come back regularly." This proved to be the case at Darlington and Hanley which have remained open. Overall, ABC found that, within months, it was deriving seventy per cent of its revenue from forty per cent of its theatres. Hit films also helped – especially, in ABC's case, *Gremlins* and *Beverly Hills Cop* – and attendances on the circuit improved twenty-four per cent in the first six months of 1985. Over the year as a whole, attendances nationally climbed by nearly one quarter to approximately 71 million.

Money continued to be invested in upgrading some cinemas and Dartnall decided to reinstate the old ABC triangle logo, if in a more modest fashion than before. The Embassy Crawley,

The ABC Fulham Road in December 1984 with its restored upper frontage and experimental design of ABC lettering.

The eight-screen Cannon (now MGM) at Salford Quays, Manchester, was the second multiplex to appear in Britain. Opened in December 1986, it had been originated by ABC and would have displayed a new adaptation of the old triangle logo. The intended position of the triangles on the upper facade can be seen but they were fitted with the Cannon trademark after that company took over ABC.

a former Shipman and King property which had been tripled in 1979/80 at a cost of £250,000, was further refurbished at a declared cost of £270,000 and renamed ABC in December 1985. The ABC triangle appeared within a circular back-lit box high on the front of the cinema. New staff uniforms had a Thirties look.

Similar treatment to that at Crawley was planned at other cinemas, while a bold decision had been taken to follow American Multi-Cinema's lead by building multiplex cinemas even before AMC's first in the UK, the Point at Milton Keynes, had opened. Construction of a £3.5 million eight-screen complex began at Salford Quays, Manchester – a location that was regarded with derision by some of the veterans at Golden Square headquarters. Dartnall's multiplex plans, as he described them in March 1985, consisted initially of six theatres, each with six screens (two 500-seaters, two 350-seaters and two 250-seaters) on sites leased in new out-of-town shopping centres in partnership with an American chain.

The company's Development Executive at that time, Ian N. Riches, recalls now: "EMI were first to follow the lead set by AMC. In fact, at the time, EMI held talks with at least one major US circuit with a view to joint venturing on UK multiplex development, but these talks came to nothing. The attitude at the time became one of wait and see, and the company was in a state of flux with the arrival of Gary Dartnall. Although I was actively looking at sites (including the Merryhill Centre Dudley and the MetroCentre Gateshead), it was impossible to actually get a deal done." EMI were reported to be interested in a site at Lea Valley, Enfield, but Riches recalls merely looking at an EMI factory site nearby.

While Dartnall was asking the board of Thorn EMI for a sum approaching £50 million to develop multiplexes, the parent company was moving towards disposing of the only mildly profitable Screen Entertainment division. In poor financial shape overall, the conglomerate was anxious to raise money by disposing of TESE, claiming that it was a bad fit with the rest of the group. Thorn EMI's interest in Thames Television and in cable were to be retained.

Gary Dartnall proposed a management buy-out of TESE for £110 million, and his offer was accepted by Thorn EMI in December 1985 with completion set for February 1986. Part of Dartnall's backing came from Australia's Bond

Corporation, headed by Alan Bond. Rival bids were reportedly made by Rank, and by the Cannon Group in association with Heron International. A drawback to both these bids was the likelihood of intervention by the Monopolies Commission to prevent an undue concentration of cinemas in one company's hands – especially Rank's, which would have amalgamated the two biggest cinema circuits.

When Dartnall was unable to raise the purchase price and working capital, even after the deadline was extended to April, the Bond Corporation on its own acquired TESE for £125 million. Dartnall decided not to stay with Bond and resigned. Rather than find someone else to run the company, Bond sold it for a handsome profit to Cannon, who were willing to pay £175 million in cash and stock. Cannon already owned the former Classic and Star chains (all renamed Cannons in December 1985) and had a total of 95 cinemas with 216 screens and 55,063 seats. The addition of the 106 ABC cinemas gave it 201 cinemas with 485 screens.

Cannon began giving all the ABCs its own name on 11 October 1986 and completed the task in March 1987. The ABC circuit finally lost its separate identity. (It would have made better business sense – and saved money – to have retained the familiar ABC name instead of giving the cinemas one derived from an obscure Hollywood film company best known for making *The Happy Hooker*.)

This is not the place to trace the turbulent history of the Cannon company. It is worth noting, though, that the Cannon name has been giving way to a new set of three initials, MGM. Cannon was taken over by Pathe Communications, which then acquired Metro-Goldwyn-Mayer. It was decided that the MGM name and lion trademark would enhance the British circuit. After Pathe had changed its own name to Metro-Goldwyn-Mayer Cinemas, it began applying the new name and initials to the circuit, beginning with the West End cinemas *en bloc* in March 1992.

Another significant development was Cannon's take-over of the Canadian circuit Cineplex Odeon's programme of multiplex development in the UK in addition to its own schemes. As a result, former ABC cinemas have been replaced by new Cannon/MGM multiplexes at Chester, Eastbourne, Gloucester, Southampton and Swindon, although at Brighton the ABC cinema continues in business as the Cannon (minus

its largest auditorium) along with the MGM multiplex at the Marina. At the time of writing, the former ABC in Belfast is the latest to give way to a new MGM multiplex. Other former ABC cinemas at Newcastle, Peterborough and Basingstoke have been forced to close by the competition from nearby multiplexes operated by rival companies.

Despite this, nearly seventy former ABC cinemas survive within the MGM circuit in the early summer of 1993 as its largest single component (others remain open in independent hands at the Elephant and Castle, Turnpike Lane, Blyth, Carlisle, Cirencester, Horsham, Kings Lynn, Lowestoft, Wigan and Belfast). The ABCs that carry on as Cannons and MGM cinemas are to be found in the West End of London at Fulham Road and Shaftesbury Avenue; in the London suburbs at Beckenham, Catford, Croydon, Ealing, Enfield, Ewell, Hammersmith, Harrow, Putney, Romford, Sidcup, Streatham and Woodford; in the rest of England at Aldershot, Basildon, Bath, Blackpool, Bournemouth, Brighton, Bristol (two), Cambridge, Canterbury, Chatham, Darlington, Gravesend, Grimsby, Halifax, Hanley, Hereford, Leeds, Leicester, Liverpool, Luton, Mansfield, Newbury, Northampton, Norwich, Nottingham, Oxford (two), Plymouth, Portsmouth, Reading, St. Helens, Southend, Staines, Stevenage, Sunderland, Wakefield and Walsall; in Scotland at Aberdeen, Dumfries, Dundee, Edinburgh, Falkirk, Glasgow (three), Kilmarnock and Kirkcaldy; in Wales at Cardiff and Newport; and in Ireland at Dublin.

The best survivors of the purpose-built ABCs in cinema usage, ones retaining much or most of their original auditorium decoration, are the Cannon Liverpool (listed), Cannon Halifax and Cannon Northampton, all drop wall conversions to triple screens (there may be others of equal interest with which I am not familiar). Northampton has even had an organ reinstated, but Halifax (with a massive but well-handled sandstone exterior) offers a richer decorative scheme with elaborate lattice grille work in the proscenium arch creating an appropriate effect of a picture frame. The Cannon Wakefield is still operating but its little-altered auditorium was one of W. R. Glen's earlier, less intricate designs while his more interesting entrance hall has been altered beyond recognition. At Rochdale, the former ABC/Cannon is being de-tripled for bingo with promised restoration of much of the original decorative scheme, although this also was not one of Glen's most striking interiors.

Some of W. R. Glen's most impressive work lingers in a kind of limbo. The splendid auditorium at Ilford is now a nightclub after bingo failed. The auditoria at Hackney, Holloway and Stoke Newington house snooker on the former stalls floor but are largely wasted, especially regrettable in the case of Stoke Newington. The former ABC at Mile End is derelict but there has been talk of its re-opening as a cinema: if any were to be saved and restored to indicate the appealing qualities of a Glen ABC of the late Thirties, this would do nicely.

The Circuit Releases 1937-1979

This is a listing of main features released on the principal ABC circuit (beginning in North or Northwest London) from 1937, the year it reached full strength with the takeover of the Union circuit. It continues to the end of 1979 when films were being released across London and most ABC cinemas had been subdivided and were in non-competitive situations, selecting from the full range of new releases (but naturally giving priority to those films taken for the ABC circuit). Films may have been shown earlier at ABC cinemas outside London as pre-releases, while in London itself the ABCs Edgware Road and Fulham Road became pre-release theatres in 1962. ABC opened its own London West End first-run house, the ABC 1 & 2 Shaftesbury Avenue, to show films ahead of general release.

In the 1940s and 1950s, other programmes were widely shown on the 'B' circuit of surplus cinemas (while certain halls played the Odeon or Gaumont release).

Films are listed in the order they went out. For space reasons, precise dates and B features have been omitted, but co-features on double bills or emphasised supporting attractions have been included. There are more than fifty-two releases for some years when additional programmes were put out at Christmas to provide seasonal fare at more theatres; there are less than fifty-two releases for some years because of the double Christmas openings the previous year or where weeks were devoted to various reissues or where films ran (as noted) for two weeks.

From 1947 onwards, when the year's top box-office attractions were announced, those in the top ten (or top eight in 1970) that received an ABC circuit release are denoted by an asterisk *.

By the 1970s the rigid policy of playing the circuit release at virtually all cinemas had broken down and many films were booked only to the more suitable locations. Sometimes two features would go out in the same week on a split release or would open on different screens at cinemas converted to more than one auditoria. Some films would be released primarily to the smaller cinemas within these conversions. Some lesser programmes would be slotted in over the circuit over a period of several months. Major attractions were often released to key theatres in the London suburbs and the regions either simultaneously or very soon after their West End opening and would play a full circuit release later. At multi-screen cinemas, top box-office hits sometimes played for several months, starting off in the largest auditorium and finishing off in the smaller ones.

1937

To Mary with Love; San Francisco; Bullets or Ballots + Rhythm on the Range; His Brother's Wife; The Road to Glory; Piccadilly Jim; The Texas Rangers; Devil Takes the Count + Dusty Ermine; The Great Ziegfeld; Craig's Wife; The Plough and the Stars; Manhattan Madness; Dimples; Theodora Goes Wild; Beloved Enemy; This'll Make You Whistle; Winterset; Tarzan Escapes; Sensation + The Smartest Girl in Town; Aren't Men Beasts + Sinner Take All; Banjo on My Knee; More Than a Secretary; Tainted Money + Under Your Spell; That Girl from Paris; Charlie Chan at the Opera + White Hunter; Devil's Playground + Beauty and the Barge; Bulldog Drummond at Bay + Criminal Lawyer; Espionage; Maid of Salem; The Magnificent Brute; Please Teacher + The Girl on the Front Page; Michael Strogoff; Nancy Steele Is Missing + Kathleen Mavourneen; One in a Million + The Good Old Soak; The Dominant Sex; Camille; Shall We Dance; Born to Dance; On the Avenue + Swing High, Swing Low; God's Country and the Woman; Waikiki Wedding; Maytime; Slave Ship; Night Must Fall + Fifty Roads to Town; I Met Him in Paris + Marked Woman; Parnell; Glamorous Night; The Emperor's Candlesticks; Last Train from Madrid + French Leave; Married Before Breakfast; Under the Red Robe; Captains Courageous

1938

The Good Earth; Broadway Melody of 1938; Easy Living + Another Dawn; You Can't Have Everything + Between Two Women; Let's Make a Night of It + Exclusive; Stella Dallas; Souls at Sea; Over She Goes + Wife, Doctor and Nurse; The Life of Emile Zola; The Bride Wore Red + The Toast of New York; The Prisoner of Zenda; Stage Door; Lancer Spy + Double or Nothing; The Awful Truth; Marie Walewska; Heidi; Angel; The Last Gangster; I'll Take Romance; Man Proof; Hitting a New High; Dead Men Tell No Tales + You're Only Young Once; Damsel in Distress; Every Day's a Holiday; True Confession; Romance for Three; The Buccaneer; The Big Broadcast of 1938; Love and Hisses; Boy of the Streets + Checkers; Housemaster; Penitentiary + Of Human Hearts; The Baroness and the Butler; Port of Seven Seas; Vessel of Wrath; A Yank at Oxford; Happy Landing; Bluebeard's Eighth Wife; Test Pilot; Joy of Living; Her Jungle Love; You and Me; Four Men and a Prayer + Cocoanut Grove; Woman Against Woman + The Terror; Vivacious Lady; Shopworn Angel; Always Goodbye; The Crowd Roars; Three Blind Mice; Love Finds Andy Hardy; Sing You Sinners; Little Miss Broadway

1939

The Adventures of Robin Hood; Three Loves Has Nancy; Alexander's Ragtime Band; Too Hot to Handle; St. Martin's Lane; If I Were King; Free to Live; The Shining Hour; I Am the Law; The Citadel; Submarine Patrol; Four Daughters; Keep Smiling; Gangster's Boy; The Dawn Patrol; Out West with the Hardys; Zaza; Sweethearts; Angels with Dirty Faces or Four's a Crowd; Young Dr. Kildare; Charlie Chan in Honolulu + Comet Over Broadway; Dramatic School; They Drive By Night; Persons in Hiding + Burn 'Em Up O'Connor; They Made Me a Criminal; Honolulu; Wings of the Navy; Fast and Loose; Midnight; Within the Law; The Three Musketeers; Sergeant Madden; East Side of Heaven + Hotel Imperial; The Oklahoma Kid; The Outsider + You Can't Get Away with Murder; Ice Follies of 1939; Made for Each Other + The Gang's All Here; The Hardys Ride High; Dark Victory; Jamaica Inn; Beau Geste; Invitation to Happiness; Confessions of a Nazi Spy; It's a Wonderful World; Only Angels Have Wings; Dodge City; This Man in Paris + Sandy Takes a Bow; Spies of the Air; Let Us Live + Naughty But Nice; Andy Hardy Gets Spring Fever

1940

Rulers of the Sea; Daughters Courageous; Juarez; Lady of the Tropics; Poison Pen + Good Girls Go to Paris; Golden Boy; Melody of Youth + The Cat and the Canary; Marx Bros. at the Circus + Coastguard; French Without Tears; The Women; The Old Maid; The Real Glory; The Wizard of Oz; Mr. Smith Goes to Washington; Angels Wash Their Faces; Another Thin Man; Gulliver's Travels; Balalaika; Raffles; The Middle Watch; The Roaring Twenties; Judge Hardy and Son; Ten Days in Paris; The Shop Around the Corner; The Amazing Mr. Williams; Arouse and Beware; We Are Not Alone; The Dark Command; Everything Happens at Night; The House Across the Bay; His Girl Friday; I Take This Woman; Dead End Kids on Dress Parade; Broadway Melody of 1940; My Son My Son; Night Train to Munich; Northwest Passage; Forty Little Mothers + Bulldog Sees It Through; The Magic Bullet; The Westerner; The Private Lives of Elizabeth and Essex; The Mortal Storm; The Doctor Takes a Wife; Andy Hardy Meets Debutante; Virginia City; Busman's Honeymoon + Three Faces West; My Love Came Back; Maryland; George and Margaret + Three Cheers for the Irish; Waterloo Bridge; Lady in Question; The Gay Mrs. Trexel; The Sea Hawk

1941

Four Sons + Sporting Blood; Strike Up the Band; He Stayed for Breakfast + Gold Rush Maisie; Saturday's Children; Freedom Radio; Torrid Zone; Bad Man of Wyoming; Tin Pan Alley; Arizona; The Man Who Talked Too Much + Hit Parade of 1941; Third Finger Left Hand; All This and Heaven Too; Little Nellie Kelly; Angels Over Broadway + A Modern Hero; Down Argentine Way; The Road to Frisco + The Farmer's Wife; Comrade X; The Prime Minister; The Fighting 69th; Married But Single; Hudson's Bay + Night Train to Munich (revival); City for Conquest + Spring Meeting; The Trial of Mary Dugan + The Tree of Liberty; Escape to Glory + The Lone Wolf Keeps a Date; Boom Town; Four Mothers; Come Live with Me; Bitter Sweet; The Lady Eve; The Letter; Men of Boys' Town; Penny Serenade; Rage in Heaven + Target for Tonight; Road to Zanzibar; A Woman's Face; Atlantic Ferry + Love Thy Neighbour; Dangerous Moonlight + I'll Wait for You; Ziegfeld Girl; Adam Had Four Sons + Two Gun Cupid; Love Crazy; The Big Store + South of Suez; High Sierra; The Great Lie; Underground; Lady Be Good; Blossoms in the Dust; She Knew All the Answers + Cash and Carry; Ice Capades + The Wagons Roll at Night; Whistling in the Dark + They Dare Not Love; Our Wife; Life Begins for Andy Hardy; South American George

1942

When Ladies Meet; Meet John Doe; Here Comes Mr. Jordan; International Squadron + Unholy Partners; Honky Tonk; Sergeant York; The Chocolate Soldier; The Black Sheep of Whitehall; Santa Fe Trail; Two-Faced Woman; Dr. Jekyll and Mr. Hyde; You'll Never Get Rich; Dive Bomber; Smilin' Through; Tarzan's Secret Treasure; Manpower + Somewhere in Camp; Design for Scandal + Texas; Ladies in Retirement + Banana Ridge; Johnny Eager; Good Morning Doctor + The Bugle Sounds; They Died with Their Boots On; Navy Blues + This Was Paris; We Were Dancing + This Gun for Hire; Woman of the Year; The Foreman Went to France; The Man Who Came to Dinner; The Fleet's In + Nazi Agent; Captains of the Clouds; The Maltese Falcon + Bedtime Story; Rio Rita + The Remarkable Andrew; The Courtship of Andy Hardy; Unpublished Story + Ship Ahoy; The Bride Came C.O.D; Mrs. Miniver; Alibi + The Lady Is Willing; Gone with the Wind (two weeks); Flying Fortress; Tarzan's New York Adventure + A Yank in Dutch; All Through the Night; Much Too Shy + Dangerously They Live; In This Our Life; I Married an Angel; Tortilla Flat; They All Kissed the Bride; The Gay Sisters; Crossroads; The Big Shot + Calling Dr. Gillespie; San Francisco (revival); Always in My Heart; Bambi; A Yank at Eton

1943

In Which We Serve; Somewhere I'll Find You; We'll Meet Again + Seven Sweethearts; Talk of the Town; Desperate Journey; Thunder Rock; For Me and My Gal; Orchestra Wives + Flight Lieutenant; Squadron Leader X; Random Harvest; White Cargo; Across the Pacific; Flying Tigers + Cairo; Panama Hattie + Tomorrow We Live; Journey for Margaret + Ice Capades Revue of 1943; Casablanca; Yankee Doodle Dandy; Keeper of the Flame; Tales of Manhattan; Captain Blood (revival, excluding Northwest London); The Bells Go Down; Mademoiselle France; Tarzan Triumphs; Hitler's Children + Happidrome; Cargo of Innocents; Slightly Dangerous; Air Force; The Great Waltz (revival) + The Vanishing Virginian; Edge of Darkness; Assignment in Brittany + Silver Skates; Theatre Royal + Three Hearts for Julia; The Human Comedy; Presenting Lily Mars; They Got Me Covered; Mission to Moscow; The Youngest Profession + Hit Parade of 1943; Above Suspicion; Action in the North Atlantic; Du Barry Was a Lady; Watch on the Rhine; New Moon; Kings Row + Air Raid Wardens; Salute to the Marines; My Learned Friend + Pilot No. 5; The Four Feathers (revival) + The Girl in Overalls; Gentleman Jim; Adventures of Tartu; The Yellow Canary + Young Ideas; The Man from Down Under; By Hook Or By Crook; A Lady Takes a Chance; Girl Crazy

The World's Greatest Films
ELEPHANT & CASTLE THEATRE
REGAL OLD KENT RD
REGAL STREATHAM
REGAL CAMBERWELL
PALLADIUM BRIXTON

Commencing Sunday Next
September 20th

DAVID O. SELZNICK'S

GONE WITH THE WIND

1,500 UNRESERVED SEATS
AVAILABLE AT ALL PERFORMANCES AT ALL THEATRES AS USUAL at 2/6, 3/- or 4/- incl. tax

TWICE DAILY AT		SUNDAY
Elephant & Castle		AT
Regal, Streatham	1.55	
Regal, Old Kent Road	AND	4.0
Palladium, Brixton	6.30	
Regal, Camberwell,		

Metro-Goldwyn-Mayer

Metro-Goldwyn-Mayer GUARANTEE--

that "G.W.T.W." will be presented in suburban and provincial cinemas everywhere **EXACTLY AS IT IS BEING SHOWN IN THE WEST END AFTER 2½ YEARS' RUN.**

NOT ONE FOOT HAS BEEN OR WILL EVER BE CUT OUT OF ITS 3 HOURS and 40 MINUTES OF PERFECT ENTERTAINMENT.

Nor will it be shown anywhere except at advanced prices — at least until 1944

DAVID O. SELZNICK'S
Technicolor Miracle

GONE WITH THE WIND

starring

CLARK GABLE

LESLIE HOWARD · OLIVIA De HAVILLAND
and
VIVIEN LEIGH.

Directed by Victor Fleming. A Metro-Goldwyn-Mayer Release (Cert. A)

Starting GENERAL RELEASE:
SOUTH OF THE THAMES— SUNDAY, SEPTEMBER 20
AND NOW SHOWING THROUGHOUT GREAT BRITAIN.

Gone with the Wind was first generally released on the ABC circuit in 1942.

1944

Now, Voyager; Cry 'Havoc'; Best Foot Forward; Mutiny on the Bounty (*revival*); Thank Your Lucky Stars; Lassie Come Home; North Star; San Demetrio London; This Is the Army; Goodbye Mr. Chips! (*revival*); Candlelight in Algeria + North West Rangers; Thousands Cheer; Northern Pursuit; The £100 Window + In Old Oklahoma; Madame Curie; The Cross of Lorraine; The Hard Way + Cabin in the Sky; The Heavenly Body; Song of Russia; A Guy Named Joe; The Desert Song; Andy Hardy's Blonde Trouble; The Halfway House + The Oklahoma Kid (*revival*); Gone with the Wind (*revival*); Destination Tokyo; See Here, Private Hargrove + Women in Bondage; Princess O'Rourke; The Fighting Seabees + Rose Marie (*revival*); Hotel Reserve + Meet the People; Broadway Rhythm; In Our Time; Two Girls and a Sailor; Up in Arms; Uncertain Glory + Three Men in White; It Happened One Sunday + Action in Arabia; The Murder in Thornton Square; Passage to Marseille; The Canterville Ghost + Man from Frisco; The Adventures of Mark Twain; The White Cliffs of Dover; Rebecca (*revival*); Show Business; The Road to Frisco (*revival*) + Make Your Own Bed; The Seventh Cross; Champagne Charlie; Lost in a Harem; The Mask of Dimitrios; Dragon Seed; Between Two Worlds + Whistling in Brooklyn; Marriage Is a Private Affair; The Thief of Bagdad (*revival*) + You Can't Do That to Me; Bathing Beauty

1945

Old Acquaintance: An American Romance; Western Approaches + Lady, Let's Dance!; Kismet; Shine On Harvest Moon; Thirty Seconds Over Tokyo; Janie + Twilight Hour; Mrs. Parkington; Brazil + Nothing But Trouble; The Thin Man Goes Home; The Constant Nymph; Meet Me in St. Louis; Arsenic and Old Lace; Music for Millions; The Man from Morocco; This Man's Navy + Atlantic City; The Very Thought of You; Keep Your Powder Dry; Hotel Berlin; Farewell My Lovely + Blonde Fever; Flight from Folly + Between Two Women; Under the Clock; Great Day + Rationing; The Picture of Dorian Gray; Hollywood Canteen; Without Love; Experiment Perilous; The Right to Live + The Town Went Wild; To Have and Have Not; 29 Acacia Avenue + The Great Flamarion; The Doughgirls; National

Velvet; Waltz Time; The Conspirators; The Hidden Eye + The True Glory; I Live in Grosvenor Square; Mr. Skeffington; Dillinger + Twice Blessed; Roughly Speaking; Week-End at the Waldorf; The Great Lie; Perfect Strangers; Murder in Reverse; Son of Lassie; Conflict + Burma Victory; The Valley of Decision; God Is My Co-Pilot; Her Highness and the Bellboy; Escape in the Desert + Bewitched; The Wizard of Oz (revival) + Irene (revival); Indiscretion; Our Vines Have Tender Grapes; Rhapsody in Blue

1946

Abbott and Costello in Hollywood; Confidential Agent; The Trojan Brothers; Forever in Love; Thrill of a Romance; Latin Quarter + Too Young to Know; They Were Expendable + Don't Fence Me In; Pillow to Post; Anchors Aweigh; Three Strangers + Up She Goes; What Next, Corporal Hargrove?; The Last Chance; Night Boat to Dublin; Saratoga Trunk; Adventure; The Corn Is Green; The Harvey Girls; Kings Row (revival) + Cinderella Jones; The Postman Always Rings Twice; Lisbon Story; Ziegfeld Follies; Mildred Pierce; Bad Bascomb; Danger Signal + I'll Turn to You; Two Sisters from Boston; San Antonio; The Hoodlum Saint + A Woman's Face (revival); Gaiety George; Yolanda and the Thief; Quiet Week-End; Easy to Wed; My Reputation; Courage of Lassie; One More Tomorrow + Boys' Ranch; Meet the Navy; Devotion; Two Smart People + Michael Strogoff; Her Kind of Man + Jesse James (revival); Piccadilly Incident; Three Wise Fools; A Girl in a Million; The Big Sleep; No Leave No Love + The Walls Came Tumbling Down; Appointment with Crime + Blossoms in the Dust (revival); Holiday in Mexico; The Man I Love + Faithful in My Fashion; This Man Is Mine; The Verdict + Little Mister Jim; Spring Song + Shadow of a Woman; The Wife of Monte Cristo + The Enchanted Forest; Conspirator; Night and Day

1947 (* denotes film in Box Office Top Ten)

The Green Years; Suspense; A Stolen Life; Lady in the Lake; The Laughing Lady; Woman to Woman + Janie Gets Married; Love Laughs at Andy Hardy + The First of the Few (revival); The Secret Heart; Cloak and Dagger; The Shop at Sly Corner + My

Brother Talks to Horses; The Sea of Grass; Never Say Goodbye; While the Sun Shines; Till the Clouds Roll By; Of Human Bondage; It Happened in Brooklyn; Temptation Harbour; White Cradle Inn + Cynthia's Secret; Nobody Lives Forever + The Jungle Princess (revival); The Other Love; The Time, The Place and the Girl; Green Fingers + Undercover Girl; The Beginning or the End; That Way with Women + The Turners of Prospect Road; High Barbaree + Hit Parade of 1947; Her Sister's Secret + Dual Alibi; Humoresque; Gallant Bess + Bonnie Scotland (revival); Royal Flush + I Met a Murderer (revival); Stallion Road; The Hucksters; Paula + The Rich, Full Life; They Made Me a Fugitive; Monte Cristo's Revenge + Ramrod; Nora Prentiss; *The Courtneys of Curzon Street; The Yearling; Fiesta; The Two Mrs. Carrolls; Song of the Thin Man + 2000 Women (revival); *Duel in the Sun; Deception; Random Harvest (revival); A Man About the House; Pursued; Song of Love; The Ghosts of Berkeley Square + This Gun for Hire (revival); Love and Learn + Will Tomorrow Ever Come?; The Black Swan (revival) + The Silver Darlings; It Happened on Fifth Avenue + Dillinger (revival); The Sea Hawk (revival) + The Sea Wolf (revival); Gone with the Wind (revival)

1948

Mr. Fitzherbert; Possessed; The Private Affairs of Bel Ami + Cottage to Let (revival); Brighton Rock; Each Dawn I Die (revival) + Bad Men of Missouri (revival); Mine Own Executioner; An Ideal Husband; The Unfaithful; Mrs. Miniver (revival); The Swordsman; Cry Wolf + The Ghost of St. Michaels (revival); Just William's Luck + Merton of the Movies; *My Brother Jonathan; Marked Woman (revival) + Manpower (revival); Night Beat + Unfinished Business (revival); Northwest Passage (revival) + Nothing But Trouble (revival); Idol of Paris + The Trespasser (revival); Lady Hamilton (revival) + In Which We Serve (revival); Broadway Melody (revival) (replaced by Pride and Prejudice [revival]); Dark Passage; City for Conquest (revival) + Wild Bill Hickok Rides; The First Gentleman; Fanny by Gaslight (revival) + Pittsburgh (revival); Counterblast + Her Husband's Affairs; This Was a Woman + Pardon My Sarong (revival); The Beast with Five Fingers + The Man Who Came to Dinner (revival); Uneasy Terms + Black Gold; The Bride Goes Wild + The Flame; Deep Valley; Body

and Soul; Bond Street; Cheyenne; The Jungle Book (revival) + Call of the Blood; High Wall; Woman in White + The Gangster; Green Dolphin Street; *Spring in Park Lane; The Unsuspected; Anna Karenina; The Pirate; *Life with Father; Noose; The Fallen Idol; Homecoming; The Winslow Boy; Silver River; No Room at the Inn; The Small Voice; Desire Me; That Hagen Girl + Calling Paul Temple; My Wild Irish Rose; The Voice of the Turtle + Smart Girls Don't Talk

1949

This Time for Keeps + Tenth Avenue Angel; Bonnie Prince Charlie; Rope; The Guinea Pig; Cass Timberlane; Elizabeth of Ladymead; *Johnny Belinda; The Small Back Room; Forbidden + My Dear Secretary; The Glass Mountain; Julia Misbehaves + They Passed This Way; Silent Dust; Things Happen at Night + The Scar; Treasure of Sierra Madre; The Queen of Spades; *Easter Parade; Edward My Son; April Showers + Flaxy Martin; For Them That Trespass + The Dude Goes West; Arch of Triumph; The Golden Madonna + Jack of Diamonds; John Loves Mary + Whiplash; Man on the Run; On an Island With You; June Bride; Now Barabbas Was a Robber; The Story of Shirley Yorke + Don't Trust Your Husband; Master of Lassie + Tuna Clipper; The Last Days of Dolwyn; It's Magic; Key Largo; Words and Music; Saints and Sinners; Private Angelo; Conspirator; That Dangerous Age; Flamingo Road; *Maytime in Mayfair; The Three Musketeers; *The Third Man; My Dream Is Yours; The Interrupted Journey; The Barkleys of Broadway; *The Hasty Heart; The New Adventures of Don Juan; Landfall; In the Good Old Summertime; The Fountainhead; Any Number Can Play; Scene of the Crime + Border Incident; Colorado Territory; Little Women

1950

Under Capricorn; White Heat; East of the Rising Sun; The Twenty Questions Murder Mystery + The Masked Pirate; Look for the Silver Lining; The Cure for Love; *The Forsyte Saga; No Place for Jennifer + Northwest Stampede; Task Force; Your Witness + The Man in Black; Neptune's Daughter; The Angel with the Trumpet + The Adventures of

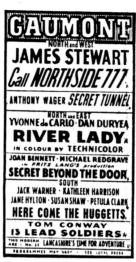
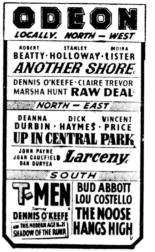

Competing attractions at the three major circuits in the London area in the winter of 1948.

Gallant Bess; It's a Great Feeling; Chain Lightning; *The Happiest Days of Your Life; Guilt Is My Shadow + Mickey; Adam's Rib; Double Confession + Stampede; South of St. Louis + Kiss in the Dark; Last Holiday + Room to Let; Battleground; Young Man of Music; The Girl Who Couldn't Quite + Without Honor; Pride of Kentucky + The Girl from Jones Beach; East Side West Side; Ambush + Side Street; One Sunday Afternoon + Barricade; *The Third Man (revival) + *The Courtneys of Curzon Street (revival); Key to the City; Montana + Always Leave Them Laughing; Too Dangerous to Love + Embraceable You; On the Town; Cairo Road + Quiet Week-End; My Daughter Joy + Someone at the Door; Stage Fright; The Dancing Years; State Secret; The Inspector General; *Father of the Bride; *Odette; *Annie Get Your Gun; *The Wooden Horse; The Damned Don't Cry; The Miniver Story; Gone to Earth; Portrait of Clare + Rocketship X-M; Sands of Iwo Jima; Caged!; The Asphalt Jungle + A Lady without Passport; Colt .45 + Night Unto Night; Three Little Words; The Daughter of Rosie O'Grady

1951

The Elusive Pimpernel; If You Feel Like Singing; Three Secrets; Two Weeks with Love + Forgery; The Woman with No Name + They Made Me a Fugitive (revival); The Glass Menagerie; Murder without Crime + Four Days Leave; Grounds for Marriage + Watch the Birdie; The Flame and the Arrow; The Franchise Affair; The Breaking Point + The Lady Takes a Sailor; Kiss Tomorrow Goodbye; *King Solomon's Mines; Vengeance Valley + Inside Straight; Mr. Drake's Duck + Thunder in the Dust; Flesh and Blood; Three Guys Named Mike + The Next Voice You Hear; A Walk in the Sun + The Naked Heart; Wedding Bells; Tea for Two; Jennie + High Venture; Father's Little Dividend; The Late Edwina Black + Paul Temple's Triumph; Return of the Frontiersman + Pretty Baby; The Toast of New Orleans + The Happy Years; One Wild Oat + The Sun Sets at Dawn; Bright Leaf; Talk of a Million + The Last Outpost; Teresa + Excuse My Dust; Storm Warning; Rich, Young and Pretty; The Galloping Major; Rocky Mountain + Backfire; *Worm's Eye View; Operation Pacific; *The Great Caruso; Happy Go Lucky; Strangers on a Train; Show Boat; *Captain Horatio Hornblower R.N.;

ABC releases on their way around London in the middle of 1951 and the choice offered by the major circuits in December 1952 and early 1953.

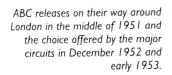

*Laughter in Paradise; Fine and Dandy; *The Great Caruso (re-run); The Lady with the Lamp; I Was a Communist for the F.B.I. + Canyon Pass; Young Wives' Tale; The People Against O'Hara; The Tales of Hoffman or Highway 301; Dallas; Texas Carnival; Along the Great Divide; An American in Paris; Lullaby of Broadway

1952

Lady Godiva Rides Again; The Light Touch; The Magic Box; Murder Inc.; Westward the Women; *Reluctant Heroes; Only the Valiant; Outcast of the Islands; Lone Star; *The African Queen; Remember That Face + Home at Seven; A Streetcar Named Desire; Invitation + Just This Once; Starlift + Fort Worth; The Belle of New York + The Sellout; Distant Drums; The Happy Family + Never Take No for an Answer; Singin' in the Rain; So Little Time + Marshmallow Moon; On Moonlight Bay; Hoodlum Empire + The Wonder Kid; Bugles in the Afternoon; Carbine Williams + Young Man with Ideas; The Highwayman + The Woman's Angle; The Star Said No + So Bright the Flame; Who Goes There!; The Wild North; Man of Bronze + The San Francisco Story; *The Quiet Man; Skirts Ahoy!; *Angels One Five; Mara Maru; Gone with the Wind (revival); Castle in the Air; Derby Day; *Ivanhoe; I'll See You in My Dreams; Scaramouche; Objective, Burma!; Where's Charley? + The Winning Team; *The Sound Barrier; Lovely to Look At; 24 Hours of a Woman's Life; Carson City + About Face; Cry, The Beloved Country; The Merry Widow; Father's Doing Fine; The Story of Will Rogers + The Devil Makes Three; Pat and Mike + The Red Badge of Courage; Big Jim McLain; The Holly and the Ivy; *Because You're Mine

1953

Jack and the Beanstalk; Top Secret; The One-Piece Bathing Suit; She's Working Her Way Through College; Trent's Last Case; The Prisoner of Zenda; The Crimson Pirate; Women of Twilight; The Iron Mistress; Plymouth Adventure; Springfield Rifle; Above and Beyond; South of Algiers; April in Paris; The Bad and the Beautiful; The Yellow Balloon; The Miracle of Fatima; Cosh Boy; The Naked Spur; Retreat, Hell! + Cattle Town; Never Let Me Go; I Confess; Elizabeth Is Queen; Jeopardy + Time Bomb; Battle Circus; Stop, You're Killing Me + Operation Secret; I Love Melvin + Remains To Be Seen; Dream Wife + The Girl Who Had Everything; The Story of Three Loves; The Lion and the Horse + A Slight Case of Larceny; The Captain's Paradise; Young Bess; She's Back on Broadway; Will Any Gentleman?; Lili; The Story of Gilbert and Sullivan; By the Light of the Silvery Moon; *Moulin Rouge; *Quo Vadis; The Beggar's Opera (but replaced by Sombrero and others at most situations after first London week); The Beast from 20,000 Fathoms; The Master of Ballantrae; Scandal at Scourie; The Man Between; Island in the Sky + The Blue Gardenia; Isn't Life Wonderful?; The Intruder; The Conquest of Everest + The Good Beginning; Ride, Vaquero + Monsoon; Dangerous When Wet; Blowing Wild + Spaceways; Abbott and Costello Meet Captain Kidd

1954

Mogambo; Beat the Devil; The Grace Moore Story + The Moonlighter; The Big Heat (after first London week) + The Heart of the Matter; All the Brothers Were Valiant; So Big + Thunder Over the Plains; The Band Wagon; Front Page Story; Torch Song; They Who Dare; *Calamity Jane; Julius Caesar or The Moon Is Blue; The Weak and the Wicked; The Charge at Feather River; Kiss Me Kate; Hobson's Choice; Eight O'Clock Walk + Devil on Horseback; Easy to Love; Hondo; Arena + Latin Lovers; Life with the Lyons; The Boy from Oklahoma + The Diamond Queen; The Long Long Trailer + My Man and I; The Naked Jungle; Knave of Hearts; Take the High Ground + Saadia; Escape from Fort Bravo; Phantom of the Rue Morgue; The Sleeping Tiger + Three Young Texans; His Majesty O'Keefe; *Happy Ever After; Executive Suite; Seagulls over Sorrento; Dial 'M' for Murder; Valley of the Kings; Duel in the Jungle; The Command; Flame and the Flesh; Lucky Me; Knights of the Round Table; Rose Marie; Her Twelve Men + Men of the Fighting Lady; Them; The High and the Mighty; Betrayed + Jennifer; Riot in Cell Block 11 + Arrow in the Dust; For Better For Worse + The Raid; To Dorothy a Son; Golden Ivory; The Jazz Singer + Riding Shotgun; Beau Brummell + Athena; King Richard and the Crusaders

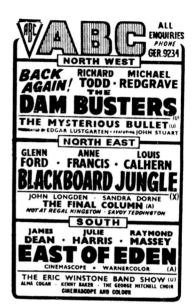

The Dam Busters was such a smash hit on the ABC circuit in 1955 that it made a return trip.

1955

*The Student Prince; Carrington V.C.; Ring of Fear; Lilacs in the Spring; Rogue Cop + Tennessee Champ; The Man Who Loved Redheads; Dragnet + The Bounty Hunter; *Seven Brides for Seven Brothers; The Human Jungle + Break in the Circle; Drum Beat; The Love Match + Invaders from Mars; Unchained + A Lion Is in the Streets; Green Fire; Bad Day at Black Rock; Young at Heart; *Raising a Riot + The Angel Who Pawned Her Harp; The Track of the Cat + The Sheep Has Five Legs; Deep in My Heart; Orders Are Orders + Make Me an Offer; The Constant Husband; The Last Time I Saw Paris; A Star Is Born; Many Rivers to Cross; Contraband Spain + King of the Coral Sea; New York Confidential + Jump into Hell; Brigadoon; See How They Run + Crashout; Jupiter's Darling; Confession + Moonfleet; Rhapsody + Bedevilled; Hit the Deck; John and Julie; The Silver Chalice; The Sea Chase; Interrupted Melody; *The Dam Busters; The Prodigal; Battle Cry; Love Me Or Leave Me; Geordie; East of Eden; Blackboard Jungle; *The Dam Busters (re-run); Pete Kelly's Blues; I Am a Camera; The King's Thief; Confidential Report + Tall Man Riding; Rififi + The Quatermass Xperiment; The Wizard of Oz (revival) + The Glass Slipper; Wichita; Tiger in the Sky; It's Always Fair Weather; Storm Over the Nile

1956

The Big Combo + Oh, Rosalinda!!; Mister Roberts; King's Rhapsody; The Tender Trap; Trial; Sincerely Yours; The Phenix City Story + You Can't Escape; Ransom; Rebel Without a Cause; *Private's Progress; Helen of Troy; The Adventures of Quentin Durward; Now and Forever; I Died a Thousand Times; Illegal; Tribute to a Bad Man + The Scarlet Coat; 1984; One Man Mutiny; Charley Moon + Shotgun; The Swan; Hell on Frisco Bay; The Last Hunt; It's Never Too Late + Gunpoint; Miracle in the Rain; Forever Darling; The Extra Day + Thunderstorm; The First Texan + It's Magic (revival); Forbidden Planet; Gaby; Ramsbottom Rides Again; *It's Great to Be Young!; Land of the Pharaohs; Wedding Breakfast; My Teenage Daughter; Serenade; Yield to the Night; Viva Las Vegas!; *The Searchers; *The Baby and the Battleship; I'll Cry Tomorrow; *Sailor Beware!; *The Bad Seed; Bhowani Junction; The

Fiends + X the Unknown; The Burning Hills; Somebody Up There Likes Me; The Gun Runner; Cell 2455, Death Row + The Slave Woman; The Fastest Gun Alive + These Wilder Years; Satellite in the Sky + The Animal World; Guys and Dolls; Friendly Persuasion

1957

Brink of Hell; Loser Takes All; *Three Men in a Boat; Moby Dick; *High Society; My Wife's Family; Man in the Sky; Baby Doll; The Opposite Sex; The Wrong Man; Kismet; *Giant; The Barretts of Wimpole Street; Rock Rock Rock + Seven Men from Now; Julie; The Good Companions; Their Secret Affair; The Smallest Show on Earth; Ten Thousand Bedrooms; The Curse of Frankenstein + Woman of Rome; The Wings of Eagles; Stampeded; Designing Woman; And Woman...Was Created + Quatermass 2; *The Tommy Steele Story; This Could Be the Night; Carry On Admiral; Something of Value; Let's Be Happy; The Teahouse of the August Moon; The Spirit of St. Louis; *The Shiralee; The Abominable Snowman + Untamed Youth; These Dangerous Years; Silk Stockings; No Time for Tears; Action of the Tiger + House of Numbers; *Yangtse Incident; *War and Peace; The Prince and the Showgirl; Tea and Sympathy; Band of Angels; Woman in a Dressing Gown; A Face in the Crowd; The Little Hut; No Sleep Till Dawn; Night of the Demon + 20 Million Miles to Earth; The Birthday Present + Dragoon Wells Massacre; Gun Glory + Time for Action; Les Girls; Both Ends of the Candle

1958

Barnacle Bill; The D.I. + The Story of Mankind; The Flesh Is Weak; The Pajama Game; Davy; The Man Who Wouldn't Talk; Jailhouse Rock; Disc Jockey Jamboree; *Happy Is the Bride; The Deep Six; Don't Go Near the Water; Chase a Crooked Shadow; The Duke Wore Jeans; Sayonara; Hell Bent for Glory; The Tall Stranger + The Golden Disc; The Safecracker + Saddle the Wind; Old Yeller; The Young Invaders; Seven Hills of Rome; *Dunkirk; The Sheepman + Cry Terror!; *The Camp on Blood Island + Young Girls Beware; Up the Creek; Marjorie Morningstar; The Law and

Jake Wade + Tarzan and the Lost Safari; Heaven Fell That Night + The Snorkel; Too Much, Too Soon + Fort Dobbs; The Brothers Karamazov; Perri + Westward Ho The Wagons!; The Moonraker; Battle of the V.1; No Time for Sergeants; Wonderful Things! + Quantrill's Raiders; *A Cry from the Streets; Raintree County; Imitation General + The High Cost of Loving; The Left-Handed Gun + Wind Across the Everglades; Merry Andrew; *Ice Cold in Alex; A Question of Adultery; *Indiscreet; *Carry On Sergeant; The Proud Rebel; Onionhead; The Revenge of Frankenstein; Cat on a Hot Tin Roof; She Didn't Say No! + Bullwhip; The Trollenberg Terror + Call Girls; The Badlanders + The Decks Ran Red; *Tom Thumb + Andy Hardy Comes Home; Girls at Sea + Gunsmoke in Tucson

1959

What Lola Wants!; Torpedo Run + Nowhere to Go; I Was Monty's Double; The Old Man and the Sea; *The Reluctant Debutante; I Only Arsked! + Buchanan Rides Alone; Party Girl + I Accuse!; Home Before Dark; Love Is My Profession + Blood of the Vampire; The Angry Hills + Tarzan's Fight for Life; The Lady Is a Square; *Carry On Nurse; Auntie Mame; The Hanging Tree; *Room at the Top; The Journey; No Trees in the Street; Life in Emergency Ward 10 + Man from God's Country; Up Periscope! + Westbound; Some Came Running; The Doctor's Dilemma + Watusi; Passport to Shame + Horrors of the Black Museum; The City Jungle; Alive and Kicking; Look Back in Anger; For the First Time; Serious Charge; Count Your Blessings; *Rio Bravo; The Mating Game; *Operation Bullshine; The Ugly Duckling; Tunnel of Love; The Big Circus; The Scapegoat; Left, Right and Centre; Yellowstone Kelly; Jack the Ripper + Temptation Island; Carry On Teacher; Jet Storm; The Siege of Pinchgut; Yesterday's Enemy; The Rough and the Smooth; The Mummy; Deadline Midnight + Never Love a Stranger; The Case of Dr. Laurent + The Last Mile; John Paul Jones; The Man Who Could Cheat Death; Behemoth the Sea Monster + Girls Disappear; The Treasure of San Teresa + Friends and Neighbours; Don't Panic Chaps + Edge of Eternity; Tommy the Toreador; The F.B.I. Story

1960

Expresso Bongo; The Stranglers of Bombay; Please Turn Over; A Summer Place; The Scarface Mob; Tamango + Comanche Station; *Two-Way Stretch; Moment of Danger; The Wreck of the Mary Deare; The Bramble Bush; Bluebeard's Ten Honeymoons + The Purple Gang; The Angry Silence; Inn for Trouble + And the Same to You; *Carry On Constable; Bottoms Up!; Cash McCall + Guns of the Timberland; Let's Get Married; School for Scoundrels; Hell Is a City; The Rise and Fall of 'Legs' Diamond + Born Reckless; The Trials of Oscar Wilde; Goliath and the Barbarians; Peeping Tom; Sergeant Rutledge + Tall Story; Circus of Horrors; The Flesh and the Fiends + Rififi and the Women; The Last Voyage + Girls Town; Follow That Horse! + Dust in the Sun; The Gazebo; Sands of the Desert; *Hercules Unchained; The Adventures of Huckleberry Finn; Ice Palace; *Dentist in the Chair; Light Up the Sky; The Nun's Story; A French Mistress; Never Take Sweets from a Stranger + Come Dance with Me; Hannibal; *Oceans 11; Home from the Hill; Watch Your Stern; The Dark at the Top of the Stairs; The Two Faces of Dr. Jekyll + Hot Hours; Village of the Damned; The Mobster + The City of the Dead; The Plunderers + Pay or Die!; Beat Girl + Nights of Temptation; The Crowded Sky; Too Hot to Handle; No Kidding; Sword of Sherwood Forest + Visa to Canton

1961

The Miracle; The Criminal; His and Hers; *Saturday Night and Sunday Morning; *Butterfield 8; The Night We Got the Bird + Offbeat; The Full Treatment; *The Sundowners; *The Long and the Short and the Tall; *Carry On Regardless; Cimarron; *The Rebel; Konga + The Hellfire Club; Fury at Smugglers Bay; Operation Eichmann + Hell to Eternity; The Sins of Rachel Cade; The Fall of the House of Usher; World by Night + Jet Over the Atlantic; Week-End with Lulu + Rag Doll; Where the Boys Are + The Green Helmet; Payroll; A Taste of Fear; Strangers on a Train (revival) + A Fever in the Blood; Go Naked in the World + The Lawbreakers; All in a Night's Work; Dentist on the Job; Portrait of a Mobster + Girl of the Night; Don't Bother to Knock; One Eyed Jacks; Gold of the Seven Saints + The White Warrior; Watch It, Sailor! + The Treasure of Monte Cristo; On the Double; Parrish; The Ladies' Man; What a Carve Up!; The Secret Partner + Ring of Fire; Raising the Wind; Two Women + The Frightened City; Murder She Said + The Honeymoon Machine; East of Eden (revival) + Armoured Command; On Friday at 11 + Nothing Barred; The Pleasure of His Company; On the Fiddle + Master of the World; What a Whopper; Breakfast at Tiffany's; The Terror of the Tongs + Homicidal; Gorgo; Too Late Blues + Love in a Goldfish Bowl; Gigi; Bachelor in Paradise; Petticoat Pirates

1962

*Blue Hawaii; The Errand Boy + Hey, Let's Twist!; Go to Blazes; The Pit and the Pendulum + Island of Shame; *The Young Ones; Fanny; *Only Two Can Play; Splendour in the Grass; My Geisha; Susan Slade + Samar; Go to Blazes; The Roman Spring of Mrs. Stone; A Thunder of Drums + The Colossus of Rhodes; A View from the Bridge; Twice Round the Daffodils; Summer and Smoke; King of Kings; *Carry On Cruising; Operation Snatch + Jungle Street; Summer and Smoke; A Majority of One; The Night of the Eagle + She'll Have to Go; *A Kind of Loving; The Man Who Shot Liberty Valance; All Fall Down + Postman's Knock; The Pot Carriers + Spin of a Coin; Hell Is for Heroes + Man-Trap; Sweet Bird of Youth; Lovers Must Learn + The Deadly Companions; Merrill's Marauders + European Nights; Boys' Night Out + The Crimebusters; Play It Cool + Seven Keys; Escape from Zahrain; Some People; The Pirates of Blood River + Mysterious Island; Guns of Darkness; I Thank a Fool; Mix Me a Person; Jigsaw; The Music Man; The Pigeon That Took Rome; The Premature Burial + Ordered to Love; Term of Trial; Two Weeks in Another Town; The Dock Brief; The Counterfeit Traitor; The Loneliness of the Long Distance Runner; The Chapman Report; The Password Is Courage; Constantine the Great + Mrs. Gibbons' Boys; Crooks Anonymous; A Prize of Arms; The Wonders of Aladdin + Tarzan Goes to India; The Thief of Bagdad + The Savage Guns; We Joined the Navy

1963

The Main Attraction; Lolita; Gypsy; Live Now – Pay Later; The Iron Maiden; Hatari!; *Summer Holiday; Critic's Choice; *Girls! Girls! Girls!; The Thief of Bagdad + The Savage Guns; Sparrows Can't Sing; The Mind Benders; It's Only Money + Who's Got the Action?; The Punch and Judy Man; Jumbo; *The Wrong Arm of the Law; The Courtship of Eddie's Father + Follow the Boys; What Ever Happened to Baby Jane?; A Girl Named Tamiko + My Six Loves; Maniac + The Damned; Porgy and Bess; Nurse on Wheels; Come Fly with Me + The Hook; Tales of Terror + Panic in Year Zero; Hud; Days of Wine and Roses; *It Happened at the World's Fair + Swordsman of Siena; The Small World of Sammy Lee; Spencer's Mountain; Donovan's Reef; The Cracksman; The Scarlet Blade + The Son of Captain Blood; Come Blow Your Horn; Tamahine; PT109; *Heavens Above!; Billy Liar!; *The V.I.P.s; Rampage; The Raven + Dr. Crippen; Mutiny on the Bounty; Station Six – Sahara; A New Kind of Love; West 11; Carry On Cabby; The World Ten Times Over + Black Zoo; Murder at the Gallop + Guns of Wyoming; Wives and Lovers; The Man Who Finally Died; Ben-Hur; Fun in Acapulco; Son of Spartacus + Flipper

1964

Palm Springs Weekend + World by Night No. 2; What a Crazy World + Gunfight at Comanche Creek; The Haunting; Kiss of the Vampire + Paranoiac; Who's Minding the Store? + Who's Been Sleeping in My Bed?; The Servant; 4 for Texas; This Is My Street; The Prize; The Leather Boys; Nothing But the Best; *Love in Las Vegas + Gladiators Seven; *Zulu; *Carry On, Jack!; Mary Mary; The Charge Is Murder + Children of the Damned; A Place to Go; Dead Image; A Distant Trumpet; *The Bargee; The Nutty Professor; Evil of Frankenstein + Nightmare; Seven Days in May; Night Must Fall + Two Are Guilty; French Dressing; Hide and Seek + Just for You; Paris When It Sizzles; The Masque of the Red Death + The Man with the X-Ray Eyes; Separate Beds + Island of Love; Kissin' Cousins + Never Put It in Writing; Carry On Spying; The Devil-Ship Pirates + The Invincible Seven; Crooks in Cloisters + Beach Party; Tarzan's Three Challenges + Flipper

and the Pirates; The Unsinkable Molly Brown; *Wonderful Life; Love with the Proper Stranger; The System + Strait-Jacket; Robin and the 7 Hoods; The Night of the Iguana; Yesterday, Today and Tomorrow; The Gorgon + The Curse of the Mummy's Tomb; Murder Most Foul + Rhino!; Rattle of a Simple Man + Cry of Battle; *The Carpetbaggers (two weeks); A House Is Not a Home + Young Fury; Of Human Bondage + West of Montana; The Tomb of Ligeia + Black Sabbath; 36 Hours + Honeymoon Hotel; Roustabout; Cheyenne Autumn

1965

Every Day's a Holiday + Duel of Champions; Sunday in New York + Company of Cowards?; *Carry On Cleo; Sex and the Single Girl; *The Yellow Rolls Royce; King and Country; Where Love Has Gone; The Patsy + Robinson Crusoe on Mars; Dr. Terror's House of Horrors + He Rides Tall; Becket; Young Cassidy + The Rounders; The Killers + Fanatic; None But the Brave; Joey Boy; Girl Happy + Sandokan the Great; She; I've Gotta Horse (double-billed second to Carry On revivals from South London); Marriage Italian Style; Dear Heart + My Blood Runs Cold; The Americaniz- ation of Emily + To Trap a Spy!; Ring of Spies + Two Left Feet; Three Hats for Lisa + Blood on the Arrow; How the West Was Won; The Secret of Blood Island + The Night Walker; Sylvia; The Hill; Tickle Me + Soldier in the Rain; Harlow; In Harm's Way; Catch Us If You Can + Bikini Beach; Battle of the Villa Fiorita (cancelled after North London with revivals substituted); The Brigand of Kandahar + Vendetta; The Spy with My Face + Son of a Gunfighter; Dr. Who and the Daleks; *Operation Crossbow; Rotten to the Core; The Third Day; *The Amorous Adventures of Moll Flanders; The Big Job; The Sandpiper + Murder Ahoy; The Disorderly Orderly + Crack in the World; Darling; City Under the Sea + The Face of Fu Manchu; Marriage on the Rocks; The Nanny; The Sons of Katie Elder; The Cincinnati Kid + Quick, Before It Melts; Dingaka; The Pleasure Girls + The Wild Affair; The Family Jewels + Town Tamer; The Secret of My Success + Once a Thief; Harem Holiday

1966

Sands of the Kalahari; Dracula, Prince of Darkness + The Plague of the Zombies; Up Jumped a Swagman; Lady L + The Money Trap; He Who Rides a Tiger + The Great Sioux Massacre; Ten Little Indians + The Captive City; The Spy Who Came in from the Cold; Monster of Terror + The Haunted Palace; *One Spy Too Many + Your Cheatin' Heart; Rasputin – The Mad Monk + The Reptile; Judith; Four Kinds of Love + Blood and Black Lace; Where the Spies Are + Joy in the Morning; The Great St. Trinian's Train Robbery; Carry On Cowboy; The Singing Nun + A Global Affair; Stop the World I Want to Get Off + Brainstorm (withdrawn by South London); *Alfie (two weeks); Morgan – A Suitable Case for Treatment; Our Man in Marrakesh; A Patch of Blue + Made in Paris; Inside Daisy Clover + Two on a Guillotine; Boeing Boeing; Island of Terror + Run with the Wind; Around the World Under the Sea + Captain Sindbad; The Moving Target + Kisses for My President; The Oscar; The Glass Bottom Boat + The Alphabet Murders; The Wonderful World of the Brothers Grimm; Paradise – Hawaiian Style; Daleks – Invasion Earth 2150 A.D.; One of Our Spies Is Missing; *The Great Race; *Nevada Smith; A Fine Madness; Carry On Screaming; Big Deal at Dodge City + The Old Dark House; Assault on a Queen; The Liquidator; Kaleidoscope; *Battle of the Bulge; California Holiday + Hercules, Samson and Ulysses; See You in Hell, Darling + Chamber of Horrors; The Idol + The Skull; The Naked Prey + Red Line 7000; Where the Bullets Fly + The Night of the Grizzly; This Property Is Condemned + The Psychopath; The Love Cage + 7 Women; The Witches; Tarzan and the Valley of Gold + The Brides of Fu Manchu; The Venetian Affair + The Dangerous Days of Kiowa Jones; *One Million Years B.C.

1967

The Ten Commandments (revival); *My Fair Lady (two weeks); Not With My Wife, You Don't!; The Spy in the Green Hat + When the Boys Meet the Girls; Drop Dead! Darling + Promise Her Anything; *The Family Way (two weeks); Danger Grows Wild + One Potato, Two Potato; Who's Afraid of Virginia Woolf?; Penelope + Return of the Gunfighter; The Viking Queen; Funeral in Berlin; Hotel (mostly cancelled after start); Is Paris

Burning?; The Peking Medallion + Bachelor Girl Apartment; The 25th Hour + Maya; The Spy with the Cold Nose; Blow-Up + Doctor, You've Got to Be Kidding!; The Double Man + First to Fight; Easy Come, Easy Go; Mister Ten Per Cent (*mostly cancelled after start*); Chuka + Warning Shot; Frankenstein Created Woman + The Mummy's Shroud; The Pistolero of Red River + Three Bites of the Apple; Barefoot in the Park; The Shuttered Room + You're a Big Boy Now; Africa – Texas Style! – *largely replaced by* The Swinger + Seconds; Jules Verne's Rocket to the Moon; Zulu (*revival*); *El Dorado; Double Trouble + Hondo and the Apaches; The Naked Runner + Countdown; The Karate Killers + Don't Make Waves; Triple Cross; The Bobo; Up the Down Staircase (*limited*); Hurry Sundown; *Bonnie and Clyde (*two weeks*); Our Mother's House; *The Dirty Dozen (*two weeks*); *Robbery; Grand Prix; Quatermass and the Pit; Waterhole 3 + Gunn; Sumuru + The Vengeance of Fu Manchu; Theatre of Death + The Deadly Bees; The Last Safari + Carnival of Thieves; A Challenge for Robin Hood + Ringo and His Golden Pistol; Cool Hand Luke

1968

[*In weeks when assorted programmes were shown, Seventeen and Helga had soon played most theatres*]

The Dirty Dozen (*revival, London only*); Will Penny + Tarzan and the Great River; *Poor Cow; Point Blank; Smashing Time; The Anniversary; The Helicopter Spies + The Fastest Guitar Alive; The Comedians; *Up the Junction; The Mercenaries; The Heroin Gang + The Eye of the Devil; Sebastian; The Vengeance of She; Firecreek; Guns for San Sebastian; Day of the Evil Gun + The Power; Reflections in a Golden Eye; Witchfinder General + The Blood Beast Terror; Counterpoint + The Pink Jungle; No Way to Treat a Lady + The Slender Thread; *The Fox + Chubasco; The Penthouse + Grand Slam; Only When I Larf + The Spirit Is Willing; The Devil Rides Out + Slave Girls; The Lost Continent; Blue; How to Steal the World + Speedway; Villa Rides!; The Odd Couple; Where Were You When the Lights Went Out? + The Biggest Bundle of Them All; *The Green Berets; Camelot; Wait Until Dark; The Impossible Years; The Strange Affair; Petulia + Flaming Frontier; *Girl on a Motorcycle; *Barbarella; 5 Card Stud; Far from the Madding Crowd; How

Sweet It Is!; Hot Millions; The Split + Woman Without a Face; Dracula Has Risen from the Grave + A Covenant with Death; Love in Our Time + Curse of the Crimson Altar; The Bliss of Mrs. Blossom; With Six You Get Eggroll; *Half a Sixpence

1969

[*Doctor Zhivago was presented as a special attraction on varying dates and Ice Station Zebra had some advance presentations*]

Stay Away Joe + Battle Beneath the Earth; *Till Death Do Us Part; The Brotherhood; *Till Death Do Us Part (*re-run*); Shalako; Twisted Nerve; *Bullitt; Rosemary's Baby; If....; Great Catherine; The Stalking Moon; Finian's Rainbow; 2001: A Space Odyssey; What's Good for the Goose; Rachel, Rachel + The Chastity Belt; Lock Up Your Daughters!; They Came to Rob Las Vegas + Sweet November; All Neat in Black Stockings; The Assassination Bureau; Crooks and Coronets; Benjamin + Riot; Frankenstein Must Be Destroyed + Sons of Satan; The Killing of Sister George; Dance of the Vampires + The Girl and the General; A Place for Lovers + Heaven with a Gun; I Love You, Alice B. Toklas + The Sergeant; Where's Jack?; *The Italian Job; Monte Carlo or Bust!; One Million Years B.C. (*revival*) + She (*revival*); 3 in the Attic + The Devil's 8; Once Upon a Time in the West; *Oh! What a Lovely War; The Smashing Bird I Used to Know; The Best House in London + The Green Slime; Goodbye, Columbus + Targets; *Mayerling; Alfred the Great; A Touch of Love; Moon Zero Two; Daddy's Gone A-Hunting + The Name of the Game Is Kill; Ice Station Zebra; The Gypsy Moths + Marlowe; The Good Guys and the Bad Guys + The Valley of Gwangi; Me, Natalie + A Fine Pair; Revenge in El Paso + Diamonds for Breakfast; Captain Nemo and the Underwater City + The Trouble with Girls; True Grit

1970

*Where Eagles Dare (*two weeks*); The Five Man Army + Flare Up; Bonnie and Clyde (*revival*) + Bullitt (*revival*); Last Summer + Paddy; Scream and Scream Again + Hell's Angels '69; The Wild Bunch; Easy Rider; The Lawyer + Stuntman; The

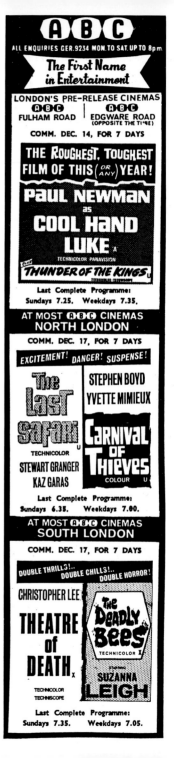

Magic Christian; The Madwoman of Chaillot (limited); Spring and Port Wine; Goodbye, Mr. Chips; Zabriskie Point; *Women in Love (two weeks); Every Home Should Have One; Alice's Restaurant; The Molly Maguires; Entertaining Mr. Sloane; Taste the Blood of Dracula + Crescendo!; The Strawberry Statement; The Adventurers; The Damned; Gone with the Wind ('scope version); The Arrangement; The Oblong Box + The Dunwich Horror; Kes; And Soon the Darkness; Hoffman; The Man Who Haunted Himself; All the Way Up; Chisum; El Condor; Bob and Carol and Ted and Alice; "Z" (limited); A Man Called Horse; The Vampire Lovers + Angels from Hell; Eye Witness; The Walking Stick + Tick...Tick...Tick; When Dinosaurs Ruled the Earth + The Great Bank Robbery; The Reivers; Scars of Dracula + Horror of Frankenstein; The Cheyenne Social Club; My Lover My Son + The Moonshine War; The Boys in the Band; Count Yorga Vampire + Cry of the Banshee; Dirty Dingus Magee; *The Railway Children

1971

Rio Lobo; Lust for a Vampire + The Losers; Monte Walsh; House of Dark Shadows + The Travelling Executioner; *There's a Girl in My Soup (two weeks); Loot; *Percy (two weeks); Ben-Hur (revival); Jane Eyre; *Up Pompeii (two weeks); Creatures the World Forgot; Get Carter (two weeks); The McMasters; The Raging Moon (limited); Zeppelin + Start the Revolution Without Me; Bloody Mama + A Bullet for Pretty Boy; The Dirty Dozen (revival); The Babymaker (limited); Little Big Man; Wuthering Heights; S.W.A.L.K.; Big Jake; *On the Buses; Little Big Man (re-run); Le Mans; Villain; Kelly's Heroes; The Abominable Dr. Phibes (limited); The Go-Between; A Gunfight; Puppet on a Chain; Dr. Jekyll and Sister Hyde + Blood from the Mummy's Tomb; Pretty Maids All in a Row (limited); Murders in the Rue Morgue + The Return of Count Yorga; Naughty (limited); Willy Wonka and the Chocolate Factory (afternoons only); Up the Chastity Belt; The Magnificent 7 Deadly Sins

1972

Something Big; The Last Run; *The Devils; Klute; Play Misty for Me; *Ryan's Daughter; The Deserter + Little Fauss and Big Halsey; Blue Water White Death; Love Story; Gumshoe; Embassy; Man in the Wilderness or She'll Follow You Anywhere; Paint Your Wagon or Zulu (revival); *Steptoe and Son; The Omega Man or Fright + I, Monster; Raid on Rommel or Such Good Friends + A Date with a Lonely Girl; *Dirty Harry; Never Give an Inch; The Boyfriend; Sitting Target; Pocket Money + Cup Glory; The Revengers; Frogs + The Hard Ride or Plaza Suite or various; The Carey Treatment + Cool Breeze; Straight On Till Morning + Fear in the Night; King Elephant; Mutiny on the Buses; Skyjacked; What's Up Doc?; Up the Front; Shaft's Big Score + Evel Knievel; Frenzy; The Garnett Saga; *A Clockwork Orange (selective); Joe Kidd; *The Godfather (selective); Mary, Queen of Scots; Prime Cut; Dr. Phibes Rides Again; Where Does It Hurt? + There's a Girl in My Soup (revival); Deliverance; Tower of Evil + Demons of the Mind or Strange Messiah + Fortune and Men's Eyes; Made; Asylum + Duel; Dracula A.D. 1972 + Trog

1973

Our Miss Fred; Fear Is the Key; *A Clockwork Orange (full release); Henry VIII and His Six Wives (limited); Portnoy's Complaint or Danish Dentist on the Job; Ulzana's Raid; The Getaway; The Valachi Papers; The Triple Echo; The Wrath of God; *The Godfather (full release); Slaughter + Boxcar Bertha; The Life and Times of Judge Roy Bean; The Ten Commandments (revival); The House in Nightmare Park; King Boxer; *That'll Be the Day; The Thief Who Came to Dinner; Bluebeard or Bequest to the Nation; Dirty Harry (revival) + Klute (revival); The Wild Bunch (revival) or Love Story (revival); England Made Me (limited release); Cold Sweat + The New One-Armed Swordsman; Soylent Green; Lady Sings the Blues; Deaf Smith and Johnny Ears + Slither; *Lady Caroline Lamb; Call of the Wild + Treasure Island; Badge 373 + Coogan's Bluff (revival)/Play Misty for Me (revival); Steptoe and Son Ride Again; Love Thy Neighbour + Cancel My Reservation; High Plains Drifter; The Last of Sheila; Man at the Top + The Chinese Connection; Shaft in Africa + Private Parts; O Lucky Man!; The Final Programme + Intimate Confessions of a Chinese Courtesan; Pat Garrett and Billy the Kid + Wicked Wicked;

This newspaper listing of ABC London area programmes in January 1972 shows how varied the bookings had become by this time.

Jesus Christ Superstar; Charley Varrick + The Great Northfield Minnesota Raid; Doctor Zhivago; The Mackintosh Man + Cahill; The Friends of Eddie Coyle + Gunfight at the O.K. Corral (revival); Ssssnake + The Boy Who Cried Werewolf; Secrets of a Door-to-Door Salesman + Climax; Take Me High

1974

Holiday on the Buses + Fear Is the Key (revival); *Enter the Dragon; Heavy Traffic; Magnum Force; Steelyard Blues; *The Day of the Jackal; The Legend of Frenchie King + Not Now, Darling; Walking Tall; *The Sting (selective); The Serpent; The Beguiled; McQ; The Don Is Dead; That Man Bolt; Westworld; The Satanic Rites of Dracula; American Graffiti; Swallows & Amazons; *The Sting (main release); Paper Moon; Serpico; King of Kung Fu; Black Belt Jones + The Deadly Trackers; The Best of Benny Hill; Craze + Cat and Mouse; Chinese Vengeance + Death Kick; Callan; Newman's Law; Dracula + The Arena; Dillinger + Slaughter's Big Rip Off; From Beyond the Grave; Blazing Saddles (two weeks) + Alvin Purple; The Dove; *The Great Gatsby; Mame (very limited); S.P.Y.S.; Percy's Progress; Sunshine; *The Exorcist (two weeks); The Legend of the 7 Golden Vampires; The Black Windmill; *Stardust; Chinatown; The Marseille Contract; Golden Needles + Whoever Slew Auntie Roo?; The Amazons; Madhouse; Man About the House; *Airport 1975 (selective)

1975

Freebie and the Bean; Sunday in the Country + Big Bad Mama; Eskimo Nell or The Super Cops + Wild Rovers; *Airport 1975 (full release – two weeks); The Prisoner of Second Avenue; The Mean Machine or Death Wish + Bad Company; The Spiral Staircase; Flesh for Frankenstein or The Front Page + Sugarland Express/Breezy; *The Towering Inferno (selective); Death Wish (two weeks); The Parallax View or The Stunt Man or Bad Company; Remember Me This Way + Brother of the Wind; That's Entertainment; *Murder on the Orient Express (two weeks); Alfie Darling; The Gambler + Phase IV (limited); Flesh Gordon (limited); Lepke + Blood Money; The Great Waldo

Pepper; Monty Python and the Holy Grail; It's Alive + Badlands; Uptown Saturday Night; Blood for Dracula (limited); Barry McKenzie Holds His Own; The Day of the Locust or The Groove Tube + Where's Poppa?; The Godfather Part II; Enter the 7 Virgins + Girls Come First; The Man Who Loved Cat Dancing + Mr. Ricco or The Yakuza; Doc Savage – The Man of Bronze + How To Destroy the Reputation of the Greatest Secret Agent; All Creatures Great and Small + Beautiful People; Where Eagles Dare (revival); The Godfather Part II (re-run); Never Too Young to Rock; *The Towering Inferno (two weeks); The Land That Time Forgot + The Tender Warrior; Massacre in Rome (limited); *Earthquake (selective); Posse + Diagnosis: Murder; The Drowning Pool; Mandingo (two weeks); *Emmanuelle; The Eiger Sanction; Black Christmas + Out of Season; Inside Out + Uptown Saturday Night (re-run); Three Days of the Condor or Alice Doesn't Live Here Anymore; Night Moves + Petersen; Lisztomania (selective); Stardust (revival) + That'll Be the Day (revival) or Macon County Line + Law and Disorder; Permission to Kill + The Ultimate Warrior; Bug + Framed; *Jaws (selected); Mister Quilp

1976

*Earthquake (full release); Gone with the Wind (revival); And Then There Were None + Guns Across the Veldt; Lisztomania (selective); Spanish Fly or The Man from Hong Kong; Once Is Not Enough; A Window to the Sky; Hustle; Aloha – Bobby and Rose + Cleopatra Jones and the Casino of Gold; Operation Daybreak + Master Gunfighter; To the Devil... A Daughter; The Bawdy Adventures of Tom Jones; The Sunshine Boys; Dog Day Afternoon; Zulu (revival); *It Shouldn't Happen to a Vet; The Slipper and the Rose; The Likely Lads; The Hindenburg; *Jaws (pre-release); *Emmanuelle; Freebie and the Bean (revival); Mahogany; Death Race 2000; Shivers; I'm Not Feeling Myself Tonight; Black Emmanuelle; Kelly's Heroes; Adventures of a Taxi Driver + Blondy; Won Ton Ton The Dog Who Saved Hollywood; Buffalo Bill and the Indians; St. Ives; Lipstick + Lifeguard; Aces High; Benji + e'Lollipop; *The Outlaw Josey Wales; *All the President's Men; Family Plot; Drum; Seven Nights in Japan; *Jaws (extended run); The Gumball Rally + Let's

Do It Again; Futureworld + The Optimists of Nine Elms/Bunny O'Hare; Logan's Run; The Shootist; Survive; The Bad News Bears + Posse; Goodbye Norma Jean; Death Weekend; Emmanuelle 2; The Way of the Dragon; Schizo; The Scarlet Buccaneer

1977

Victory at Entebbe; The Enforcer; *King Kong (pre-release); The Big Bus; Sweeney!; Two Minute Warning; *When the North Wind Blows (two weeks); Marathon Man; Cross of Iron; The Great Scout and Cathouse Thursday; The Squeeze; Ben-Hur (revival); *King Kong; The Eagle Has Landed (two weeks); Stand Up Virgin Soldiers; The Sentinel; Zoltan...Hound of Dracula; The Food of the Gods; *Airport '77 (pre-release); Car Wash + Crusin'; Fire + Crash; *A Star Is Born; Adventures of a Private Eye; Squirm; The Car + Day of the Animals; The Outlaw Josey Wales (revival) + Magnum Force (revival); Battle of Midway; It Shouldn't Happen to a Vet (revival) + All Creatures Great and Small (revival); The People That Time Forgot; *Airport '77 (full release); Orca...Killer Whale; Smokey and the Bandit; The Greatest; Are You Being Served?; Black Sunday; Mean Streets; Exorcist II The Heretic; The Island of Dr. Moreau; Young Lady Chatterley; Slap Shot; Outlaw Blues; Demon Seed + The Super Cops; *The Adventures of the Wilderness Family; Jaws (revival); Operation Thunderbolt; Crime Busters; Voyage of the Damned; The Amsterdam Kill + Fist of Fury; The Pack + Blue Sunshine; The Sting (revival); The Godfather (revival); Young Emmanuelle; The Last Remake of Beau Geste; Suspiria; The Gauntlet; Rollercoaster (pre-release)

1978

Come Play With Me; Rabid + Dead of Night; The White Buffalo; Bobby Deerfield; One on One + Greased Lightning; The Choirboys; First Love; Rollercoaster (full release); Viva Knievel + Watch Out We're Mad/Grizzly; *Abba – The Movie; Wages of Fear + The Last Dinosaur; The Silver Bears + Breakheart Pass (revival); The Boys in Company C; Looking for Mr. Goodbar; Gone in 60 Seconds + Clones; Skateboard + The Bad News Bears in Breaking Training; *Saturday Night Fever; The Goodbye Girl; The Twelve Tasks of

Asterix; Telefon; *The Stud; The Black Panther + 21 Hours at Munich; Oh God; Enter the Dragon (revival) + Death Race 2000 (revival); MacArthur The Rebel General; Sweeney 2; Heroes; A Piece of the Action; Gray Lady Down; The Duellists; Let's Get Laid!; Kingdom of the Spiders + The Redeemer; Adventures of a Plumber's Mate + Cain's Way; Full Circle + The Car (revival); The Comeback + Legend of the Lawman; The Medusa Touch + Russian Roulette; Mitchell + Three the Hard Way; I Wanna Hold Your Hand + American Hot Wax; 2001 A Space Odyssey (revival); Game of Death; Leopard in the Snow; Straight Time + The Late Show; The Terror of Dr. Chaney + Revenge of the Dead; Warlords of Atlantis + Crash (revival); Emmanuelle 2 + Emmanuelle in Tokyo; The Swarm; House Calls + Paper Moon (revival); Jesus Christ Superstar (revival); Bilitis + You're Driving Me Crazy; The One and Only + Race for Your Life, Charlie Brown; International Velvet; Fist of Fury Part II + Special Cop in Action; Convoy; The Silent Partner; Heaven Can Wait; *Grease; The Playbirds; The Big Sleep; Driver; Slavers; *Watership Down; Shipwreck; The Greek Tycoon; Death on the Nile; Hooper; Coma; Ruby + Satan's Slave; It Lives Again; The Other Cinderella + Adventures of a Taxi Driver (revival); Hot Dreams + Man Hungry; *Superman – The Movie; Killer's Moon + The Last Hard Men; *Every Which Way But Loose; *Jaws 2

Breaking Training (revival); Emmanuelle and the White Slave Trade + Jet Sex; Blazing Saddles (revival) + Monty Python and the Holy Grail (revival); Players (limited); The Champ; Confessions from the David Galaxy Affair + Confessions of a Sex Slave; What's Up Superdoc? + The Cop in Blue Jeans; Arabian Adventure; Buck Rogers in the 25th Century; Convoy (revival) + Sweeney 2 (revival); Beyond the Poseidon Adventure; Porridge + To Russia with Elton; Boulevard Nights (limited) + The Enforcer (revival); Elvis – The Movie; The Brink's Job + The Land That Time Forgot (revival); The Main Event; Dracula; Bloodline; Home Before Midnight + Sweeney! (revival); The Bitch; The In-Laws; The Ghoul (revival) + Legend of the Werewolf (revival); Airport '80 – The Concorde; Bloodbrothers; *Quadrophenia; Rabid + Shivers; Cheech & Chong's Up in Smoke; Phantasm + The Groove Tube; Prophecy; The Frisco Kid; Mad Max + From Hell to Victory; Close Encounters of a Handyman + King Dick; Smokey and the Bandit; Scum; Yesterday's Hero; Moment by Moment + The Eiger Sanction (revival); The Golden Lady; The Jericho Mile (limited); The Getaway (revival) + The Legacy; Meteor; *Star Trek – The Motion Picture; The Slipper and the Rose; The Prisoner of Zenda

1979

Capricorn One; The Last Snows of Spring; Foul Play; The Amazing Captain Nemo; Sgt. Pepper's Lonely Hearts Club Band; Too Many Chefs; National Lampoon's Animal House; Same Time Next Year; *The Deer Hunter; Brass Target; The Hills Have Eyes; The Boys from Brazil; Superman – The Movie (revival); The Water Babies; Battlestar Galactica; The Goodbye Girl (revival) + You Light Up My Life; Movie Movie (limited); Kentucky Fried Movie + Adventures of a Private Eye; The Class of Miss MacMichael + The Little Girl Who Lives Down the Lane; The Warriors; Big Wednesday + Drive-In (limited); In Praise of Older Women (limited); The World Is Full of Married Men + Can I Come Too?; Escape to Athena; The Towering Inferno (revival); The Music Machine + The Gumball Rally; The Kids Are Alright; Oliver's Story + The Bad News Bears in

An A to Z of ABC

In this listing of all the ABC cinemas, information in brackets usually refers to details outside the period of cinema operation by ABC. I have indicated if a cinema was part of the circuit as formed in 1928 or when it became part of the circuit and whether it was acquired from a major chain. Cinemas operated in Eire through associated companies are listed but Shipman and King cinemas, which eventually came under the same ownership as ABC, are only included in the cases of the Embassy Crawley and Empire Watford, the two theatres which were renamed ABC. Cinemas opened by Cannon/MGM are also excluded, except for the Salford Quays multiplex which was initiated by ABC.

Many of the ABC cinemas surviving as Cannons were having their names changed to MGM/Metro-Goldwyn-Mayer Cinemas while this book was being finalised and the listings may not be completely up to date in this respect at the time of publication.

Cinemas are listed by the district in which they were located and with which they were usually associated in advertising, and by the name they had at the time they were taken over or opened by ABC. Thus the ABCs in the Reading area outside the town centre appear under local districts like Tilehurst, with cross references under the listing for Reading. However, in a few instances – Belfast and Hull, for example – cinemas that probably should have been entered under local areas remain under main town headings for lack of information regarding the correct names of the neighbourhoods.

Where ABC had more than one cinema at a place, they are listed in the order they became part of the circuit or, if more than one was acquired at the same time, in order of original opening (where such information is known).

Seating figures vary from different sources and, of course, were often changing: those given here are from ABC opening programmes, other company publications, or the *Kinematograph Year Book*. In the case of cinemas opened by ABC, the break-down in seating between stalls and balcony is given where available. Quite often slightly different figures appear in different sources: priority has been given to figures taken from opening programmes as these represent the most official source (it is possible this information was supplied to the printers before the final seating figures had been determined, although this was usually worked out on the architect's plans). Seating would vary over the years in any case and would have been reduced at most cinemas in the mid-1950s following the installation of CinemaScope and by more generous row spacing. Where drastic changes resulted from converting the stalls to "luxury lounges" or through major structural sub-division, new seating figures are given.

Dates of ABC take-over are for the most part from company sources and, in one or two instances, may refer to when a take-over was announced rather than when the building was physically transferred to the company. Sometimes several months could elapse between the two, although transfers of ownership were usually rapid.

I have given all the information known to me on the history of cinemas before being taken over by ABC and after ABC gave them up as cinemas (including what replaced them when demolished), but I have not been able to resolve some contradictions or carry out much further investigation.

Opening dates given for former theatres always refer to when they became full-time cinemas, not when they opened as live theatres or music halls.

This listing would not have been possible without information contained in the CTA Bulletin, the *Kinematograph Year Books*, and many details supplied by the late Gordon Coombes. Many CTA members rushed to provide post-ABC information that I requested in the *CTA Bulletin* and their names are listed in the Acknowledgments.

SCVT refers to Scottish Cinema and Variety Theatres, one of the companies that made up ABC in the beginning.

I have not included Union cinemas that were closed at the time of the ABC take-over and not re-opened. Some periods of closure during World War Two may not have been recorded.

While I hope the information contained here will be useful to local historians, they should check the dates and details in newspaper sources.

ABERDEEN Grampian

REGAL Union Street (rear entrance on Shiprow) (on site of Palladium). Opened 26.7.54 by ABC, architect: C. J. Foster (adaptation of W. R. Glen scheme started in 1939), 1914 seats. Renamed ABC 24.3.62. Closed 5.5.74 for tripling. ABC 1 opened 3.6.74, 600 seats. ABC 2 & 3 opened 8.7.74, 153 & 147 seats. (Renamed Cannon 6.87. Open.)

ABINGDON Oxfordshire

PAVILION. (Taken over c1936 by Union.) Taken over 10.37, part of Union circuit. Closed c1939. (Demolished. Offices.)

REGAL The Square (High Street, Ock Street and Bath Street). (Opened 8.6.35 by Union, architect: Harold S. Scott, 900 seats, stadium plan.) Taken over 10.37, part of Union circuit. Closed 13.4.69. (Bingo. Partweek films from 5.5.69. Taken over by Star 30.6.69. Closed 28.1.76 for fulltime bingo. Re-opened c7.84 as part-week cinema. Closed 12.85. Re-opened as fulltime cinema 7.2.86. 326 seats. Part-time bingo. Re-opened 4.87 as cinema only. Closed 14.9.89. Derelict.)

ACTON West London

SAVOY Old Oak Road and Western Avenue, East Acton. (Opened 13.4.31, architect: George Coles, 1721 seats.) Taken over 12.35. Closed 29.12.62. (Interior gutted for bowling alley. Bingo.)

ALDERSHOT Hampshire

RITZ High Street. (Opened 13.5.37 by Union, architects: Verity and Beverley, 1747 seats.) Taken over 10.37, part of Union circuit. Renamed ABC c1961. Closed 28.5.77 for tripling and bingo. ABC 1, 2 & 3 opened 6.10.77, 313 & 187 & 150 seats. (Renamed Cannon. Open.)

ALL SAINTS' Manchester

LA SCALA 207 Oxford Road. (Opened 1922.) Taken over 22.8.32, 2300 seats. (Taken over by independent 7.10.45 and renamed Roxy, 1861 seats. Modernised and re-opened 27.2.58 as Plaza, 1704 seats. Taken over by Star 1.4.62. Closed c1963. Bingo. Twinned for bingo in balcony and cinema in stalls. Re-opened c8.63, 1100 seats. Closed c1966. Bingo only.)

ALTRINCHAM Greater Manchester

REGAL Manchester Road. (Opened 13.5.31, architects: Drury and Gomersall, 1750 seats. Taken over by Union 24.2.36.) Taken over 10.37, part of Union circuit. Closed 6/7.1.56 by fire. (Demolished. Office block – Regal House.)

AMMANFORD Dyfed

PALACE. (Opened pre-1914. 847 seats.. Taken over by Union 3.37.) Taken over 10.37, part of Union circuit. (Taken over by independent 30.9.56. Closed 4.6.77.)

ANCOATS Manchester
see also Beswick

TOWER Piercy Street. (Opened pre-1914. 700 seats. Taken over by Union 7.36.) Taken over 10.37, part of Union circuit. 562 seats. Closed 30.5.53.

ANFIELD Liverpool

ROYAL Breck Road. (Opened 11.11.20, former Theatre Royal music hall. 1100 seats.) Taken over c1932. Leased to Regent c5.33. (Purchased by Regent 12.33, taken over 3.5.34. Taken over by Southan Morris 1938. Taken over by Essoldo 26.8.54. Closed 16.1.65. Bingo.)
POPULAR Netherfield Road North. (Opened 12.25, 1508 seats.) Taken over c8.35. Closed 8.12.56. (Derelict. Demolished.)
BELMONT Belmont Road. (Opened 17.1.14, 717 seats.) Taken over 17.11.30. Leased out to 10.34. Closed 19.11.37. (Taken over by Levy circuit 20.11.37, closed for improvements and re-opened 24.1.38 as Lido, 766 seats. Closed 6.6.59. Club. Public house.)

ARBROATH Tayside

PALACE James Street. Part of original circuit, from SCVT. Closed c4.39. (Demolished for new Palace.)
PALACE James Street (site of old Palace). Opened 7 or 13.5.40 by ABC, architect: W. R. Glen, 1488 seats. (Taken over by independent 30.9.63. Closed c1985. Re-opened. Stalls converted to roller skating rink c1988, balcony continuing as cinema. Closed. Demolished c1991.)

ARDWICK Manchester

ARDWICK Ardwick Green. (Opened c1911 as Victoria. 1500 seats.) Taken over 1.7.29. Closed by war-time bomb damage. (Demolished. Apollo car park.)
APOLLO Stockport Road and Hyde Road, Ardwick Green. (Opened 29.8.38, architects: Peter Cummings and Alex M. Irvine, decorative design: Mollo and Egan, Holophane lighting director: R. Gillespie Williams, 2631 seats.) Taken over 31.1.43. Renamed ABC c1962. (Taken over by independent 30.1.77 for live shows/occasional films, and renamed Apollo. Open.)

ARMAGH Co. Armagh

RITZ Market Square. Opened 6.12.37 by ABC (Union). 782 seats. Closed 23.2.74. (Taken over by independent. Closed.)

ASHTON-IN-MAKERFIELD Greater Manchester

PALACE Bryn Street. Taken over 27.2.36. 483 seats. Closed 2.4.66.

ASHTON-UNDER-LYNE Greater Manchester

EMPIRE. (Opened 22.8.32, former Empire Hippodrome live theatre. Closed 15.7.33 for modernisation, architects: Drury and Gomersall and re-opened 4.11.33, 1600 seats. Taken over by Union 31.12.34.) Taken over 10.37, part of Union circuit. Live shows 11.39 to 5.40. Renamed ABC c1963. Closed 5.4.75. (Re-opened 31.5.76 as Tameside Theatre with some film shows. Summer film seasons until 1986.)

ASTON Birmingham

GAIETY Coleshill Street. (Former concert hall/music hall. Cinema from 1920.) Taken over c1.29. Closed 9.36 by explosion in projection room. (Demolished c8.38. New Gaiety on site.)
ASTORIA Lichfield Road. (Opened 12.12.27, former Theatre Royal with interior entirely rebuilt, architects: Satchwell and Roberts, 1271 seats.) Taken over 7.1.29. Taken over by Regent c5.33 to 1935. Closed 26.11.55. (Alpha Television Studios. Demolished. BRMB Radio HQ and Showroom.)
ORIENT High Street, Six Ways. Opened 4.8.30 by ABC, architects: Satchwell and Roberts, scenic artist: George Legg, 1541 seats. Renamed ABC 3.2.64. Closed 23.8.69. (Asian cinema. Demolished for housing estate.)
GAIETY Coleshill Street (site of old Gaiety). Opened 18.11.39 by ABC, architect: W. R. Glen, 1480 seats: 1030 stalls & 450 balcony. Closed 5.63 for modernisation. Re-opened 4.8.63 as ABC. 1348 seats. Closed 10.10.64 for 70mm installation. Re-opened 22.10.64. Closed 29.11.69 by Compulsory Purchase Order. (Demolished 1970. University of Aston open space.)

ASTON CROSS Birmingham

PICTURE HOUSE Lichfield Road. (Opened c1913, architect: A. Hurley Robinson. 900 seats.) Taken over c1.29. 891 seats. Closed 3.8.63. (Asian cinema. Derelict. Demolished.)

ATHERSTONE Warwickshire

REGAL Long Street. (Opened 28.8.37, architect: Harold S. Scott, 744 seats, stadium plan.) Taken over 30.8.43 from Mayfair circuit. (Taken over by independent 27.3.60. Closed 1987. Demolished. Housing.)

BAKER STREET Central London

TUSSAUD'S CINEMA Madame Tussaud's, Marylebone Road. (Opened 26.4.28, architect: F. Edward Jones, 1714 seats.) Booked by ABC after John Maxwell became chairman of owning company in 2.29, but not otherwise part of ABC circuit. Closed 9/10.9.40 by bomb damage in air raid. (Demolished. Planetarium.)

BALHAM South London

PICTURE HOUSE 172 High Road. (Opened 1911 by Amalgamated Cinematograph Theatres as Pyke's. Renamed Picture House 1912. Enlarged by architect Clifford Aish and re-opened 5.9.27.) Taken over c1933. 1259 seats. Front rebuilt, auditorium refurbished, and re-opened 12.10.53 as RITZ. Closed 7.9.68. (Bingo. Asian cinema. Demolished. Shops.)

BALSALL HEATH Birmingham
see Moseley Road

BANBURY Oxfordshire

PALACE Market Square. (Former Palace Theatre. Operated as cinema from c1924. Taken over by Union c5.32. 794 seats.) Taken over 10.37, part of Union circuit. Closed 10.6.61. (Converted to commercial use.)

GRAND Broad Street. (Former Grand Theatre. Operated as cinema pre-1916.) Taken over 30.8.43, from Mayfair circuit. 837 seats. Closed 14.12.68. (Bingo.)

BANKHALL Liverpool

COMMODORE Stanley Road. (Opened 22.12.30, architects: Gray and Evans, 1906 seats.) Taken over 6.4.31. Closed 30.11.68. (Bingo. Funeral premises.)

BARKING East London

CAPITOL East Street. (Opened 21.10.29, archi-tect: J. Aldridge, 1266 seats.) Taken over 19.5.30. Closed 12.12.59. (Demolished.)

BARKINGSIDE Northeast London

STATE Fairlop Road. (Opened 10.38, architect: George Coles, 2194 seats. Closed c10.40 by bomb damage. Requisitioned for use by War Office and local authorities.) Taken over 9.47. Restored and re-opened 16.2.48. Renamed ABC 1964. Closed 19.8.72 for stalls bingo and smaller cinema in balcony. Re-opened 23.11.72, 626 seats. Closed 4.12.76. (Taken over by Ace and re-opened 17.9.78 as Ace State. Video cinema added 15.5.82. Closed 30.8.84. Disused.)

BARNSLEY Yorkshire

RITZ Peel Street. (Opened 22.3.37 by Union, architects: Verity and Beverley, 2007 seats.) Taken over 10.37, part of Union circuit. Renamed ABC c1961. Closed 16.3.74. (Demolished.)

BARROW-IN-FURNESS Cumbria
see also Walney Island

COLISEUM Abbey Road. (Opened 9.14. Taken over by Union 8.36.) Taken over 10.37, part of Union circuit. (Taken over by Essoldo 21.3.48. 1070 seats. Closed c1966. Demolished c1977.)

PAVILION. (Opened c1.20 as Salthouse Pavilion. Taken over by Union 8.36. 944 seats.) Taken over 10.37, part of Union circuit. Closed 24.10.59.

GAIETY Abbey Road. (Closed 5.33. Re-opened 1.1.34. Taken over by Union 8.36.) Taken over 10.37, part of Union circuit. Closed 11.38. (Taken back by Brennan circuit. Taken over by Essoldo 2.48. 1,000 seats. Renamed Essoldo c1950. Closed c1968. Demolished c1973.)

PALACE Duke Street. (Opened 10.21 as Palace Theatre, former Hippodrome music hall with some film shows. Closed 11.30 for modernisa-tion. Re-opened 8.8.31, 1356 seats. Taken over by Union 8.36.) Taken over 10.37, part of Union circuit. (Taken over by Essoldo 21.3.48. Closed c1968. Bingo.)

REGAL 47 Forshaw Street. (Former Star, then Tivoli music hall. Enlarged c7.31, architect: F. J. Parker, 1050 seats. Renamed Regal 9.31. Taken over by Union 8.36.) Taken over 10.37, part of Union circuit. Closed 29.12.56.

RITZ Abbey Road and Holker Street. (Opened 14.9.36 by Union, architects: Drury & Gomersall and F. J. Parker, 1735 seats.) Taken over 10.37, part of Union circuit. Renamed ABC c1961. Closed 15.1.77. (Taken over by independent, re-opened 4.77 as Astra. Triple from 5.6.77, 640 & 260 & 260 seats. Open.)

BASILDON Essex

ABC 1 & 2 Town Square. Opened 5.9.71 by ABC. 644 & 455 seats. ABC 3 (video) opened 5.7.79, 91 seats. ABC 3 closed. (Renamed Cannon. Open.)

BASINGSTOKE Hampshire

GRAND Wote Street. (Opened c6.13, former Corn Exchange. Taken over by Union c1937. 598 seats.) Taken over 10.37, part of Union circuit. 598 seats. Closed c1939. (Theatre. Renamed Haymarket Theatre 1951. Closed 6.92 for recon-struction.)

PLAZA Sarum Hill. (Former drill hall. Taken over by Union c1937.) Taken over 10.37, part of Union circuit. 670 seats. Closed 26.6.54. (Co-Op furniture store. Demolished 1981. Office block.)

WALDORF Wote Street. (Opened 1935. 863 seats. Taken over by Union 18.3.37.) Taken over 10.37, part of Union circuit. Closed 27.2.71 for conversion to "luxury lounge". Re-opened 8.3.71, 568 seats. Closed 25.6.77 for twinning. ABC 1 & 2 opened 15.9.77, 420 & 218 seats. (Renamed Cannon. Closed 21.2.91. Derelict.)

BATH Avon

BEAU NASH 22-23 Westgate Street. (Opened pre-1914 as Electric. Closed 18.4.20 for recon-struction, architect: Alfred J. Taylor, re-opened as Beau Nash. 744 seats. Later enlarged. 1,088 seats.) Taken over 8.29. Modernised 12.71. (Open under Cannon/MGM. 733 seats.)

ASSEMBLY ROOMS Alfred Street. (Cinema from c1924, former ballroom. Taken over by Savoy Cinemas c1926.) Part of original circuit. (Leased to Regent c5.33. Closed 23.6.34. Taken over by National Trust.)

BATTERSEA South London
see Wandsworth

BATTLEFIELD Glasgow

MAYFAIR 33 Sinclair Drive, Langside. (Opened 22.1.34, architect: Eric A. Sutherland, 1340 seats.) Taken over c9.35. Closed 30.6.73. (Warehouse. Demolished 1980.)

BAYSWATER West London

QUEENS 98 Bishops Bridge Road, corner of Queensway. (Opened 3.10.32, architects: J. Stanley Beard and Clare, 1428 seats.) Taken over 19.2.35. Renamed ABC 1962. Closed 28.6.75 for tripling. ABC 1, 2 & 3 opened 2.10.75, 436 & 224 & 213 seats. (Closed 11.8.88. Derelict.)

BECKENHAM Southeast London

REGAL 296 High Street and Croydon Road. (Opened 22.9.30, architect: Robert Cromie, 1980 seats. Briefly associated with County. Taken over by Union 1936.) Taken over 10.37, part of Union circuit. Renamed ABC 22.1.62. Closed 11.11.78 for tripling. ABC 1 opened 21.12.78, 587 seats (old balcony). ABC 2 & 3 opened 11.2.79, 295 & 124 seats. (Renamed Cannon. Open.)

BEDMINSTER Bristol

REX North Street. Opened 9.12.40 by ABC (Union), architect: W. R. Glen, 1250 seats, one floor. Balcony added in 1950s: 1634 seats. Renamed ABC c1963. (Taken over by independent 12.2.78, renamed Rex. Closed 16.8.80. Bingo.)

BELFAST Antrim

ROYAL HIPPODROME Great Victoria Street. Opened 7.31 by ABC, former variety theatre. 1800 seats. (Taken over by independent 12.38. Taken over by Rank 28.11.60. Modernised and re-opened 10.61 as Odeon, 1150 seats. Bombed 1974. Taken over by independent and renamed New Vic. Bingo.)

STRAND 152/4 Holywood Road. (Opened 7.12.35 by Union, architect: J. McBride Neill, 1141 seats.) Taken over 10.37, part of Union circuit. (Taken over by independent. Closed 19.11.83. Re-opened. Open.)

MAJESTIC 204/222 Lisburn Road. (Opened 25.5.36 by Union, architect: J. McBride Neill, 1369

seats.) Taken over 10.37, part of Union circuit. Closed 4.10.75. (Furniture store.)

RITZ College Square East (now 1-11 Fisherwick Place) and Grosvenor Road. (Opened 9.11.36 by Union, architect: Leslie H. Kemp, 2219 seats.) Taken over 10.37, part of Union circuit. Renamed ABC c1963. Closed 22.9.77 by arson. Re-opened as quad. (Renamed Cannon. 551, 444, 281 & 215 seats. Closed 1.7.93.)

BENWELL Newcastle

ADELAIDE 385 Elswick Road. (Taken over 1928 by Union.) Taken over 10.37, part of Union circuit. Closed 1.2.43. (Woolworth's. Shop.)

MAJESTIC. (Opened 10.27 as live theatre with projection facilities unused until re-opened 6.30 as cinema. 1142 seats. Taken over by Union 7.30.) Taken over 10.37, part of Union circuit. Closed 20.5.61. (Bingo.)

BERMONDSEY South London

RIALTO 146 St. James's Road. (Opened as Colleen 4.9.26. Taken over by Abrahams. Renamed Rialto 1929.) Taken over 10.30. (Taken over by Eric Rhodes 1931. Taken over by other independents. Closed by bomb damage 1940. Re-opened. Closed 11.2.61. Bingo from 16.4.61.)

BESWICK Greater Manchester

DON Beswick Street. (Opened pre-1914. Taken over by Union 7.36. 839 seats.) Taken over 10.37, part of Union circuit. Closed 8.2.58.

BEVERLEY Humberside

REGAL Norwood. (Opened 2.11.35 by local company in association with County, incorporating old Assembly Rooms extension with new entrance and foyer.) Taken over 8.11.37. 946 seats. Closed 22.6.68. (Bingo. Snooker club. Listed building. Derelict.)

BEXHILL East Sussex

RITZ Buckhurst Road. (Opened 18.1.37 by Union, architects: Verity & Beverley and B. A. Stevens, 1142 seats.) Taken over 10.37, part of Union circuit. Closed 2.12.61. (Bingo. Demolished. Telephone exchange.)

BEXLEYHEATH Southeast London

REGAL Broadway. (Opened 3.9.34, architect: Robert Cromie, 1947 seats. Taken over by Union c1935.) Taken over 10.37, part of Union circuit. Renamed ABC 29.1.62. (Bowling alley built over car park.) Closed 28.1.78 for quadrupling. ABC 1, 2, 3 & 4 opened 25.5.78, 506 & 350 & 230 & 216 seats. (Closed 19.3.87. Demolished 1987. Supermarket.)

BICESTER Oxfordshire

REGAL London Road. (Opened 9.34 by Union, architect: Harold S. Scott, 504 seats.) Taken over 10.37, part of Union circuit. Partweek bingo from 1968. Taken over by Star 1.7.69. Taken back 2.3.75. Closed 3.12.75. (Fulltime bingo.)

BIRKENHEAD Merseyside

see also Tranmere

(LA) SCALA Argyle Street. (Opened 18.4.21, conversion of Theatre Royal, architect: James Stoneman Bramwell, 1000 seats.) Taken over 2.30. Closed 6.2.37. (Demolished for Savoy.)

SAVOY Argyle Street (site of Theatre Royal/ Scala). Opened 10.10.38 by ABC, architect: W. R. Glen, 2016 seats: 1248 stalls & 768 balcony. Closed 1940 by bomb damage to ceiling. Re-opened 16.12.40. Renamed ABC c1961. Closed 14.11.70 for "luxury lounge" treatment. Re-opened 7.12.70, 600 seats, stalls only. Closed 27.3.82. (Snooker club.)

BIRMINGHAM West Midlands

see also Aston, Aston Cross, Bordesley Green, Edgbaston, Erdington, Hall Green, Handsworth, Harborne, Hay Mills, Ladywood, Moseley Road, Saltley, Selly Oak, Sparkbrook, Stirchley and Yardley

METROPOLE Snow Hill. (Former music hall.) Taken over c1.29. (Leased to Regent 5.33 to 1935.) (Taken over by independent 11.7.38. Taken over by Clifton 8.39. Closed 1941 by war damage. Demolished c1952. YMCA.)

SELECT 47 Station Street. (Opened 30.7.10 as Electric Theatre by Electric Theatres circuit, architect: Bertie Crewe. Renamed Select 1921, repertory cinema. May have been an ABC theatre briefly in 1928 – listed in *Kine Year Book* 1929 under company heading as part of circuit. (Closed 1931. Amusement arcade. Rebuilt and re-opened 20.3.37 as Tatler News Theatre, architect: Cecil E.

M. Fillmore. Taken over by Jacey, renamed Jacey c1962. Taken over by Classic 1980, renamed Classic. Twinned. Closed 27.9.84. Taken over by independent, re-opened as Tivoli. 105 & 142 seats. Closed 1988. Re-opened 1988.)

FORUM New Street and Ethel Street. Opened 1.11.30 by ABC, architect: W. R. Glen, constructed within walls of Regent, ex-Masonic Hall, 1259 seats: 501 stalls, 348 balcony, 410 upper circle. Renamed ABC c1961. Closed 9.4.83. (Video games centre with offices above.)

BRISTOL Bristol Road. (Opened 16.5.37, architect: Hurley Robinson, 1712 seats. Taken over 1.1.44. Renamed ABC 8.59. Closed 4.5.63 for conversion to Cinerama. Re-opened 14.9.63 as ABC CINERAMA, 1232 seats. Closed 5.2.72 for tripling. ABC 1, 2 & 3 opened 27.7.72, 482 & 353 & 175 seats. (Renamed Cannon. Closed 24.9.87. Demolished 1987. MacDonald's.)

BLACKBURN Lancashire

SAVOY Bolton Road. (Opened 11.22.) Taken over 23.2.31. (Leased to Regent c5.33 to 1935.) (Taken over by independent c1935. 1017 seats. Closed 28.12.57. Bingo.)

MAJESTIC King William Street. (Opened pre-1914 as Exchange, former Exchange Hall. Re-opened 31.3.24, named Majestic.) Taken over, modernised and re-opened 3 or 10.10.32. 1582 seats. (Taken over by independent 27.9.53, modernised and re-opened 2.11.53. Taken over by Essoldo 12.55. Renamed Essoldo 1.56. Taken over by Classic 1.4.72, renamed Classic. Triple from 5.3.76. Taken over by Unit Four, renamed Unit Four. 315 & 256 & 186 seats. Taken over by Apollo. Open.)

BLACKHEATH Southeast London

ROXY 3 Old Dover Road. Opened 11.2.35 by ABC, architects: Bertie Crewe and Marshall & Tweedy, 1342 seats. Closed by wartime bomb damage. Re-opened 6.1.47. Renamed ABC 1963. Closed 16.2.74. (Demolished. Supermarket.)

BLACKLEY Manchester

see Higher Blackley

BLACKPOOL Lancashire

HIPPODROME Church Street and King Street. (Opened pre-1914, former variety theatre.)

Taken over 12.4.29. 2820 seats. Much live use. Closed autumn 1937. Re-opened 6.38. Closed 28.10.39. Re-opened 29.1.40. Reduced to 1,878 seats in 1949. Closed c1960. (Largely demolished for ABC.)

PRINCESS Promenade. (Opened 12.12.12. 900 seats. Improved, architect: H. Best, re-opened 7.22.) Taken over 10.4.29. 1770 seats. Renamed ABC (NORTH SHORE) c1960. Renamed PRINCESS 1963. Closed 1981. (Converted to The Venue for music concerts. Indoor market. Entertainment venue: Bizness Puberama.)

ABC Church Street and King Street (site of Hippodrome, some walls retained). Opened 31.5.63 by ABC, 1934 seats. Mostly live shows. Closed 31.1.81 for tripling. ABC 1, 2 & 3 opened 30.4.81, 728 & 321 & 231 seats, cinema use only. (Renamed Cannon. Renamed MGM 14.5.93. Open.)

BLOOMSBURY Central London

BLOOMSBURY Brunswick Square. (Opened 19.1.72 by Walter Reade, 490 seats, one floor underground.) Taken over 4.5.74 and renamed ABC. Renamed EMI INTERNATIONAL FILM THEATRE 27.1.77. Closed 15.2.78. (Taken over by Cinegate and re-opened 23.3.78 as Gate Two. Twinned from 24.9.81 and renamed Gate Bloomsbury 1 & 2, 266 & 266 seats. Closed 30.10.85. Taken over by Artificial Eye and re-opened as Renoir. Open.)

BLYTH Northumberland

WALLAW Union Street. (Opened 1937, architect: Percy L. Browne and Son, 1600 seats.) Taken over 24.3.55. (Taken over by independent 21.6.70. Taken over by Classic 2.1.72. Taken over by independent 24.6.77. Closed 11.12.82. Re-opened 27.12.82. Tripled & re-opened 10.7.87, 850 & 150 & 80 seats. Open.)

BOLTON Greater Manchester

PALLADIUM Higher Bridge Street. (Opened 1.22.) Taken over c1930. (Leased to Regent 5.33 to 1935. 1250 seats.) (Taken over by independent c1935. Closed 1958. Wrestling stadium.)

REGAL Spa Road. (Former Olympia skating rink, then music hall, converted to Regal cinema 1931.) Taken over c1932. 2380 seats. (Taken over c1945

by independent. Closed c1955. Dance hall and/or skating rink.)

CAPITOL Churchgate. (Opened 13.2.29, architects: Gray and Evans.) Taken over 26.7.35. 1642 seats. Structurally altered and re-opened 2.7.56. Renamed ABC 20.8.62. Closed 1.10.77. (Bingo. Sports centre – squash courts in stalls, balcony disused.)

BOOTLE Merseyside

GAINSBOROUGH Knowsley Road. (Opened 18.2.22.) Taken over 1.6.31. 1311 seats. Closed 12.11.60. (Bingo from 25.9.62.)

BORDESLEY GREEN Birmingham

ELITE Bordesley Green and Crown Road. (Opened 1917. Taken over by Savoy Cinemas.) Part of original circuit. 1327 seats. (Leased to Regent 5.33 to 1935.) Closed 1942 by bomb damage. (Scrapyard. Disused. Lower walls remain.)

PALACE, High Street. Taken over 10.28, former live theatre, 2148 seats. Reconstructed? 1296 seats. Closed c1942. (Demolished.)

RITZ Bordesley Green East. (Opened 7.11.27, architect: Hurley Robinson.) Taken over 19.5.30. 1442 seats. Closed 29.9.62. (Bingo. Demolished c1989/90.)

BOSCOMBE Bournemouth

CARLTON 677 Christchurch Road. Opened 27.7.31 by ABC, architects: Reynolds and Tomlin, 1650 seats. Closed 14.4.71, stalls into "luxury lounge", and re-opened 29.4.71, renamed ABC. Closed 10.7.74. (Bingo to c1987. Derelict.)

BOTLEY Oxford

MAJESTIC. (Taken over by Union.) Taken over 10.37, part of Union circuit. Closed 10.9.40. (Accommodation for war evacuees. Cooper's "Oxford" marmalade factory. Furniture/DIY shop. Demolished c1990. Furniture shop.)

BOURNEMOUTH Dorset

see also Boscombe and Westbourne

WESTOVER Westover Road. (Taken over 23.6.28 by Savoy Cinemas.) Part of original circuit. Closed 1937. (Forte's cafe.)

WESTOVER 27 Westover Road. Opened 19.6.37

by ABC, architect: W. R. Glen, 2515 seats: 1605 stalls & 910 balcony. Renamed ABC 3.58. Closed 24.9.69 for twinning. ABC 1 & 2 opened 13.6.70, 644 & 982 seats. ABC 2 closed 24.1.73 for twinning. ABC 2 re-opened 19.4.73 as ABC 2 & 3, 587 & 223 seats. (Renamed Cannon. Renamed MGM 22.5.92. Open.)

BOWES ROAD North London
RITZ 174 Bowes Road, New Southgate. Opened 21.12.33 by ABC, architect: W. J. King, 1870 seats. Closed 11.4.70, stalls into "luxury lounge" (balcony closed). Re-opened 2.5.70 as ABC, 588 seats. Closed 16.2.74. (Assembly Hall of Jehovah's Witnesses.)

BRACKNELL Berkshire
REGAL High Street. (Opened 1930. 396 seats. Taken over by Union c1936.) Taken over 10.37, part of Union circuit. (Taken over by independent 10.4.60. Closed 6.63.) Re-opened 23.8.65 by ABC. Closed 9.2.74. Re-opened 17.3.74. Closed 4.9.76 for twinning. ABC 1 & 2 opened 12.12.76, 300 & 200 seats. Closed 30.10.82. (Demolished c1989.)

BRADFORD Yorkshire
SAVOY Darley Street. (Opened 29.3.20, two balconies.) Part of original circuit, from Savoy Cinemas. 1517 seats. Closed 15.4.39. (Bought by Marks and Spencer 7.39 and demolished for store extension.)
REGENT Manningham Lane. (Opened 10.14. Taken over 1924 by Savoy Cinemas.) Part of original circuit. (Leased to Regent 5.33 to 1935.) Closed 3.12.38. (Re-opened by independent 26.12.38. 1384 seats. Taken over by Essoldo 7.47. Renamed Essoldo 12.49. Closed 1965. Bingo. Asian cinema. Closed 3.75 by fire. Demolished. Road.)
RITZ Broadway and Leeds Road. Opened 8.5.39 by ABC, architect: W. R. Glen, 2037 seats. Renamed ABC c1968. Closed 3.8.74 for tripling and Painted Wagon pub in old Leeds Road entrance. ABC 1 opened 6.10.74, 732 seats. ABC 2 & 3 opened 18.11.74, 174 & 163 seats. (Renamed Cannon. Closed 17.9.87. Demolished 1989.)

BRIDGETON Glasgow
ARCADIA 484 London Road, Bridgeton Cross. (Opened 31.12.30, architect: William Beresford Inglis. Taken over c1929. 1409 seats. (Taken over by independent c1939. Closed 7.53 by ceiling collapse. Taken over by Green's 1.11.54. Re-opened. Closed 4.62. Bingo. Demolished 1971.)
OLYMPIA Bridgeton Cross. (Opened 1924 by SCVT, former music hall.) Part of original circuit. Interior reconstructed and re-opened 21.11.38, 1689 seats. Renamed ABC c1963. Closed 9.3.74. Listed building.

BRIDGNORTH Salop
MAJESTIC Whitburn Street. (Opened 22.11.37 by Lou Morris, architects: J. Owen Bond and Son, 1030 seats.) Taken over 30.8.43 from Mayfair circuit. (Taken over by Star 30.6.69. Partweek bingo.) Taken back by ABC 2.3.75. Closed 3.12.77. (Taken over by independent and re-opened 29.10.78. Twinned c1982, 500 & 200 seats. Tripled, 500 & 86 & 86 seats. Open.)

BRIDLINGTON Humberside
REGAL Promenade. (Opened 28.7.38 by Lou Morris, architect: C. Edmund Wilford, 1489 seats.) Taken over 30.8.43, from Mayfair circuit. (Taken over by Star 30.6.69. Closed 24.12.71. Bingo.)

BRIGHOUSE West Yorkshire
RITZ Bonegate Road and Bradford Road. Opened 3.37 by Union, architect: J. H. Freer, 986 seats, stadium plan.) Taken over 10.37, part of Union circuit. Closed 24.6.61. (Bingo to 9.61. Ballroom from 1981.)

BRIGHTON West Sussex
SAVOY 75/79 East Street & corner of Pool Valley and The Parade. Opened 1.8.30 by ABC, architect: W. R. Glen, interior decorations: H. H. Martyn and Co., 2567 seats: 1508 stalls & 1059 balcony. Closed 5.2.58 for modernisation and re-opened 27.3.58, 2304 seats. Renamed ABC 26.4.61. Closed 15.11.75 for quadrupling. ABC 1, 2, 3 & 4 opened 3.4.76, 820 in former balcony & 346 & 284 & 231 seats. (Renamed Cannon. Cannon 1 in former balcony closed 5.91, others open.)

ASTORIA 10/17 Gloucester Place and Blenheim
Place. (Opened 21.12.33, architect: E. A. Stone and Partners, 1823 seats.) Taken over 2.35. Reconstructed 1958 for 70mm presentations. Closed 7.5.77. (Bingo. Open.)

BRISTOL Avon
see also Clifton, Filton, Fishponds and St. George
KING'S Old Market Street. (Opened pre-1914. 700 seats. Closed 7.20 for reconstruction and re-opened 5.21. Closed 20.3.26 by fire. Reconstructed and re-opened 4.9.26.) Taken over 11.3.29. Modernised 1931. 1485 seats. Closed 4.12.76. (Demolished. Office block.)
EMPIRE Old Market Street. (Opened 13.4.31, former variety theatre with some films.) Taken over c10.32. 1437 seats. Closed 24.6.39. (Taken over by Odeon 25.6.39. Closed 9.12.39. Re-opened as live theatre 26.12.39. BBC studios mid-1950s to 1962. Demolished 1963. Pedestrian underpass.)
ABC New Bristol Centre, Frogmore Street. Opened 17.11.66 by ABC, 806 seats, stadium. Closed 13.9.80 for twinning. ABC 1 & 2 opened 11.12.80, 411 & 301 seats. (Renamed Cannon. Open.)

BRIXTON South London
PALLADIUM Brixton Hill. (Opened 20.3.13, architect: Gilbert Booth.) Taken over 10.29. 1200 seats. Closed 28.4.56 for reconstruction of front. Re-opened 24.9.56 as REGAL, 1156 seats: 878 stalls & 278 balcony. Renamed ABC 20.10.63. (Taken over by independent 23.10.77 and renamed Ace. Closed 28.3.81. Re-opened 8.6.85 as the Fridge nightclub. Open.)

BROUGHTON Salford
see Higher Broughton

BURNLEY Lancashire
PALACE St. James Street. (Former live theatre with some cinema use.) Taken over 2.31. (Leased to Regent 5.33 to 1934.) 1614 seats. (Leased out c12.37 to 4.9.39.) Taken back. (Taken over by independent and returned to variety from 3.11.41. Cinema from 13.1.47. Modernised and re-opened 22.11.54. 1100 seats. Taken over by Star 12.58. Closed 1962. Bingo. Demolished 1973.)

BURNSIDE Glasgow

RHUL Stonelaw Road. (Opened 27.4.32, architect: Neil C. Duff, 1250 seats.) Taken over 12.36. Closed 5.11.60. (Demolished. Safeways supermarket.)

CAMBERWELL South London

PALACE 23/31 Denmark Hill. Former Palace Theatre, taken over 9.32. 1396 seats. (Taken over by independent 1940. Taken over by Hyams by 1.42. Closed 18.4.43. Re-opened 26.4.43 as variety theatre. Closed 28.4.56. Demolished.)

REGAL 254/272 Camberwell Road and Medlar Street. Opened 17.6.40 by ABC, architect: Leslie H. Kemp, 2600 seats. Closed 9.40 by enemy action. Re-opened 6.10.40. Renamed ABC 17.12.61. Closed 27.10.73. (Bingo. Open.)

CAMBRIDGE Cambridgeshire

REGAL 37 St. Andrews Street. Opened 3.4.37 by ABC, architect: John S. Quilter and Son, 1869 seats. Closed 28.8.71 for twinning. ABC 1 & 2 opened 13.1.72, 452 & 736 seats. ABC 1 closed 6.9.84 by fire. Re-opened 16.11.84. (Renamed Cannon. Renamed MGM 23.4.93. Open.)

PLAYHOUSE Mill Road, corner of Covent Garden. (Opened 13.5.13, architect: George Baines and Son, 769 seats. Taken over by Union 31.12.34.) Taken over 10.37, part of Union circuit. 686 seats. Closed 24.11.56. (Fine Fare supermarket. Salvation Army shop.)

TIVOLI 16 Chesterton Road. (Opened 19.3.25, architect: G. P. Banyard. Taken over by Union 31.12.34.) Taken over 10.37, part of Union circuit. 580 seats. Closed 24.11.56. (Warehouse.)

CENTRAL 21 Hobson Street (site of old Central). (Opened 11.10.30, architect: G. P. Banyard. Taken over by Union 31.12.34. 1069 seats.) Taken over 10.37, part of Union circuit. Closed 25.4.39 by fire. Re-opened 11.11.40. Closed 15.1.72. (Bingo.)

THEATRE CINEMA 48/50 St. Andrews Street. (Opened 11.9.33, former New Theatre, 900 seats. Taken over by Union 31.12.34. Variety and films.) Taken over 10.37, part of Union circuit. Closed 8.1.38. Re-opened 10.7.39. Requisitioned 10.40. Re-opened 13.10.47 as NEW THEATRE. 618 seats. Stage shows from 29.3.48. Closed as live

theatre 17.3.56. (Warehouse. Demolished 1961. Janus House.)

VICTORIA 9/11 Market Hill. (Opened 28.8.31, architects: Hoare and Wheeler, decorative painter: Baron Avild Rosencrantz, 1430 seats. Taken over by Union 14.10.35.) Taken over 10.37, part of Union circuit. Closed 3.6.67 for modernisation. Re-opened 7.10.67 with stalls as "luxury lounge", 924 seats. Restaurant space converted to second screen and opened 4.12.72, 139 seats. Closed 4.12.83 by fire. Re-opened 10.2.84. (Renamed Cannon Victoria. Closed 14.1.88. Demolished, except frontage, for Marks and Spencer home furnishings store.)

CAMBUSLANG Strathclyde

RITZ Main Street. Opened 12.5.30 by ABC, architect: W. Inglis, 1595 seats. Closed 2.7.60. (Demolished 1962. Shops and offices.)

CAMDEN TOWN North London

BEDFORD 93/95 High Street. Former live theatre, taken over 1933. 1259 seats. Closed 24.6.39. (Taken over by Odeon or independent. Closed 11.12.39. Variety theatre. Closed. Demolished 1962.)

CANTERBURY Kent

CENTRAL St. Margaret's Street (site of St. Margaret's Hall/Empire Music Hall). (Opened 7.11.27, architects: Dore and Anderson, 735 seats.) Taken over c1933. (Leased to Regent 5.33 to 1935.) Closed 6.42 by bomb damage. Re-opened 28.9.42. Closed c10.42. Re-opened 22.3.43. Closed 9.7.49 by Compulsory Purchase Order from Council. (Marlowe Theatre from 29.5.50. Closed. Demolished. Shops.)

REGAL 43/45 St. George's Place. (Opened 5.8.33 by County, architect: Robert Cromie, 1685 seats. Relinquished by County 4.4.35.) Taken over 29.4.35. Closed 31.10.42 by bomb damage. Re-opened 2.43. Renamed ABC 8.63. Closed 5.8.72 for split into stalls bingo and balcony cinema. Re-opened 26.10.72, 536 seats. (Renamed Cannon. Stalls bingo converted to Cannon 2, 404 seats, opened 5.8.88. Renamed MGM 16.4.93. Both open.)

CARDIFF South Glamorgan

QUEEN'S Queen Street, opposite Park Place. (Opened pre-1914 as Cardiff Cinema Theatre. Renamed Queen's 9.25.) Part of original circuit. 1253 seats. Closed 29.10.55. (Demolished. Wyman's.)

PAVILION St. Mary Street. (Opened c5.16, former Philharmonic Hall and Panopticon. 1600 seats.) Part of original circuit. (Taken over by independent 11.6.45. 1216 seats. Modernised and re-opened 6.61 as Gala Pavilion by Gala, 568 seats. Closed 1968. Bingo.)

OLYMPIA 63 Queen Street. (Opened 1912, former Andrews Hall for variety/exhibitions. Modernised, architect: Howard Williams, and re-opened 11.35.) Taken over 10.36. 2047 seats. Closed 3.4.76 for tripling. ABC 1 opened 27.5.76, 617 seats. ABC 2 & 3 opened 24.6.76, 318 & 150 seats. (Renamed Cannon. Refurbished and renamed MGM 29.5.92. Open.)

CARLISLE Cumbria

CITY PICTURE HOUSE English Street. (Taken over by Union.) Taken over 10.37, part of Union circuit. 881 seats. Closed 30.6.60. (Demolished. Littlewoods store.)

PUBLIC HALL Chapel Street. (Converted church hall. Taken over by Union.) Taken over 10.37, part of Union circuit. 695 seats. Closed 17.11.56. (Carpet warehouse.)

LONSDALE Warwick Road. (Opened 21.9.31, architect: Percy L Browne and Son, 1880 seats. Taken over by Union c1935.) Taken over 10.37, part of Union circuit. Renamed ABC 15.1.62. Closed 19.2.72 for split into bingo & cinema. Re-opened 25.5.72, 578 seats. (Taken over by independent 9.7.78 and renamed Lonsdale. Twinned and re-opened 19.12.78, 410 & 230 seats. Closed c4.87. Re-opened. Third screen added c9.87, 50 seats. Open as triple.)

CASTLEFORD West Yorkshire

ALBION PICTURE PALACE Albion Street. (Opened 31.1.27.) Taken over 6.6.32. 904 seats. (Taken over by Star 3.11.57. Closed 1.3.75 for tripling. Re-opened 9.6.75 as Studio 1, 2 & 3, 350 & 110 & 100 seats. Taken over by Cannon. Renamed Cannon. Closed c4.87. Night club: Escapades.)

CATFORD Southeast London

PLAZA Central Parade, 1 Bromley Road & Sangley Road. (Opened 23.12.13 as Central Hall Picture House, architect: E. A. Stone, 1046 seats. Renamed Plaza 21.11.32. Taken over by Union c1935.) Taken over 10.37, part of Union circuit. Closed 27.5.61 for modernisation. Re-opened 26.11.61 as ABC, 925 seats. Closed 10.10.81 for twinning. ABC 1 & 2 opened 20.12.81, 519 & 259 seats. (Renamed Cannon. Open.)

CATHCART Glasgow

RIALTO 15 Old Castle Road. (Opened pre-1920 as Picture House. Renamed Rialto. Enlarged and re-opened 5.11.28.) Taken over 3.30. 1311 seats. (Taken over by independent c1946. Re-opened 23.12.48 as George. Closed c1961. Kingdom Hall of Jehovah's Witnesses.)

CAVERSHAM Reading

REGAL Church Street. (Opened 3.10.38, architect: E. Norman Bailey, 857 seats.) Taken over 30.8.43, from Mayfair circuit. Closed 7.6.58. (Warehouse and offices. Demolished. Supermarket.)

CHATHAM Kent

REGENT High Street. (Opened 1914 as Imperial Picture Palace, 1674 seats. Renamed Regent 1927.) Taken over 18.3.29. Closed 9.1.37. (Demolished for new Regent.)

RITZ 324 High Street. (Opened 22.3.37 by Union, architect: Robert Cromie, 2322 seats.) Taken over 10.37, part of Union circuit. Closed 20.5.72. (Bingo. Open.)

REGENT 385 High Street (site of old Regent). Opened 11.7.38 by ABC, architect: W. R. Glen, 1906 seats: 1151 stalls & 755 balcony. Renamed ABC 30.10.61. Closed 22.1.72 for tripling. ABC 1, 2 & 3 opened 15.6.72, 528 & 366 & 172 seats. (Renamed Cannon. Open.)

CHEADLE Cheshire

ELECTRA High Street. Taken over 4.36. 868 seats. (Let from 5.4.54. Operated by Snape circuit. Closed 11.63, end of lease. Demolished.)

CHEETHAM HILL Manchester

PREMIER Cheetham Hill Road (site of old

Premier). (Opened 2.8.25, architect: John Knight, 1850 seats.) Taken over 21.1.29. Renamed ABC c1965. Closed 25.7.70.

CHELTENHAM Gloucestershire

REGAL The Promenade, junction of St. George's Road and Royal Well Walk. Opened 2.1.39 by ABC, architects: W. R. Glen and Leslie C. Norton, 1839 seats: 1165 stalls & 674 balcony. Renamed ABC 28.8.62. Closed 14.11.81. (Demolished 1985. Office block.)

CHESTER Cheshire

REGAL Love Street and Foregate Street. Opened 30.10.37 by ABC, architect: W. R. Glen, 1973 seats: 1196 stalls & 777 balcony. Renamed ABC 6.59. Closed 28.1.80 for twinning balcony plus bingo on former stalls floor. Re-opened as ABC 1 & 2, 470 & 252 seats. (Renamed Cannon. Closed 16.12.90. Derelict.)

CHESTERFIELD Derbyshire

REGAL Cavendish Street. Opened 12.10.36 by ABC, architect: J. Owen Bond with modifications by W. R. Glen, 2048 seats. Renamed ABC c1961. Closed 12.6.71. Re-opened 5.9.71 with smaller ABC in old balcony, 484 seats, plus Painted Wagon pub in stalls area. (Renamed Cannon. Taken over by independent and re-named Regal. Closed 18.4.03.)

CHORLEY Lancashire

THEATRE ROYAL Market Street. Taken over c1932. 896 seats. (Taken over by independent c1938. Closed c1957. Demolished 1960.)

CHORLTON-CUM-HARDY Greater Manchester

SAVOY Manchester Road and Nicholas Road. (Opened 8.11.20 as Picture House by PCT. Taken over by Savoy Cinemas and renamed Savoy.) Part of original circuit. 1500 seats. (Taken over 26.3.46 by Gaumont and re-opened 1.4.46 as Gaumont. 1250 seats. Closed 6.1.62. Co-Op Funeral Centre with new frontage.)

CIRENCESTER Gloucestershire

REGAL Kewis Lane. (Opened 29.11.37, architect: Harold S. Scott, 1008 seats.) Taken over 1943,

from Mayfair Circuit. Renamed ABC 1963. Partweek bingo. (Taken over 30.6.69 by Star and renamed Regal.) Taken back 2.3.75. Closed 28.3.77. (Fulltime bingo.) Two video cinemas opened by EMI 1981, 150 & 150 seats. Video cinemas converted to conventional projection. (Taken over by independent. Open.)

CLAPTON North London

RITZ 217a Lower Clapton Road. Opened 23.10.39 by ABC, architect: W. R. Glen, 1884 seats. Renamed ABC 1962. Closed 15.9.73. (Demolished. Car park.)

CLEETHORPES Humberside

RITZ Grimsby Road. (Opened 31.7.37 by Union, architect: Robert Cromie, 1429 seats.) Taken over 10.37, part of Union circuit. Renamed ABC c1959. Closed 12.8.72 for split into stalls bingo and balcony cinema. Re-opened 26.10.72, 483 seats. Closed 10.9.82. Serious fire in 4.85. Demolished 1993.)

CLIFTON Bristol

TRIANGLE Queens Road. (Opened 1.12.13 as Triangle Picture Hall, conversion of roller skating rink, architect: W. H. Watkins, 1400 seats.) Taken over 8.29. Closed by bomb damage 24.11.40. (Demolished. University building.)

WHITELADIES Whiteladies Road. (Opened 29.11.21.) Taken over 8.29. 1314 seats. Closed 27.4.57 to enlarge balcony. Re-opened 26.8.57, 1411 seats. Closed 22.8.59 for modernisation. Re-opened 5.9.59. Renamed ABC c1965. Closed 10.6.78 for tripling. ABC 1, 2 & 3 opened 7.9.78, 380 & 259 & 126 seats. (Renamed Cannon. Renamed MGM 16.4.93. Open.)

CLIFTONVILLE Margate

ASTORIA Northdown Road. (Opened 4.8.34, conversion of large garage, architect: E. A. Stone, 1680 seats.) Taken over 2.35. Closed 20.7.40. (Twice bombed. Demolished. Garage.)

CLYDEBANK Glasgow

EMPIRE. (Opened 1.14 and taken over by SCVT. 1150 seats.) Part of original circuit. Closed 21.6.59 by fire. (Demolished.)

BANK 385 Glasgow Road. (Opened 11.27 by

SCVT, former Gaiety Theatre. 1071 seats.) Part of original circuit. Closed 30.9.61. (Demolished except gable end. Furniture warehouse.)
GAIETY. Part of original circuit, from SCVT. Closed c1929. (Demolished c1960.)
PALACE Kilbowie Road. Part of original circuit, from SCVT. 800 seats. (Taken over by independent 6.40. Never re-opened.)
LA SCALA Graham Avenue. (Opened 14.2.38 by Alexander King, architect: Lennox Paterson, 2648 seats. Closed 1941. Re-opened 1944.) Taken over 31.8.59. Renamed ABC c1965. Closed 12.4.69 for splitting into stalls bingo and new cinema in balcony. Re-opened 31.7.69, 776 seats. Closed 19.2.83. (Disused. Bingo open.)

COATBRIDGE Strathclyde
REGAL The Cross. Opened 17.2.36 by ABC, architect: Charles J. McNair, 1958 seats. Renamed ABC c1963. Closed 9.12.72 for splitting into stalls bingo and new cinema in balcony. Re-opened 15.3.73, 510 seats. Closed 22.1.83. (Bingo continued.)

COLCHESTER Essex
PLAYHOUSE St. John's Street. (Opened 1929, former garrison theatre.) Taken over 2.5.32. Gallery removed, balcony enlarged, reseated and re-opened 6.4.35. 1158 seats. Modernised, architect: C. J. Foster, and re-opened 20.10.62 as ABC, 963 seats. Closed 8.81. (Bingo. Disused.)

COMMERCIAL ROAD East London
see Stepney

CONSETT Durham
REX Harvey Street (site of Tivoli ballroom). (Opened 5.12.38, architect: J. W. Father, 1434 seats.) Taken over 15.3.43. Closed 11.6.66 by fire. (Demolished.)

CORK Co. Cork, Eire
SAVOY Patrick Street. Opened c6.32 by Associated Irish Cinemas, architects: Moore and Crabtree, 2285 seats. (Taken over by Irish partners or separate company c1935. Closed. Shopping arcade.)

COSHAM Hampshire
CARLTON High Street. (Opened 28.2.34, architect: R. A. Thomas, 1298 seats.) Taken over 26.12.37. Closed 5.12.40 by bomb damage. Re-opened 31.12.41. (Taken over by Essoldo 27.12.49. Renamed Essoldo c1950. Modernised 1968, 559 seats. Taken over by Classic 2.4.72 and renamed Classic. Triple from 20.11.82, 559 & 120 & 106 seats. Renamed Cannon. Open.)

COVENTRY West Midlands
EMPIRE Hertford Street. (Variety theatre, ex-Corn Exchange, with films. Destroyed 23.4.31 by fire.) Taken over, reconstructed, architects: W. R. Glen and (resident) Satchwell & Roberts, and re-opened 2.9.33, 1547 seats. Renamed ABC c1969. Closed 3.7.71. (Demolished for new ABC.)
ABC Hertford Street Precinct (site of Empire). Opened 24.5.73 by ABC. 840 seats (stadium). Mezzanine bar area converted to ABC 2, opened 20.10.77, 86 seats. (Renamed Cannon 1 & 2. Closed 21.4.88. Shop.)

COWLEY Oxford
REGAL Cowley Road and Magdalen Road. (Opened 19.4.37 by Union, architect: Robert Cromie, 1674 seats.) Taken over 10.37, part of Union circuit. Closed 7.70. (Bingo.)

CRAWLEY West Sussex
EMBASSY High Street. (Opened 1.8.38 by Shipman and King/H. Bancroft, architect: Robert Cromie, 1014 seats. Closed 8.12.79 for tripling. Embassy 1, 2 & 3 opened 20.3.80, 332 & 234 & 118 seats. Taken over by EMI.) Modernised and renamed ABC 12.85, 297 & 214 & 106 seats. (Renamed Cannon. Renamed MGM 18.6.93. Open.)

CRAYFORD Southeast London
PRINCESSES THEATRE. (Opened 7.15, former Vickers' works theatre. Taken over by Union c1935. 1024 seats.) Taken over 10.37, part of Union circuit. Run of live shows c1949-50. Renovated (balcony converted to projection suite) and re-opened 3.9.51 as RITZ, 900 seats, one floor. Closed 1.12.56. (Demolished. Shops and flats.)

CREWE Cheshire
EMPIRE Heath Street. Taken over c1.29. (Taken over by independent c9.41. 938 seats. Closed late 1950s. Bingo. Closed 3.84. Demolished.)

CROSBY Liverpool
REGENT Liverpool Road. (Opened 1919.) Taken over 25.11.35. 1100 seats. Closed 30.11.68. (Bingo.)

CROYDON South London
HIPPODROME Crown Hill. (Opened Spring 1918, former music hall. 1250 seats.) Taken over 2.2.31. (Leased to Regent from 5.33 to c1935.) Closed 18.4.42. (Taken over by Odeon and re-opened 4.5.42. Closed 3.11.56. Demolished. British Home Stores. Converted to Classic 1, 2 & 3, later Oscar 1, 2 & 3, then Focus 1, 2 & 3. Closed 14.8.82. Converted to fitness centre & snooker club.)
SAVOY Broad Green, West Croydon. Opened 9.3.36 by ABC, architect: W. R. Glen, 2276 seats. Closed 30.3.53 by fire. Re-opened 27.12.53. Closed 5.7.58 for modernisation. Re-opened 19.10.58 as ABC. Closed 20.5.72 for tripling. ABC 1, 2 & 3 opened 2.11.72, 650 & 390 & 187 seats. (Renamed Cannon. Open.)

DAGENHAM Northeast London
PRINCESS New Road. (Opened 8.10.32 by Lou Morris, architect: Robert Cromie, 1987 seats, stadium plan.) Taken over 28.8.33. Closed 23.4.60. (Bowling alley from 3.12.60. Open.)

DARLASTON Staffordshire
OLYMPIA Blockall. (Opened 19.10.12, conversion of skating rink, architects: Joynson Bros.) Taken over c1.29. 969 seats. Closed 10.12.55. (Car showrooms. Demolished c1965. Housing.)

DARLINGTON County Durham
REGAL Northgate (site of Theatre Royal, latterly cinema). Opened 31.1.38 by ABC, architects: Percy L. Browne, Son and Harding, 1620 seats. Renamed ABC c1961. Closed 28.5.77 for tripling. ABC 1, 2 & 3 opened 16.6.77, 590 & 220 & 149 seats. (Renamed Cannon. Open.)

DARWEN Lancashire

OLYMPIA Bolton Road. (Opened 1911, former live theatre.) Taken over 23.2.31. (Leased to Regent 5.33. to 1935.) 1325 seats. (Taken over by independent c1938. Re-opened 30.5.49 as New Olympia by Cheshire County Cinemas. Taken over by Star 15.7.61. Bingo.)

DENNISTOUN Glasgow

PICTURE HOUSE Armadale Street and Finlay Drive. (Opened c1921.) Taken over c10.29. 1373 seats. Closed 5.11.60. (Demolished.)

DENTON Greater Manchester

ROTA Ash Road and Thornley Road. (Opened 10.12.34, architect: Henry Elder, 1206 seats. Taken over by Union 4.4.36) Taken over 10.37, part of Union circuit. Closed 24.10.59. (Demolished. Houses.)

DERBY Derbyshire

WHITE HALL St. Peters Street. (Opened 14.12.14. 870 seats.) Taken over c1.29. (Taken over by Odeon 22.4.35, 913 seats. Closed 29.6.35 for modernisation. Re-opened 3.8.35 as Odeon. Closed 1.5.65. Demolished. British Home Stores.)

EMPIRE Becketts Well Lane. (Opened 10.10.10 as Victoria Electric Theatre, architect: J. H. Morton, 1000 seats. Renamed Empire c1918.) Taken over 11.30. 1254 seats. (Taken over by independent c10.40. Renamed Black Prince 1.8.49. Closed 14.3.60. Demolished. Shopping mall.)

POPULAR Mill Street. (Opened 16.8.28, architects: Naylor, Sale and Woore, 1132 seats, one floor.) Taken over 8.35. Closed 15.3.58. (Nightclub. Snooker hall.)

REGAL East Street. Opened 27.6.38 by ABC, architect: W. R. Glen, 1840 seats, 1248 stalls & 592 balcony. Renamed ABC 23.8.60. Closed 10.6.78 for tripling. ABC 1, 2 & 3 opened 5.10.78, 533 & 380 & 213 seats. Closed 14.7.84. (Demolished.)

NEW TROCADERO ENTERTAINMENTS CENTRE London Road. Opened 26.8.83 by EMI, 559 seats in balcony area of former Gaumont Palace/Gaumont/Odeon, bingo in stalls. Cinema

closed 14.12.88 after part of ceiling collapsed. (Derelict.)

DEWSBURY West Yorkshire

PLAYHOUSE Crackenedge Lane. (Opened 26.10.31, architect: Robert Cromie, 1850 seats.) Taken over 6.5.35. Renamed ABC c1963. Closed 11.4.70. (Bingo.)

REGAL SUPER, Market Place. (Opened c7.13 as Picture House. Taken over by Lou Morris, modernised and re-opened 25.12.33 as Regal Super Cinema. Taken over by Union 31.12.34, 919 seats.) Taken over 10.37, part of Union circuit. (Taken over by Essoldo 7.2.54. Renamed Essoldo c1955. Modernised 12.68, 361 seats on one floor. Taken over by Classic 2.4.72, and renamed Classic. Closed 6.5.79 for twinning. Re-opened 31.6.79, 330 seats in old balcony & 144 seats. Renamed Cannon. Taken over by Apollo, renamed Apollo, 315 & 151 seats. Closed 1993.)

DIDSBURY Greater Manchester

CAPITOL Parrs Wood Road South and School Lane. (Opened 21.5.31, architect: Peter Cummings, 1900 seats. Destroyed by fire 25.4.32 except walls and entrance. Rebuilt, architect: Peter Cummings, and re-opened 16.8.33. Taken over by Union 24.2.36. 1835 seats.) Taken over 10.37, part of Union circuit. Some live shows 1948/9. Closed 14.1.56. (ABC TV Studios. Polytechnic Theatre.)

DONCASTER South Yorkshire

PICTURE HOUSE High Street. (Opened 28.9.14, architect: E. H. Walker, 1000 seats.) Taken over c6.29. 1132 seats. Closed 28.10.67. (Bingo.)

ABC Cleveland Street. Opened 18.5.67 by ABC, architects: Morgan & Branch with C. J. Foster & Alan Morgan, 1277 seats, stadium plan. Closed 17.1.81 for tripling. ABC 1, 2 & 3 opened 9.4.81, 477 & 201 & 135 seats. (Renamed Cannon. Closed 18.6.92.)

DOVECOT Liverpool

GRANADA Prescot Road. (Opened 24.12.32, architect: A. E. Shennan, 1803 seats.) Taken over 12.6.35. Closed 30.9.61. (Bingo.)

DOVER Kent

PLAZA 20 Cannon Street. (Opened 1.7.29, conversion of bus garage, architect: A. H. Steel, 1000 seats, one floor.) Taken over 2.3.31. (Taken over by independent 15.4.51. Taken over by Essoldo c1955. Renamed Essoldo 9.7.56. Taken over independent 1.68, renamed Rio. Closed c1969. Bingo. Closed.)

GRANADA Castle Street. (Opened 8.1.30 by Bernstein Theatres, architect: Theodore Komisarjevsky, 1717 seats. Taken over by independent 12.4.31.) Taken over 19.6.35. Renamed ABC 4.60. Closed 6.6.70 for conversion to "luxury lounge". Re-opened 6.7.70, 610 seats, stalls only. Closed 30.10.82. (Nightclub.)

DUBLIN Co. Dublin, Eire

see also Dun Laoghaire

SAVOY 19 Upper O'Connell Street. Opened 29.11.29 by Associated Irish Cinemas, architect: F. C. Mitchell, interior design by W. E. Greenwood, 2792 seats. (Taken over by Irish partners or separate company c1935. Taken over by Rank. Modernised 1960. Taken over by local company c1980. Open as five-screen complex.)

ADELPHI 98/101 Middle Abbey Street. Opened 12.1.39 by ABC, architects: W. R. Glen and (local) W. R. Donnelly, 2296 seats: 1524 stalls & 772 balcony. Operated by Adelphi-Carlton subsidiary. Triple from 8.10.70, seating 614 (old balcony) & 1052 (old stalls) & 360 (former café). ABC 4 opened 23.11.73. All closed by fire 6.9.76. Adelphi 2, 3 & 4 re-opened 10.9.76. Adelphi 1 re-opened 19.11.76. (To Cannon. Open.)

CARLTON 52 Upper O'Connell Street. (Opened c1938, 1996 seats.) Taken over c1963, operated by Adelphi-Carlton subsidiary. Tripled. Carlton 1 opened 26.8.76. Carlton 2 & 3 opened 3.9.76. Carlton 1 closed by fire 6.9.76. Carlton 1 re-opened 17.9.76. Carlton 4 opened. (To Cannon. Open.)

DUMBARTON Strathclyde

PAVILION College Street. (Opened pre-1920. Taken over by Green's c1924. Taken over by independent c1925. Taken over by SCVT 1.27.) Part of original circuit. Renamed RIALTO c1928. 1245 seats. Closed 7.12.65 by fire. (Re-opened by independent. 966 seats. Re-opened by Caledonian Associated. Closed 7.5.89.)

DUMFRIES Dumfries and Galloway

PLAYHOUSE Irish Street. (Opened 1.22, former Mechanics' Institute. Taken over by SCVT.) Part of original circuit. Closed 12.31.

REGAL Shakespeare Street. Opened 14.12.31 by ABC, architects: Gordon and Scrymgeour, 1699 seats. Closed 18.3.72 for splitting into bingo and smaller cinema in former balcony. Re-opened, renamed ABC, 8.6.72, 532 seats. (Renamed Cannon. Open.)

DUNDEE Tayside

PALACE Nethergate. (Former variety theatre, cinema from 1925. Taken over by SCVT.) Part of original circuit. Closed c4.38. (Sold. Reconstructed for variety and re-opened 6.10.38. Renamed Theatre Royal 1965. Closed. Auditorium demolished for offices, facade retained.)

PLAZA Hilltown. (Opened 28.5.28, architects: Maclaren, Souter & Salmond, 1620 seats.) Taken over 9.29. (Taken over by independent 30.3.58. Closed 23.9.72. Bingo. Split for small cinema, opened 31.3.75. Closed 10.4.76, with bingo club.)

CAPITOL 7 Seagate and Gellatly Street (site of Majestic). (Opened 1956, 1400 seats, stadium plan.) Taken over 2.5.59, improved and re-opened 25.5.59 as ABC, 1238 seats. Closed 28.4.79 for twinning. ABC 1 & 2 opened 9.8.79, 618 & 319 seats. (Renamed Cannon. Open.)

DUN LAOGHAIRE Co. Dublin, Eire

ADELPHI 40/42 George Street. Opened c1948, 1601 seats. Closed 1977 or earlier.

DUNSTABLE Bedfordshire

PALACE High Street North (site of earlier cinema). (Opened c1920, architects: Franklin and Deacon, 512 seats. Taken over by Union.) Taken over 10.37, part of Union circuit. Closed c1939.

UNION High Street North. (Opened 27.9.37 by Union, architect: Leslie H. Kemp, 1432 seats: 1048 stalls & 384 balcony.) Taken over 10.37, part of Union circuit. Renamed ABC c1961. (Taken over by Star 1.7.69 and renamed Studio. Partweek bingo. Closed 14.2.73 for fulltime bingo. Open.)

DURSLEY Gloucestershire

REGAL 18 Kingshill. (Opened 16.12.37, architect: Harold S. Scott, 658 seats on one floor.) Taken over 30.8.43, from Mayfair circuit. Partweek bingo in 1960s. (Taken over by Star 30.6.69. Split for films and bingo.) Taken back 2.3.75. Cinema closed 22.6.77. (Bingo. Supermarket. Demolished c6.93.)

EALING West London

LIDO Northfield Avenue, West Ealing. (Opened 6.13 as West Ealing Kinema, architect: G. Percy Pratt. Reconstructed and extended, architect: G. Percy Pratt, re-opened 15.10.28.) Taken over 8.30, renamed LIDO, 1097 seats. (Possibly leased to Regent from 5.33 to 8.35.) (Taken over by independent c1938. Closed 13.2.65, taken over by Star. Bingo. Circle converted to Studio 1 & 2, opened 17.9.71, 160 & 161 seats. Taken over by Cannon. Open as Cannon Northfield Avenue. Stalls now snooker club.)

FORUM Uxbridge Road. (Opened 23.4.34, architects: J. Stanley Beard & Clare, and W. R. Bennett, 2175 seats.) Taken over 3.35. Renamed ABC 1961. Closed 15.3.75 for tripling. ABC 1, 2 & 3 opened 29.6.75, 764 & 417 & 210 seats. (Renamed Cannon Uxbridge Road. Renamed MGM 23.4.93.)

EASTBOURNE East Sussex

LUXOR Pevensey Road. (Opened 3.4.33, architects: J. Stanley Beard and A. Douglas Clare, 1725 seats. Taken over by Union 26.10.35.) Taken over 10.37, part of Union circuit. Renamed ABC 12.2.62. Closed 2.5.73 for twinning and Painted Wagon pub. ABC 1 opened 5.7.73, 585 seats. ABC 2 opened 9.8.73, 159 seats. (Renamed Cannon. Closed 21.2.91.)

EAST ACTON West London

see Acton

EAST HAM East London

BROADWAY 86 High Street South. (Opened 1911.) Taken over c1930. (Taken over by independent c1934. Taken over by Southan Morris. Taken over by Essoldo 26.8.54. Closed 15.6.57. Demolished.)

ECCLES Greater Manchester

BROADWAY Church Street. (Opened 29.7.32, architect: Joseph Gomersall of Drury and Gomersall, 2040 seats. Taken over by Union 24.2.36.) Taken over 10.37, part of Union circuit. Renamed ABC c1965. Closed 9.3.74. (Commercial use.)

EDGBASTON Birmingham

PICTURE HOUSE Monument Road. Opened 26.12.28 by ABC, 1660 seats. Renamed ABC c1959. Closed 16.11.68. (Bingo. Demolished.)

EDGWARE North London

RITZ Station Road, The Mall and Manor Park Crescent. Opened 2.5.32 by ABC, architect: W. J. King, decorative artist: F. L. Philie, 2190 seats. Renamed ABC 20.8.62. Closed 3.5.68 for modernisation. Re-opened 24.8.68. Closed 3.2.73 for tripling. ABC 1 opened 4.3.73, 705 seats. ABC 2 & 3 opened 16.4.73, 207 & 146 seats. (Renamed Cannon. Closed 8.4.93. Expected to be re-opened by independent.)

EDGWARE ROAD North London

REGAL 35/51 Harrow Road. Opened 12.9.38 by ABC, architect: W. R. Glen, 1980 seats, 1234 stalls & 746 balcony. Originally known as "Regal Harrow Road". Renamed ABC 27.11.61. Closed 3.2.79 for quadrupling. ABC 1, 2, 3 & 4 opened 24.5.79, 363 & 323 & 237 & 180 seats. (Renamed Cannon. Closed 11.8.88. Derelict.)

EDINBURGH Lothian

see also Stockbridge

HAYMARKET 90 Dalry Road. (Opened 13.12.12. Taken over by SCVT.) Part of original circuit. (Taken over by independent c1930. Renamed Scotia 1.9.49. Closed 30.12.62 by fire. Re-opened 14.1.63. Closed 29.2.64. Demolished. Post Office.)

RITZ Rodney Street, Canonmills. Opened 9.9.29 by ABC, architects: A. V. Gardner and W. R. Glen, 1925 seats. Modernised c2.69 with stalls becoming "luxury lounge", 1200 seats. Closed 28.11.81. (Demolished.)

LYCEUM Slateford Road and Robertson Avenue. (Opened 8.11.26, architects: Mitchell and Telfer.)

Taken over c1938. 1324 seats. Closed 8.4.61. (Bingo. Fire in 11.63. Garage.)
REGAL 120 Lothian Road and Morrison Street. Opened 10.10.38 by ABC, architect: Stewart Kaye of Stewart Kaye and Walls, 2769 seats: 1683 stalls & 1086 balcony. Renamed ABC 20.3.61. Closed 22.2.69 for tripling. ABC 1, 2 & 3 opened 29.11.69, 860 & 738 & 318 seats. (Renamed Cannon. Renamed MGM 14.5.93. Open.)

ELEPHANT AND CASTLE South London
ELEPHANT AND CASTLE THEATRE, 26/28 New Kent Road (site of Theatre Royal). Opened 22.12.32 by ABC in partnership, architect: W. R. Glen, 2315 seats. Taken over fully 10.34. Closed 10.5.41 by bomb damage. Re-opened 2.6.41. Closed 2.9.67 for modernisation and stalls into "luxury lounge". Re-opened 9.10.67 as ABC, 1431 seats. Closed 25.1.81 for tripling. Re-opened 7.5.81, 546 & 271 & 211 seats. (Became Cannon. Taken over by Coronet 8.6.86, renamed Coronet Film Centre. Open.)

ELTHAM Southeast London
PALACE 118 High Street, corner of Passey Place. (Opened 1922. Modernised, architect: Robert Cromie, re-opened 13.8.34, 1300 seats. Taken over by Union c1935.) Taken over 10.37, part of Union circuit. Renamed ABC 20.1.64. Closed 29.4.72. (Demolished. Shops and offices.)

ENFIELD North London
SAVOY Savoy Parade, Southbury Road. (Opened 28.10.35, architect: George Coles, 2242 seats.) Taken over 24.2.36. Renamed ABC 1962. Closed 1.4.78 for quadrupling. ABC 1, 2, 3 & 4 opened 20.7.78, 620 & 356 & 217 & 140 seats. (Open as Cannon.)

ERDINGTON Birmingham
PICTURE HOUSE High Street. (Former Public Hall, opened pre-1916 as cinema. Also known as West's Picture House. 621 seats.) Taken over c10.29. 540 seats. (Leased to Regent from 5.33 to 1935.) Closed 24.11.56. (Demolished. Wilton market.)
PALACE High Street. (Opened c1918. Extensively altered, architect: Horace G. Bradley,

re-opened 7.10.29.) Taken over c10.29. 1348 seats. Closed 19.8.72. (Demolished. Garage.)

ERITH Southeast London
RITZ Pier Road. (Opened as Picture House. Taken over by Union 1.12.35. Closed 25.6.37 for modernisation. Re-opened 2.8.37 as Ritz, 1170 seats on one floor.) Taken over 10.37, part of Union circuit. Closed 24.11.56. (Demolished.)

ESSEX ROAD North London
see Islington

EVERTON Liverpool
SUPER CINEMA Mere Lane. (Opened 4.11.16. 1050 seats.) Taken over c1932. (Leased to Regent 5.33. Sold to Regent 12.33. Taken over 3.5.34. Taken over by Southan Morris 1938. Taken over by Essoldo 26.8.54. Closed 14.9.63. Bingo.)

EWELL Southwest London
REMBRANDT Kingston Road. (Opened 3.10.38, architect: E. Norman Bailey, 1462 seats.) Taken over 31.1.43. Closed 18.9.71 for twinning. Re-opened 29.11.71 as ABC 1 & 2, 606 & 152 seats. (Renamed Cannon. Renamed MGM 21.5.93. Open.)

EXETER Devon
SAVOY London Inn Square, Northern Hay and New North Road. Opened 23.11.36 by ABC, architect: W. R. Glen, 1958 seats: 1224 stalls & 734 balcony. Renamed ABC c11.60. Closed 30.9.72 for stalls to bingo, two cinemas upstairs in former balcony and upper stage area. ABC 1 & 2 opened 25.1.73, 508 & 170 seats. (To Cannon. Closed 4.6.87. Demolished. Shops and offices.)

FALKIRK Central Scotland
GRAND THEATRE. (Former music hall.) Taken over c1929. Closed early 1932. (Demolished for Regal.)
PICTURE HOUSE Bank Street. (Opened 4.20. Taken over by Alexander B. King 7.20. Enlarged, architect: Neil C. Duff, re-opened 12.27.) Taken over c1930. 1115 seats. Closed 29.7.72. (Bingo.)
REGAL Princes Street. Opened 29.10.34 by ABC, architect: Charles J. McNair, 1996 seats. Renamed

ABC c1961. Stalls area closed 18.11.72 for conversion to twin cinemas under balcony (balcony kept open). Triple from 11.2.73, 704 & 126 & 128 seats. (Renamed Cannon. Open.)

FALMOUTH Cornwall
ST. GEORGE'S HALL Church Street. (Opened 4.11.12, 850 seats. Taken over by Union c1.36.) Taken over 10.37, part of Union circuit. Closed 4.3.48 by fire. (Exterior kept, auditorium demolished for shopping arcade.)
GRAND Market Street. (Opened 1929, former live theatre. Taken over by Union c1.36.) Taken over 10.37, part of Union circuit. 989 seats. Renamed ABC c1961. Closed 21.9.68. (Bingo.) Re-opened as ABC 4.5.70. (Taken over by independent 18.3.76 and renamed Grand. 815 seats. Closed 31.1.86. Demolished c1988, except facade.)

FARNWORTH Lancashire
RITZ Peel Street. (Opened 25.9.22, former Queen's live theatre. Renamed Ritz 1935. Taken over by Union 8.36.) Taken over 10.37, part of Union circuit. 900 seats. Closed 8.5.64 by fire. Re-opened 18.10.64 as ABC. (Taken over by Star 5.1.69, renamed Studio 1. Closed 30.10.71. Bingo. Demolished. Vacant site.)

FAZAKERLEY Liverpool
REO Longmoore Lane and Mosspit Lane. (Opened 31.3.33, architect: Lionel A. G. Pritchard, 1508 seats.) Taken over 27.7.36. Closed 14.1.61. (Derelict. Bingo.)

FELIXSTOWE Suffolk
RITZ 95 Crescent Road. (Opened 29.3.37 by Union, architect: Robert Cromie, 959 seats.) Taken over 10.37, part of Union circuit. Closed 13.7.63. (Bingo. Twin cinemas opened 8.8.74 in old balcony, Ladbroke's Film Centre 1 & 2, 150 & 90 seats. Taken over by Rank Bingo. Renamed Top Rank Cinemas c1987. Open.)

FILTON Bristol
CABOT Gloucester Road North. Opened 7.10.35 by ABC, architect: W. H. Watkins, 1114 seats: 746 stalls & 368 balcony. (Taken over

7.10.56 by independent. Closed 29.7.61. Demolished. Supermarket.)

FINNIESTON Glasgow

KELVIN 1073 Argyle Street. Opened 12.5.30, architect: A. V. Gardner, 1957 seats. John Maxwell was a director of the owning company and the cinema was booked by ABC for its first year or so. (Closed 1959. Sports stadium, mostly boxing and wrestling. Bingo from 22.2.73. Night club.)

FISHPONDS Bristol

VANDYCK 748/756 Fishponds Road. (Opened 5.11.26, architect: W. H. Watkins, 1200 seats.) Taken over 7.4.30. Renamed ABC 1967. Closed 28.7.73. (Bingo.)

FOLKESTONE Kent

PLEASURE GARDENS THEATRE Bouverie Road. (Taken over by Walter Bentley 8.29. Taken over by Union c11.35.) Taken over 10.37, part of Union circuit. Live show use only. (Taken over c1939. Cinema from 2.11.56. Closed 5.64. Bingo. Demolished. Office block.)

PLAYHOUSE Guildhall Street. (Opened 14.8.12, architect: A. R. Bowles, 732 seats. Taken over by Walter Bentley 8.29. Taken over by Union c11.35.) Taken over 10.37, part of Union circuit. Closed 27.7.40. (Refurbished and re-opened 1.4.46 by Essoldo. Closed 26.8.62. Demolished 5.63. Supermarket.)

CENTRAL George Lane. (Opened 23.9.12, 900 seats. Enlarged 1921, 1500 seats. Taken over by Walter Bentley 8.29. Modernised and re-opened 23.12.29, 1351 seats. Taken over by Union c11.35.) Taken over 10.37, part of Union circuit. (Taken over by independent c1940. Taken over by Essoldo 4.46. Renamed Essoldo c1956. Taken over by Classic 3.82, renamed Classic. Closed 3.11.73 for tripling. Classic 1 & 3 opened 28.3.74, 291 & 308 seats. Classic 2 opened 23.5.74, 196 seats. Taken over by Eric Rhodes 6.74, renamed Curzon. Taken back by Classic. Renamed Cannon. Closed 2.88.)

FOREST GATE East London

QUEEN'S Romford Road. (Opened c7.13. Closed 6.5.28 for reconstruction including bal-

cony, architects: Leathart and Granger, and re-opened 6.9.28, 1750 seats.) Taken over 10.29. Closed 21.4.41, destroyed by land mine. (Site cleared. Supermarket.)

FOREST HILL Southeast London

CAPITOL 11/15 London Road. (Opened 11.2.29, architect: J. Stanley Beard, 1687 seats. Taken over by London & Southern 4.29 and operated to 8.32.) Taken over 7.33. Renamed ABC 22.12.68. Closed 13.10.73. (Bingo.)

FULHAM West London

see *Walham Green*

FULHAM ROAD London

FORUM 142/150 Fulham Road, Drayton Gardens and Cavaye Place. (Opened 18.12.30, architects: J. Stanley Beard and Clare, auditorium paintings by George Murray, 2179 seats.) Taken over 8.4.35. Renamed ABC 1961. Closed 12.6.74 for quadrupling. ABC 1 & 2 opened 22.12.74, 777 & 228 seats. ABC 3 opened 1.1.75, 223 seats. ABC 4 opened 23.1.75, 222 seats in former backstage area. ABC 1 closed 5.10.77 for twinning and re-opened 22.12.77 as ABC 1 & 2, 417 & 371 seats with ABC 2, 3 & 4 renumbered 3, 4 & 5. Renovated late 1984. (Renamed Cannon. Renamed MGM 6.3.92. Open.)

GALASHIELS Borders

PLAYHOUSE Market Square. (Opened c1920.) Taken over c1936. 1201 seats. (Taken over by independent 3.5.69. Renamed Capitol 8.69. Re-opened 1972 for films and bingo as Kingsway Leisure Centre, 400 seats in cinema. Open.)

GATESHEAD Tyne and Wear

RITZ Brunswick Street. Opened 25.7.38 by ABC, architects: Percy L. Browne, Son and Harding, 1988 seats: 1214 stalls & 774 balcony. Closed 18.5.68 by Compulsory Purchase Order. (Demolished for motorway.)

GLASGOW Strathclyde

see also *Battlefield, Bridgeton, Burnside, Cathcart, Clydebank, Dennistoun, Finnieston, Govan, Govanhill, Hillhead, Muirend, Oatlands, Parkhead, Riddrie, Shawlands and Springburn*

KING'S 520 Sauchiehall Street. (Opened 1912 as Vitagraph Theatre. Renamed King's c1916. Taken over by SCVT.) Part of original circuit. Renovated and re-opened 24.9.31, 625 seats. Closed 4.1.54. (Taken over by independent and re-opened 17.3.54 as Newscine, 450 seats. Renamed Newcine 14.2.55. Renamed Curzon c3.60. Taken over by Classic 9.64. Renamed Tatler Club 29.7.73. Renamed Curzon Classic. Closed 1984. Nightclub.)

COLISEUM 97 Eglinton Street. (Opened pre-1914. Taken over by SCVT 2.3.25.) Part of original circuit. Closed 16.5.31 for improvements including removal of stage to increase seating. Re-opened 7.9.31, 3094 seats. Closed 4.5.63 for installation of Cinerama. Re-opened 26.9.63 as ABC COLISEUM CINERAMA THEATRE, 1310 seats. Renamed ABC COLISEUM for regular programming. Closed 11.10.80 by Compulsory Purchase Order for road scheme, later dropped. Bingo from 1988.)

THEATRE DE LUXE Sauchiehall Street. Part of ABC circuit in company listing, *Kinematograph Year Book 1930*. Closed 1931.

PHOENIX Sawfield Place. Taken over c1929. 980 seats. (Taken over by independent c1943. Renamed Endrick 23.12.48. Closed c1953. House of Fraser warehouse. Demolished c1972.)

REGAL 326 Sauchiehall Street (site of Hengler's Circus, later Waldorf Palais, part of structure retained). Opened 13.11.29 by ABC, architect: Charles McNair, 2359 seats. Renamed ABC c1959. Closed 23.6.79 for quadrupling. ABC 1, 3, 4 & 5 opened 13.12.79, 970 & 386 & 206 & 192 seats. (Renamed Cannon. Closed by fire 1992. Re-opened. Renamed MGM 18.12.92.)

GEORGE 101 St. George's Road, Charing Cross. (Opened 6.36 as the Norwood, architects: Laird and Napier, 1200 seats, stadium plan. Taken over by independent and re-named George c1944.) Taken over 18.12.55. Renamed ABC 4.5.58. Closed 20.9.75. (Asian cinema, renamed Dreamland. Snooker club.)

ABC 2 Sauchiehall Street (adjacent to ABC 1). Opened 19.10.67 by ABC, architect: Leslie C. Norton, 922 seats, stadium plan. (Renamed Cannon. Renamed MGM 18.12.92.)

GLOUCESTER Gloucestershire

PICTUREDROME Barton Street and Blenheim

Road. (Opened 15.1.23, 744 seats.) Taken over 1943, from Mayfair circuit. Modernised and re-named RITZ 16.5.55. Closed 8.4.61. Re-opened 11.6.61. Closed 3.3.62. (Bingo to 1984. Taken over by Gloucester Operatic and Dramatic Society. New Olympus Theatre from 3.86.)

REGAL St. Aldgate Street, King's Square. Opened 19.3.56 by ABC, architect: W. R. Farrow (after pre-war scheme by W. R. Glen), 1468 seats: 1006 stalls & 462 balcony. Renamed ABC 3.63. Closed 6.4.74 for tripling. ABC 1, 2 & 3 opened 22.7.74, 658 & 343 & 294 seats. (Became Cannon. Closed 12.12.90.)

GOLDERS GREEN North London
see also Temple Fortune

LIDO 210 Golders Green Road. (Opened 1.10.28, architect: W. J. King, decorator: Guy Lipscombe, 1953 seats.) Taken over c1929. Closed 1.6.57 for modernisation. Re-opened 7.10.57, renamed ABC, 1728 seats. Closed 8.5.71 for stalls conversion to "luxury lounge". Re-opened 29.5.71. Closed 16.7.77 for tripling. ABC 2 opened 26.9.77, 291 seats (former balcony). ABC 1 & 3 opened 27.10.77, 398 & 144 seats. (Became Cannon. Closed 19.3.87. Demolished 1987.)

GORTON Greater Manchester
COSMO Hyde Road, Wellington Street. (Opened pre-1914, 700 seats. Taken over by Union 7.36.) Taken over 10.37, part of Union circuit. 737 seats. Closed 30.7.60 by fire. (Bingo.)

GOUROCK Strathclyde
PAVILION Pier Head. (Former roller skating rink. Taken over by SCVT.) Part of original circuit. Closed c12.29. (Roller skating rink again from end 12.29.)

GOVAN Glasgow
CINEMA (or PICTURE HOUSE) 729 Govan Road, Govan Cross. (Opened 20.6.13. Opened or taken over by SCVT.) Part of original circuit. Closed 4.36. (Demolished for Plaza.)

PLAZA 727 Govan Road (site of Cinema or Picture House). Opened 21.12.36 by ABC, archi-tect: Charles J. McNair, 2280 seats. Renamed

ABC c1965. Closed 15.4.72. (Demolished Summer 1972.)

GOVANHILL Glasgow
PICTURE HOUSE, Bankhall Street. (Opened 1926, architect: Eric A. Sutherland, 1200 seats.) Taken over 4.11.29. 1148 seats. Closed 20.5.61. (Bingo. Warehouse.)

GRAVESEND Kent
PLAZA 1 Windmill Street. (Opened 19.7.11 as Cinema. Taken over by Union, improved and re-opened 1.10.34 as Plaza. Closed 7.35 by fire. Re-opened 17.2.36.) Taken over 10.37, part of Union circuit. 750 seats. Closed 12.3.55. (Shops.)

REGAL 65 New Road. (Opened 1.10.10 as Gem. Taken over by Union 23.12.33. Renamed Regal 7.5.34.) Taken over 10.37, part of Union circuit. 1260 seats. Closed 10.8.68. (Bingo.)

SUPER New Road. (Former Public Hall, films from 1910. Renamed Popular Picture Palace 1911. Renamed Empire Picture Palace 1919. Renamed Rivoli Music Hall. Renamed Regent 3.11.32. Taken over by Union, reconstructed, architect: A. H. Jones, and re-opened 16.9.33 as Super, 954 seats.) Taken over 10.37, part of Union circuit. Closed 22.11.58. (Shops. Demolished. Freezer centre.)

MAJESTIC King Street. (Opened 30.9.31, archi-tect: George E. Clay, 1774 seats. Taken over by Union 23.12.33.) Taken over 10.37, part of Union circuit. Renamed ABC 1963. Closed 5.8.72 for tripling. ABC 1, 2 & 3 opened 26.12.72, 576 & 320 & 107 seats. (Open as Cannon.)

GREAT YARMOUTH Norfolk
REGENT Regent Road. (Opened c26.12.14, archi-tect: Francis Burdett Ward. 1650 seats.) Taken over 8.29. Closed 9.82. (Listed building. Bingo.)

REGAL Regent Road (site of Theatre Royal). Opened 1.1.34, architects: F. R. B. Howard & T. S. Darbyshire of Yates, Cook & Darbyshire and Olley & Howard, 1600 seats. Taken over by Union 20.8.36.) Taken over 10.37, part of Union circuit. Summer live shows. Renamed ABC 25.12.61. (Renamed Cannon. Closed 26.5.88. Demolished.)

GREENOCK Strathclyde
PICTURE HOUSE 21 West Blackhall Street. Opened 26.11.21, 1500 seats.) Taken over, reconstructed and re-opened 12.29 as REGAL, 1700 seats. Renamed ABC 24.5.76. Triple from 21.6.79, 550 & 212 & 159 seats. (Renamed Cannon. Closed 10.9.87. Demolished. Shopping development.)

GRIMSBY Humberside
see also Cleethorpes

PRINCE OF WALES Freeman Street. Taken over 4.36. Closed c1937. (Demolished for Regal.)

TIVOLI. (Former variety theatre.) Taken over 4.36. 1217 seats. (Taken over c1936 for variety theatre.)

STRAND Park Street. Taken over 4.36. 1331 seats. Closed 1943 by bomb damage. (Dem-olished. Flats.)

REGAL Freeman Street (site of Prince of Wales). Opened 4.12.37 by ABC, architect: W. R. Glen, 1966 seats: 1280 stalls & 686 balcony. Renamed ABC c1961. Closed 2.7.66 for new ABC cinema upstairs and ground floor supermarket. Re-opened 18.3.67, 1231 seats. Closed 12.4.80 for tripling. Re-opened, 450 & 238 & 128 seats. (Renamed Cannon. Open.)

HACKNEY North London
REGAL Mare Street, corner of Well Street. Opened 16.3.36 by ABC, architect: W. R. Glen, 1846 seats. Renamed ABC 15.1.62. Closed 1.3.75. (Taken over by independent, re-opened 10.1.77 as Mayfair. Closed 8.79. Snooker centre from 10.82.)

HADLEIGH Essex
KINGSWAY. Opened 27.4.36 by ABC, architect: Leslie C. Norton, 1404 seats. Closed 20.12.58. (Taken over by independent, re-opened 7.12.59. Bingo and wrestling. Closed 1970. Demolished. Supermarket, now motor showroom.)

HALIFAX West Yorkshire
REGAL Ward's End. Opened 19.9.38 by ABC, architect: W. R. Glen, 1918 seats: 1250 stalls & 668 balcony. Renamed ABC c1961. Closed 4.9.76 for tripling. ABC 1, 2 & 3 opened 12.9.76, 670 & 200 & 173 seats. (Renamed Cannon. Open.)

HALL GREEN Birmingham

ROBIN HOOD Stratford Road. (Opened 26.12.27, architect: H. E. Farmer.) Taken over c10.29. 1517 seats. Closed 7.3.70. (Demolished. Supermarket.)

HAMILTON Strathclyde

REGAL Townhead Street and Blackswell Lane. Opened 17.8.31 by ABC, architect: Charles J. McNair. Closed 6.37 for reconstruction with new balcony, architect: Alec Cullen. Re-opened 23.9.37, 2023 seats. Renamed ABC 27.8.62. Closed 23.9.76 by fire. (Derelict.)

HAMMERSMITH West London

BROADWAY 8/14 Queen Caroline Street. (Opened 13.6.12, architect: Frank Matcham, 1200 seats. Taken over 23.12.27 by Savoy Cinemas.) Part of original circuit. Closed 12.9.77 after collapse of part of ceiling. (Demolished by 6.78.)

BLUE HALL (or BLUE HALL NO. 1) 207 King Street. (Opened 10.12.12, 1300 seats. Taken over by Favourite Cinemas.) Part of original circuit. Closed 1936. (Demolished for Regal.)

BLUE HALL EXTENSION (or BLUE HALL NO. 2) (at rear of Blue Hall). (Opened 26.12.13, architects: John Quilter and Sons, 1300 seats. Taken over by Favourite Cinemas.) Part of original circuit. Closed late 1936 (after opening of Regal). (Demolished. Regal car park.)

COMMODORE Young's Corner, King Street. (Opened 14.9.29, architect: George Coles, 2884 seats.) Taken over 24.7.33. Closed 8.6.63. (Bingo. Demolished. Office block.)

REGAL 207 King Street (site of Blue Hall). Opened 14.9.36 by ABC, architect: W. R. Glen, 2257 seats: 1283 stalls & 974 balcony. Renamed ABC 1964. Closed 1.3.75 for tripling. ABC 1, 2 & 3 opened 25.5.75, 662 & 414 & 213 seats. (Renamed Cannon. Open.)

HANDSWORTH Birmingham
see also Hockley

REGAL Soho Road and Booth Street. (Opened 13.10.29, architect: Harold S. Scott, 2096 seats.) Taken over 3.5.35. Renamed ABC c1959. Closed 16.11.68. (Bingo. Asian cinema. Demolished c1980.)

HANLEY Stoke-on-Trent Staffordshire

CAPITOL New Street. (Opened 20.7.25, reconstruction of King's Theatre, 1300 seats.) Taken over 9.12.29. 1182 seats. Closed 24.8.63. (Bingo. Demolished. Marks and Spencer store.)

ABC CINE BOWL 18 Broad Street. Opened 23.8.63 by ABC, architect: C. J. Foster, 1348 seats & bowling alley. Closed 28.5.77 for tripling. ABC 1, 2 & 3 opened 25.8.77, 573 & 233 & 162 seats. ABC 2 & 3 closed 26.8.77 by sound problems. ABC 2 & 3 re-opened 25.9.77. (Renamed Cannon. Open.)

HANWORTH West London

REX Hampton Road. (Opened 9.9.37, architect: Leslie H. Kemp, 1003 seats.) Taken over 30.8.43, part of Mayfair circuit. Closed 17.9.60. (Demolished. Petrol stations with flats above.)

HARBORNE Birmingham

ROYALTY High Street. (Opened 20.10.30, architect: Horace G. Bradley.) Taken over c3.35. 1494 seats. Closed 2.11.63. (Bingo.)

HAREHILLS Leeds

GAIETY 91 Roundhay Road. (Opened 6.7.21, architect: G. Frederick Bowman, 1046 seats.) Taken over c1936. 970 seats. Closed 22.2.58. (Demolished. Gaiety public house.)

HARRINGAY North London

RITZ Turnpike Parade, Turnpike Lane. Opened 30.12.35 by ABC, architect: W. J. King, 1850 seats: 1271 stalls & 579 balcony. Renamed ABC 9.10.61. Closed 11.6.77 for tripling. ABC 1, 2 & 3 opened 22.9.77, 625 & 417 & 316 seats. (Renamed Cannon. Taken over by Coronet 17.7.88, renamed Coronet. Open.)

HARROGATE South Yorkshire

REGAL Cambridge Road and Oxford Road. Opened 18.9.37 by ABC, architects: W. R. Glen and H. Linley Brown, 1646 seats: 1120 stalls & 526 balcony. Renamed ABC c1961. Stalls closed 25.1.73 for splitting into Painted Wagon pub and second cinema. ABC 2 opened 14.5.73, 130 seats (ABC 1 now 494 seats). Closed 26.2.83. (Demolished.)

HARROW North London
see also North Harrow

DOMINION Station Road. (Opened 9.1.36, architect: F. E. Bromige, 2014 seats.) Taken over 24.2.36. Renamed ABC 1962. Closed 4.3.72 for splitting into balcony cinema and stalls bingo. Re-opened 4.6.72, 612 seats. ABC 2 opened 6.8.81 in former café space, 133 seats. (Renamed Cannon Station Road. Open.)

HARROW ROAD West London
see also Edgware Road

PRINCE OF WALES 331 Harrow Road (site of old Prince of Wales). (Opened 27.10.34, architects: J. Stanley Beard and W. R. Bennett, 1750 seats.) Taken over 19.2.35. Closed 23.11.68. (Bingo.)

HASTINGS East Sussex

RITZ Cambridge Road. Opened 19.3.38 by ABC (Union), architects: Verity and Beverley, 1906 seats: 1212 stalls & 694 balcony. Renamed ABC 5.4.62. Closed 6.10.71. (Demolished. Sainsbury's supermarket.)

HAY MILLS Birmingham

ADELPHI Coventry Road (site of Picture House). (Opened 10.10.27, architects: Satchwell and Roberts.) Taken over 7.1.29. 1243 seats. Closed 31.8.68. (Disco. DIY centre – Adelphi House.)

HAYWARDS HEATH West Sussex

BROADWAY The Broadway. (Opened 12.9.32. Taken over by Union 8.37, 701 seats.) Taken over 10.37, part of Union circuit. Closed 31.1.48. Re-opened 25.10.48. Closed 27.1.52. (Furniture store. Demolished.)

PERRYMOUNT Perrymount Road. (Opened 30.5.36. 800 seats. Taken over by Union 8.37.) Taken over 10.37, part of Union circuit. 744 seats. Closed 11.11.72. (Demolished. Entrance to office block.)

HELENSBURGH Strathclyde

TOWER Colquhoun Square. (Opened c1928.) Taken over 3.35. 809 seats. Closed 16.1.68.

HEREFORD Hereford and Worcester

GARRICK Widemarsh Street. (Taken over by

Union c1933.) Taken over 10.37, part of Union circuit. (Taken over by independent c1938. Closed c1941.)

KEMBLE Broad Street. (Former Corn Exchange and live theatre. Taken over by Union c1932.) Taken over 10.37, part of Union circuit. 807 seats. Live shows in 1948. Closed 19.7.52 on expiry of lease. (Re-opened c7.53 by independent. Closed 1961. Demolished 1963. Office block.)

RITZ Commercial Road. Opened 10.1.38 by ABC (Union), architect: Leslie H. Kemp, 1012 seats, stadium plan. Renamed ABC 19.6.61. Closed 19.8.72 for splitting into front stalls bingo and new ABC in rear section. Re-opened 16.11.72, 378 seats. Closed 10.12.77. (Bingo. Cinema at rear re-opened 7.12.84 as Classic, 340 seats. Renamed Cannon. Open.)

HERNE BAY Kent
CASINO 55 Central Promenade. (Opened 26.5.19. Taken over by Union c1.36. Modernised and re-opened 26.12.36, 708 seats, one floor.) Taken over 10.37, part of Union circuit. Temporary closures from flooding. Closed 30.10.54. (Amusement arcade.)

HIGHER BLACKLEY Manchester
AVENUE Victoria Avenue East and Rochdale Road. (Opened 8.32 as Victoria, decorative artist: Sherwood-Edwards, 1414 seats. Renamed Avenue c1940.) Taken over 30.10.55. Renamed ABC 13.1.64. Closed 31.3.73. (Demolished 1985.)

HIGHER BROUGHTON Salford
(NEW) RIALTO Bury New Road. (Opened 24.10.27, architects: Gray and Evans, 1400 seats, one floor.) Taken over 28.12.31. Renamed ABC c1965. Closed 3.2.73. (Bingo. Closed. Stage used for disco.)

HIGHGATE North London
(ELECTRIC) PALACE 17 Highgate Hill. (Opened 1909. Taken over by Union c1935.) Taken over 10.37, part of Union circuit. 730 seats, one floor. Closed 12.4.58. (Demolished.)

EMPIRE 643 Holloway Road. (Opened 4.10 as Pavilion. Improved 1914, renamed Empire. Taken over by Union c1935.) Taken over 10.37, part of

Union circuit. 644 seats, one floor. Closed 10.2.57. (Gresham Ballroom.)

HILLHEAD Glasgow
GROSVENOR 194 Byres Road. (Opened 3.5.21, architects: Gardner and Glen.) Taken over c10.29. 1257 seats. (Taken over by Caledonian Associated Cinemas 24.5.76. Stalls twinned and re-opened 12.80, 276 & 265 seats; balcony disused. Entrance at rear on Ashton Lane. Open.)

HOCKLEY Birmingham
(NEW) PALLADIUM Soho Hill (site of Hockley Picture House). (Opened 11.22, architect: L. L. Dussault.) Taken over 22.10.36. 917 seats. Closed 13.2.65. (Bingo. Derelict.)

HOLLOWAY North London
SAVOY 338 Holloway Road. Opened 5.2.40 by ABC, architect: W. R. Glen, 1826 seats. Renamed ABC 12.2.62. (Taken over by Coronet 18.2.79, renamed Coronet. Closed 22.6.83. Foyer into amusement arcade – closed. Stalls into snooker centre – open.)

HORSHAM West Sussex
CAPITOL London Road. (Opened 7.11.23. Taken over by Union 14.10.35.) Taken over 10.37, part of Union circuit. 632 seats. Closed 21.8.54. (Community centre, live theatre and, later, Regional Film Theatre. Frequent film shows. Closed 3.1.83 for new Arts Centre at former Ritz. Demolished.)

RITZ North Street. (Opened 13.6.36 by Union, architect: L. H. Parsons of Goodman and Kay, consultants: Verity and Beverley.) Taken over 10.37, part of Union circuit. 1086 seats. Renamed ABC 20.2.67. Closed 26.6.82. (Taken over by Council, run as Cine. Subdivided for Horsham Arts Centre, opened 21.12.84: Ritz Cinema, 126 seats, and Capitol Theatre with some film shows, 450 seats. Open.)

HOUNSLOW West London
REGAL Staines Road and Bath Road. Opened 27.11.37 by ABC, architect: W. R. Glen, 1860 seats: 1260 stalls & 600 balcony. Renamed ABC 1964. Closed 21.5.77. (Demolished.)

HOVE East Sussex
GRANADA Portland Road and School Road. (Opened 17.7.33, architect: H. L. Hemsley, 1638 seats.) Taken over 18.6.35. Renamed ABC 27.5.65. Closed 3.12.70 for stalls conversion to "luxury lounge". Re-opened 24.12.70. Closed 5.6.74. (Bingo. Open.)

HUDDERSFIELD West Yorkshire
EMPIRE John William Street. (Opened 8.3.15, architects: Stocks and Sykes.) Taken over c1933. 796 seats. (Taken over by independent and modernised c7.40. Closed 4.51 by defective ceiling. Re-opened 4.52. Closed 5.8.73.)

GRAND Manchester Road. (Opened 14.3.21, architect: Clifford Hickson of Stocks, Sykes and Hickson. Taken over by Union 7.28.) Taken over 10.37, part of Union circuit. 878 seats. Closed 6.7.57. (Nightclub. Closed.)

RITZ Market Street. (Opened 10.2.36 by Union, architect: Robert Cromie, 2027 seats.) Taken over 10.37, part of Union circuit. Renamed ABC c1961. Rear stalls split into pub and ABC 2, opened 24.2.74, 216 seats, with ABC 1 in former balcony, 648 seats. ABC 3 added. Closed 5.3.83. (Demolished.)

HULL Humberside
RIALTO Terry Street, off Beverley Road, adjacent Stepney Station. (Opened 9.12.12, part of former skating rink. Renamed Rialto 1920.) Taken over 6.31 and front modernised. 2073 seats. (Taken over by independent c1944. Renamed National, taking name of bombed cinema. Closed 22.7.61. Demolished. Car park.)

REGAL 132 Ferensway. (Opened 26.1.34 by local company in association with County, architect: Robert Cromie, 2553 seats.) Taken over 8.11.37. Renamed ABC 21.2.60. Closed 31.7.76 for quintupling. ABC 2 & 3 opened 21.10.76 in old balcony, 346 & 261 seats. ABC 1 opened in old front stalls area and ABC 4 & 5 in old back stalls 25.11.76, 571 & 166 & 97 seats. (Renamed Cannon. Closed 29.6.89.)

REX Endyke Lane. (Opened 3.8.35 by local company in association with County, architect: Robert Cromie, 1048 seats.) Taken over 8.11.37. Closed 24.10.59. (Demolished.)

ROYALTY Southcoates Lane, East Hull. (Opened

17.8.35 by local company in association with County, architect: Robert Cromie – copy of Rex preceding, 1045 seats.) Taken over 8.11.37. Closed 2.4.66. (Front demolished, auditorium into supermarket.)

REGIS Hessle Road, Gipsyville, West Hull. (Opened 5.9.35 by local company in association with County, architect: Robert Cromie – copy of Royalty and Rex preceding, 1045 seats.) Taken over 8.11.37. Closed 24.10.59. (Demolished.)

HUMBERSTONE Leicester

TROCADERO Humberstone Road, Scraptoft Lane and Uppingham Road. (Opened 1.10.31, architect: Herbert Langham, 1992 seats.) Taken over 1938. Closed 16.3.63. (Bingo. Destroyed by fire. Site cleared. Petrol station.)

HYDE Greater Manchester

RITZ Travis Street. Opened 21.2.38 by ABC (Union), architect: William T. Benslyn, 1268 seats. Closed 13.7.68. (Bingo.)

HYTHE Kent

RITZ East Street and Prospect Road. (Opened 12.6.37 by Union, architect: E. Norman Bailey, 858 seats.) Taken over 10.37, part of Union circuit. (Taken over by independent 17.3.53. Closed 1965. Bingo. Circle re-opened 27.4.71 by Classic as Vogue, 275 seats. Taken over by Mecca 15.11.73, renamed Mecca. Taken back by Classic by 1980, renamed Classic. Closed 7.8.84. Demolished. Flats.)

ILFORD East London

see also Barkingside

REGAL 300-310 High Road, corner of Green Lane. Opened 26.7.37 by ABC, architect: W. R. Glen, 1974 seats: 1274 stalls & 700 balcony. Renamed ABC 14.10.62. Closed 28.4.73 for tripling. ABC 1 opened 27.5.73, 692 seats. ABC 2 & 3 opened 16.7.73, 156 & 157 seats. Closed 28.1.84. (Bingo. Closed c1989. Concert venue, The Island, from 12.92.)

IPSWICH Suffolk

HIPPODROME St. Nicholas Street. (Former live theatre.) Taken over c1932. 1110 seats. Closed c1945. (Live theatre. Ballroom. Bingo. Closed.)

RITZ Buttermarket. (Opened 4.1.37 by Union, architect: Robert Cromie, 1689 seats.) Taken over 10.37, part of Union circuit. Renamed ABC c1962. Closed 17.3.73 for tripling. ABC 2 opened 21.5.73, 445 seats. ABC 1 & 3 opened 18.6.73, 544 & 133 seats. Closed 5.4.86. (Demolished 1988.)

ISLINGTON North London

EMPIRE 40 Upper Street (now Islington High Street). Opened 3.32 by ABC, formerly Grand Theatre (some films shown from 1897). Closed 7.2.38 by fire. Re-opened 6.2.39, 1396 seats. Closed 10.3.62. (Demolished. Office block.)

CARLTON 161/9 Essex Road, corner of River Street. (Opened 1.9.30, architect: George Coles, 2248 seats.) Taken over 2.35. Renamed ABC 1962. Closed 11.70 to 6.12.70 by heating problems. Closed 5.8.72. (Bingo. Listed building.)

KEIGHLEY West Yorkshire

RITZ Alice Street. Opened 28.2.38 by ABC (Union), architect: Sam Beverley of Verity and Beverley, 1526 seats. Renamed ABC 30.7.71. Closed 2.2.74. (Bingo.)

KENSAL RISE North London

PALACE Chamberlayne Road. (Opened 17.9.31, architects: J. Stanley Beard and Clare, interior decoration: W. R. Bennett, incorporating King's Picture Palace converted to vestibule of new cinema, 1600 seats.) Taken over 19.2.35. Renamed ABC c1970. Closed 12.1.74. (Bingo. Nightclub.)

KENSINGTON West London

see North Kensington

KENTISH TOWN North London

FORUM 9-17 Highgate Road. (Opened 17.12.34, architect: J. Stanley Beard, interior decorator: W. R. Bennett, 2175 seats.) Taken over 3.35. Renamed ABC c1963. Closed 18.7.70. (Bingo. Ballroom. Town and Country Club, concert venue. Listed building. Renamed Forum 5.93.)

KIDDERMINSTER Hereford and Worcester

EMPIRE. (Opened 7.22, architect: Harold Scott.) Taken over c1935. 566 seats. (Taken over by

independent 1938. Closed c1960. Shop.)

CENTRAL Oxford Street. (Opened 5.10.31, architects: Webb and Gray, 1290 seats.) Taken over 11.11.35. Renamed ABC 27.1.64. Closed 19.2.72 for splitting into smaller cinema and bingo. Re-opened 1.6.72, 484 seats. Closed 1.5.82. (Demolished.)

KILMARNOCK Strathclyde

KING'S Titchfield Street. (Opened pre-1914. Taken over by SCVT. Half live use in 1920.) Part of original circuit. 1268 seats. Closed 14.4.34 for reconstruction, architect: C. J. McNair. Re-opened 17.12.34 as REGAL. Renamed ABC 14.12.64. Closed 12.5.73 for spitting, stalls to bingo, balcony for films. Re-opened 17.9.73, 602 seats. Closed 1.6.75 by fire. Re-opened 18.8.75. ABC 2 & 3 opened 1.8.76, 193 & 149 seats, replacing bingo. (Renamed Cannon. Open.)

GEORGE West George Street. (Opened 21.12.22. Taken over by SCVT. Closed 20.11.27 by fire. Re-opened 16.4.28.) Part of original circuit. 1098 seats. Closed 20.5.61. (Bingo. Nightclub.)

KING'S CROSS North London

REGENT Euston Road. (Opened 26.12.32, former Theatre of Varieties, architect for alterations: Andrew Mather, 1200 seats.) Taken over 14.10.35. (Taken over by independent after 24.12.49. Taken over by Granada c1954. Renamed Century 13.9.54. Renamed Granada 6.5.67. Closed 6.4.68. (Bingo. Closed 1969. Demolished. Town Hall extension.)

KING'S LYNN Norfolk

ELECTRIC. (Taken over by Union 6.28.) Taken over 10.37, part of Union circuit. Closed 6 or 9.4.38.

MAJESTIC Tower Street and 1/2 Sedgeford Lane. (Opened 26.5.28, architects: J. L. Carnell and W. D. White. Taken over by Union c1934.) Taken over 10.37, part of Union circuit. 1149 seats. (Taken over by independent 27.4.75. Majestic 2 opened 25.6.77, 198 seats in former ballroom. Majestic 3 opened c7.91 in rear stalls, 400 seats. Majestic 1 now 450 seats. Open.)

THEATRE ROYAL (site of old Theatre Royal).

Opened 4.4.38 by ABC (Union), architect: Keeble C. Allflatt, 1030 seats. Closed 14.4.62. (Bingo.)

KINGSTON-UPON-THAMES Southwest London

UNION 22/30 Richmond Road, corner of Canbury Park Road (incorporating site of Cinema Palace). (Opened 15.2.32 as Regal, associated with County, architect: Robert Cromie, 2433 seats. Taken over by Union 1936. Renamed Union 4.3.37.) Taken over 10.37, part of Union circuit. Renamed REGAL c1939. Renamed ABC 18.8.61. Closed 17.7.76. (Bingo. Listed building. Open.)

KIRKCALDY Fife

PALACE Whytecauseway. (Opened pre-1914. Taken over by SCVT c1924.) Part of original circuit. Modernised & re-opened 6.11.39, 1000 seats. Closed 28.12.45 by fire. (Demolished.)

PICTURE HOUSE Port Brae. Part of original circuit, from SCVT. 616 seats. (Taken over by independent c1938. Closed c1940.)

PATHHEAD. Part of original circuit, from SCVT. 600 seats. (Taken over by independent c1930. Closed c1942. Demolished.)

OPERA HOUSE 260a High Street. (Opened c1928 by SCVT, former live theatre, 1311 seats.) Part of original circuit. Rebuilt, architect: C. J. McNair, and re-opened 8.37 as REGAL, 2016 seats. Renamed ABC 2.63. Closed 29.10.77 for tripling. ABC 1 opened 18.12.77, 547 seats. ABC 2 & 3 opened 29.1.78, 287 & 235 seats. (Renamed Cannon. Renamed MGM 16.4.93. Open.)

KIRKDALE Liverpool

GARRICK Westminster Road, corner of Foley Street. (Opened c1.16. 1350 seats.) Taken over c1932. (Leased to Regent 5.33, purchased by Regent 12.33, taken over 3.5.34. Taken over by Southan Morris 3.38. Taken over by Essoldo 26.8.54. Closed 14.3.59. Demolished. Houses.)

GROSVENOR Stanley Road. (Opened 14.8.22. 1040 seats.) Taken over c1932. (Leased to Regent 5.33, purchased by Regent 12.33, taken over 3.5.34. Taken over by Southan Morris 1938. Taken over by Essoldo 26.8.54. Closed 31.8.63. Bingo.)

VICTORY Walton Road and Luton Grove. (Opened 4.10.22, 1130 seats.) Taken over 9.35. Closed 29.7.61. (Demolished. Shops.)

KNOTTY ASH Liverpool

REGENT Prescot Road. (Opened 10.26, 1150 seats.) Taken over 12.6.35. Closed 7.5.38. (Car showroom. Supermarket.)

REGENT Prescot Road and Baden Road, Old Swan (adjacent to old Regent). Opened 9.5.38 by ABC, architect: W. R. Glen, 1727 seats: 1211 stalls & 516 balcony. Closed 17.2.62 for modernisation. Re-opened 25.2.62. Closed 25.3.67. (Demolished. Shops and flats.)

LADBROKE GROVE West London
see North Kensington

LADYWOOD Birmingham

CROWN Icknield Port Road. (Opened 26.12.27, architect: Harold S. Scott, 1291 seats.) Taken over 3.35. Closed 14.1.61. (Builders' merchants.)

LANCASTER Lancashire

COUNTY Dalton Square. (Former church/concert hall/music hall. Re-opened after alterations 30.6.30. Taken over by Union c1936.) Taken over 10.37, part of Union circuit. 826 seats. Closed 1.12.56. (Offices – Palatine Hall.)

GRAND St. Leonard's Gate, corner of Lodge Street. (Former live theatre. Taken over by Union c1936.) Taken over 10.37, part of Union circuit. 654 seats. Live shows c1947-9. Closed 8.1.51. (Sold to Lancaster Footlights Club. Amateur theatre. Open.)

(NEW) KINGSWAY Parliament Street. (Opened 4.23, former garage. One floor. Taken over by Union c1936.) Taken over 10.37, part of Union circuit. Closed c1939. (Mostly demolished. Garage. Discount store.)

PALACE Dalton Square (Opened 8.7.29 as Palace Theatre, architect: J. E. Derham of Derham and Kay, 1191 seats. Taken over by Union c1936.) Taken over 10.37, part of Union circuit. Closed 19.11.66 for conversion of stalls into "luxury lounge". Re-opened 26.12.66, 854 seats. Renamed ABC c1968. Closed 2.3.74. (Disco.)

LEEDS West Yorkshire
see also Harehills

SAVOY Boar Lane. (Opened 4.10.15 as City, architect: J. P. Crawford, 514 seats. Taken over by Savoy Cinemas. Closed 2.7.25 for redecoration. Re-opened 13.8.25 as Savoy. Taken over by Gaumont c9.28 and renamed Leeds Repertory Cinema.) Part of original circuit, from Savoy, but on lease to Gaumont. Taken back 30.9.29 and renamed SAVOY. Operated as news theatre from 24.11.30. (Leased to Regent c5.33. Renamed Academy 19.9.33, feature policy.) Returned to circuit 1935. (Sold. Reconstructed, architect: Peter Cummings, and re-opened 23.12.36 as Tatler, 350 seats, one floor. Closed 27.1.64. Demolished. Royal Exchange House.)

RITZ Vicar Lane and New Briggate. Opened 19.11.34 by ABC, architect: W. R. Glen, 1950 seats: 1100 stalls & 850 circle. Renamed ABC 23.5.59. Closed 19.7.69 for twinning. ABC 1 & 2 opened 4.4.70, 670 & 867 seats. ABC 2 closed 5.1.74 for twinning. Re-opened 17.3.74 as ABC 2 & 3, 474 & 236 seats. (Renamed Cannon. Renamed MGM 21.5.93. Open.)

SHAFTESBURY York Road. (Opened 20.10.28, architect: J. P. Crawford, 1603 seats.) Taken over c1939. Closed 27.6.58. (Taken over by Star. Closed 27.10.62. Bingo. Re-opened as cinema 19.10.64. Closed 28.6.75. Demolished.)

LEICESTER Leicestershire
see also Humberstone

PRINCE'S Granby Street. (Opened c1918 as Cinema de Luxe, former Temperance Hall/concert hall. Renamed Prince's c1928.) Taken over, reconstructed and re-opened 27.1.30. 1170 seats. Closed 3.2.40. (Re-opened by independent 12.2.40. Taken over by Essoldo 2.54. Renamed Essoldo c1954. Closed 23.4.60. Demolished. Shops and offices.)

MELBOURNE Nedham Street/Melbourne Road. (Opened 18.5.20.) Taken over 11.31 and modernised. (Taken over by independent 10.38. 941 seats. Closed c1961. Asian cinema, called Apsara. Live concerts in 1987.)

SAVOY Belgrave Gate. Opened 26.6.37 by ABC, architects: W. R. Glen and C. Edmund Wilford, 2424 seats. Renamed ABC c1960. Closed 24.1.70 for twinning. ABC 1 & 2 opened 31.10.70, 606 & 910 seats. ABC 2 closed 13.1.73 for twinning. Re-opened 18.3.73 as ABC 2 & 3, 410 & 232 seats. (Renamed Cannon. Open.)

LEIGH Greater Manchester

REGAL Spinning Jenny Street and King Street. Opened 25.6.38 by ABC, architect: W. R. Glen, 1566 seats: 1068 stalls & 498 balcony. Renamed ABC c1962. Closed 4.1.69. (Bingo. Closed. Derelict.)

LEVENSHULME Greater Manchester

KINGSWAY SUPER. (Opened 14.3.29, architect: John Knight, 1810 seats. Taken over by Union 24.2.36.) Taken over 10.37, part of Union circuit. Closed 25.6.57 by fire.

REGAL Stockport Road. Opened 14.12.37 by ABC, architect: W. R. Glen, 1850 seats. Closed 15.1.57 by fire in balcony. Re-opened 8.4.57. Closed 22.4.61. (Bowling alley.)

LEWISHAM Southeast London

PRINCE OF WALES 210 High Street (site of Electric Palace). (Opened 9.10.22, architect: J. Stanley Beard, 1347 seats.) Taken over 7.33. Closed 13.6.59. (Demolished. Shops.)

LEYLAND Lancashire

PALACE East Street. (Taken over by Union 8.37.) Taken over 10.37, part of Union circuit. 418 seats. Closed 18.3.51. (Taken over by independent. Closed c1961. Bingo.)

REGENT SUPER. (Opened c1931. Taken over by Union 8.37. 1002 seats.) Taken over 10.37, part of Union circuit. Closed 24.3.49, destroyed by fire. (Supermarket.)

LEYTON North London

RITZ High Road. Opened 4.7.38 by ABC, architect: W. R. Glen, 2418 seats: 1532 stalls & 886 balcony. Renamed ABC 19.10.62. (Taken over by independent 10.12.78 and renamed Crown. Closed 1.12.79. B&Q DIY centre. KwikSave supermarket.)

LEYTONSTONE North London

REX 689 High Road. Opened 21.9.36 by ABC, architect: W. R. Glen, 1954 seats: 1174 stalls & 780 balcony. Closed 18.3.61. (Bowling alley. Demolished.)

LICHFIELD Staffordshire

REGAL Tamworth Street. (Opened 18.7.32, architect: Harold S. Scott, 1235 seats. Taken over by County 11.32. Taken over by independent c1941.) Taken over 30.8.43, from Mayfair circuit. (Taken over by Star 1.7.69. Partweek bingo. Closed 10.7.74. Bingo. Closed c1979. Supermarket.)

LINCOLN Lincolnshire

PICTURE HOUSE High Street. (Opened 1.15.) Taken over 2.7.31 and renamed REGAL. 1030 seats. Closed 26.2.66. (Demolished. Littlewood's store.)

SAVOY Saltergate. Opened 14.12.36 by ABC, architect: W. R. Glen, 1970 seats. Renamed ABC c1961. Closed 3.6.72 for splitting into balcony cinema and stalls bingo. Re-opened 2.8.72, 549 seats. (Renamed Cannon. Closed 20.10.88. Demolished c4.90. Part of shopping centre.)

LITHERLAND Merseyside

REGAL Church Road and Hawthorne Road. (Opened 12.6.39. architect: George E. Tonge, 1046 seats, stadium plan.) Taken over 24.7.55. Closed 28.7.62. (Bowling alley. Nightclub/disco.)

LIVERPOOL Merseyside

see also Anfield, Bankhall, Crosby, Dovecot, Everton, Fazakerley, Kirkdale, Knotty Ash, Norris Green, Paddington, Tuebrook and Walton

PRINCE OF WALES Clayton Square. (Opened 25.11.12 by PCT as Picture House, architects: G. L. Alexander/Matthew Watson, Landless and Pearse, 700 seats. Renamed Prince of Wales 1920. Taken over by Savoy Cinemas c1923.) Part of original circuit. Closed 8.2.36. (Re-opened 10.2.36 as Prince of Wales. Taken over by Jacey and re-opened c16.12.46 as Liverpool News Theatre, 561 seats. Renamed Gala International Film Theatre 17.9.62. Renamed Jacey Film Theatre 1963. Closed 7.7.72. Church. Demolished.)

HOMER Great Homer Street. (Opened 1914. 950 seats.) Taken over c1932. (Leased to Regent 5.33, purchased by Regent 12.33 and taken over 3.5.34. Taken over by Southan Morris 3.38. Taken over by Essoldo 26.8.54. Closed 20.1.62. Demolished.)

OLYMPIA West Derby Road. (Opened 23.3.25 by Savoy Cinemas, former variety theatre, 2900 seats.) Part of original circuit. Closed 25.3.39. (Warehouse. Taken over by Mecca 1947, opened as dance hall. Bingo. Disused.)

FORUM Lime Street, corner of Elliot Street. Opened 16.5.31 by ABC, architects: W. R. Glen and [resident] A. Ernest Shennan, 1835 seats: 1035 stalls & 750 balcony. Renamed ABC 17.2.64. Closed 15.5.82 for tripling. ABC 1, 2 & 3 opened 26.8.82, 683 & 272 & 217 seats. Listed building. (Renamed Cannon. Open.)

FUTURIST Lime Street. (Opened 16.9.12 as Lime Street Picture House. Renamed City Picture House. Taken over by Sol Levy and renamed Futurist 11.20. 1029 seats. Taken over by 20th Century-Fox 1954.) Taken over 4.4.60 and re-opened 10.7.60 with Todd-AO installation, 870 seats. Closed 17.7.82. (Derelict.)

SCALA Lime Street. (Opened 31.1.16, architect: J. Goodman of Essex and Goodman, 650 seats. Taken over by 20th Century-Fox 1954. Taken over by Gala/Jacey 15.5.60.) Taken over 3.9.67. 628 seats. Closed 24.8.82. (Hippodrome dance hall and bar.)

LLANDUDNO Gwynedd

CINEMA Mostyn Stret. (Opened 1914, architect: Arthur Hewitt.) Taken over c1931. Renamed SAVOY c1932. (Taken over by independent 1.8.36. Destroyed by fire 4.6.42. New Savoy opened 8.55, architects: Arthur Hewitt and Jones, 600 seats, one floor. Closed 10.86.)

LONDON West End

see also Baker Street and Bloomsbury

for suburbs see Acton, Balham, Barking, Barking-side, Bayswater, Beckenham, Bermondsey, Bexleyheath, Blackheath, Bowes Road, Brixton, Camberwell, Camden Town, Catford, Clapton, Crayford, Croydon, Ealing, East Ham, Edgware, Edgware Road, Elephant and Castle, Eltham, Enfield, Erith, Ewell, Forest Gate, Forest Hill, Fulham Road, Golders Green, Hackney, Hammersmith, Hanworth, Harringay, Harrow, Harrow Road, Highgate, Holloway, Hounslow, Ilford, Islington, Kensal Rise, Kentish Town, King's Cross, Kingston-upon-Thames, Lewisham, Leyton, Leytonstone, Manor Park, Mile End, Mitcham, Muswell Hill, Neasden, Norbury, North Harrow, North

Kensington, Old Kent Road, Pinner, Poplar, Purley, Putney, Richmond, Romford, Rotherhithe, Shoreditch, Sidcup, Southall, Stamford Hill, Stepney, Stoke Newington, Stratford, Streatham, Teddington, Temple Fortune, Tooting, Twickenham, Upton Park, Uxbridge, Walham Green, Walthamstow, Wandsworth, Wembley, Willesden, Wimbledon, Winchmore Hill, Woodford, Woolwich and Yiewsley

REGAL Marble Arch, corner of Edgware Road. (Opened 29.11.28, architect: Clifford Aish, interior decorator: Charles Muggeridge, 2400 seats.) Taken over 28.9.29. Closed 3.1.45. (Taken over by Odeon and re-opened 9.9.45 as Odeon Marble Arch. Closed 22.3.64. Demolished. New Odeon Marble Arch, shops and office block.)

ALHAMBRA Leicester Square. (Music hall operated by Stoll.) Taken over and used as cinema from 23.12.29 to 20.12.30. (Continued under Stoll as cinema to 3.31, then variety. Closed. Demolished. Odeon Leicester Square.)

LONDON PAVILION Piccadilly Circus. (Music hall with some cinema use.) Taken over and used as cinema from 20.4.31 to 5.32. (Live shows. Closed 7.4.34. Reconstructed internally as cinema and re-opened 5.9.34, architect: F. G. M. Chancellor, 1209 seats. Closed 26.4.81. Converted to shopping mall and Rock Circus.)

RIALTO 3/4 Coventry Street. (Opened 18.3.13 as the West End, architect: Hippolyte Blanc, interior decoration: Horace Gilbert, 700 seats. Renamed Rialto 28.4.24.) Taken over 1.34. (Taken over by independent c1939. Closed 3.41 by bomb damage. Re-opened 7.9.42. Closed 1.46. Re-opened 29.11.46 by London Films. Taken over by Films de France, renovated, architect: George Coles, and re-opened 1.10.49. Taken over by 20th Century-Fox, altered, architect: Sam Beverley, and re-opened 15.10.54. Taken over by Brent Walker 9.3.77. Closed 9.1.82. Derelict. Listed building.)

ABC 1 & 2 135 Shaftesbury Avenue. Opened 21/22.12.70 by ABC, internal reconstruction of Saville Theatre, architects: William Ryder and Associates, 616 & 581 seats. (Renamed Cannon 17.10.86. Renamed MGM 6.3.92. Open.)

ABC Brunswick Square, Bloomsbury. (Opened 19.1.72 by Walter Reade as The Bloomsbury Cinema, 490 seats, underground.) Taken over 4.5.74 and renamed ABC. Renamed EMI INTERNATIONAL FILM THEATRE 27.1.77. (Taken over 15.2.78 by Cinegate, re-opened 23.2.78 as

Gate Two. Twin from 24.9.81, 266 & 266 seats, renamed Gate Bloomsbury 1 & 2. Closed 30.10.85. Taken over by Artificial Eye, re-opened 9.5.86 as Renoir Russell Square. Open.)

CASINO Old Compton Street. (Opened 30.9.54 as Casino Cinerama Theatre, former Prince Edward live theatre with some film use.) Taken over 4.5.74 for film and live theatre use. Films ended 8.4.78. (Live theatre only. Renamed Prince Edward. Open)

LONDONDERRY Londonderry

PALACE Shipquay Street. (Taken over by Union 9.36. 800 seats.) Taken over 10.37, part of Union circuit. (Taken over by independent c1944.)

RIALTO Market Street. (Opened 1918. Taken over by Union 9.36. 800 seats.) Taken over 10.37, part of Union circuit. Closed 22.8.59. (Largely demolished for new ABC.)

ABC Market Street (site of Rialto). Opened 4.6.60 by ABC, architects: C. J. Foster, Alan Morgan and Berry & Miller, 1166 seats. (Taken over by independent 2.5.76, renamed Rialto. Closed 1983. Taken over by City Council 1984 for films and live shows.)

LONGTON Stoke-on-Trent

ALEXANDRA PALACE Edensor Road. (Opened 1911 as Panopticon, former skating rink. Renamed Alexandra 5.11. Closed by fire 1927 and rebuilt, architects: Wood and Goldstraw.) Taken over 12.31. 850 seats. (Taken over by independent c1935. 1106 seats. Closed 1957. Night club.)

EMPIRE Commerce Street. (Opened 23.1.22, former live theatre.) Taken over 12.31. Variety theatre for several months to 3.7.33. (Leased to Regent to 1935.) 1350 seats. Refurbished and re-opened 28.7.52. 775 seats in 1957. Closed 2.4.66. (Bingo. Closed. Destroyed by fire 31.12.92.)

LOWESTOFT Suffolk

MARINA Off London Road North. (Opened 1930, former live theatre reconstructed for films, architect: F. Burdett Ward.) Taken over 16.2.31. 962 seats. Renamed ABC c1962. (Taken over by independent 3.8.75, renamed Marina. Re-opened 18.1.81. Second cinema added in old theatre bar area c6.82, 70 seats. Closed 12.84 or 2.85.

Refurbished for live shows and films, re-opened as Marina Theatre 1.10.88, 850 seats. Open.)

LUTON Bedfordshire

PICTUREDROME 87 Park Street. (Opened 8.4.11, 500 seats. Taken over by Southan Morris c1924. Enlarged c1928. Taken over by Union 11.30.) Taken over 10.37, part of Union circuit. Closed 10.37 by Licensing Committee (quite likely before take-over). Not re-opened. Sold. (Motorcycle showroom.)

EMPIRE 116 Bury Park Road. (Opened 29.11.21, architects: Brown and Parrott. Extended 1927, architect: R. M. Godfrey, 900 seats. Taken over by Southan Morris 8.29. Taken over by Union c1933.) Taken over 10.37, part of Union circuit. Closed 15.10.38. (Taken back by Southan Morris. Not re-opened. Synagogue.)

ALMA THEATRE Alma Street and New Bedford Road. (Opened 21.12.29, architect: George Coles, 1664 seats. Taken over by Union 24.2.36.) Taken over 10.37, part of Union circuit. Some live shows. Closed 28.3.48. (Live theatre. Ballroom. Demolished 7.60. Cresta House.)

UNION 16-42 Gordon Street. (Opened 11.10.37 by Union, architect: Leslie H. Kemp, 2104 seats.) Taken over 10.37, part of Union circuit. Renamed RITZ 7.49. Closed 25.9.71. (Discotheque.)

SAVOY 51 George Street. Opened 17.10.38 by ABC, architect: W. R. Glen, 1892 seats: 1296 stalls & 696 balcony. Renamed ABC 2.10.61. Closed 17.4.71 for tripling. ABC 1, 2 & 3 opened 23.9.71, 632 & 458 & 272 seats. (Renamed Cannon. Open.)

MAIDENHEAD Berkshire

RIALTO Bridge Avenue. (Opened 31.10.27, architect: Robert Cromie. Taken over by Union 8.28.) Taken over 10.37, part of Union circuit. 1262 seats. Renamed ABC 1960. Closed 18.5.85. (Demolished. Offices with cinema space in basement.)

PLAZA Queen Street (site of Picture House). (Opened 3.9.28, architect: T. F. Ford. Taken over by Union c1930.) Taken over 10.37, part of Union circuit. 718 seats. Closed 13.10.62. (Bingo.)

RITZ Bridge Street. (Opened 20.1.36 by Union, reconstruction of Picture Theatre, architect: A. H.

Jones, 748 seats, single floor.) Taken over 10.37, part of Union circuit. Closed c1944. (Squash club.)

MAIDSTONE Kent

RITZ Pudding Lane. (Opened 18.3.11 as Pavilion Picture Palace, conversion of skating rink. Enlarged 1920, 1350 seats, now called Pavilion. Closed for improvements. Taken over by Union 3.10.35 and re-opened 5.10.35 as Ritz.) Taken over 10.37, part of Union circuit. 1389 seats. Closed 11.1.54 by fire. (Cornwallis House: shops and offices.)

CENTRAL PICTURE PLAYHOUSE King Street. (Opened 7.2.21, architects: Ruck and Smith, 1250 seats. Taken over by Union 3.10.35.) Taken over 10.37, part of Union circuit. 1168 seats. Closed 27.6.55 by fire. Reconstructed, architects: C. J. Foster and R. J. Westaway, and re-opened 10.12.56 as RITZ, 1270 seats: 869 stalls & 401 balcony. Renamed ABC 1962. Closed 5.10.74. (Bingo. Demolished 1980. Boots store.)

PALACE THEATRE Gabriels Hill. (Opened 20.4.31, former live theatre with some films. Taken over by Union 3.10.35.) Taken over 10.37, part of Union circuit. 668 seats. Live repertory theatre use in 1948, films on Sundays. Closed 1.4.51. (Leased out for live theatre use.) Taken back 7.4.52. (Leased out 9.3.53.) Re-opened 18.7.55. Closed 19.10.57. (Demolished c1960. Sainsbury's supermarket. Robert Dyas ironmongers.)

MANCHESTER

see also All Saints', Altrincham, Ancoats, Ardwick, Ashton-under-Lyne, Beswick, Bolton, Cheetham Hill, Chorlton-cum-Hardy, Denton, Didsbury, Eccles, Gorton, Higher Blackley, Hyde, Leigh, Levenshulme, Miles Platting, Moss Side, Oldham, Old Trafford, Openshaw, Rochdale, Rusholme, Salford Quays, Stockport, Wigan and Wythenshawe

GAIETY THEATRE Peter Street. (Opened 1921, former live theatre. Taken over by Savoy Cinemas.) Part of original circuit. (Leased to Regent 5.33 to 1935.) (Taken over by independent 7.11.37, improved, architects: Roberts, Wood and Elder, and re-opened 1937 for live shows. Re-opened 24.2.40 as fulltime cinema, 1298 seats. Closed by war damage 1.6.41. Re-opened 7.41. Closed 31.3.48 for structural alter-

ations. Re-opened 4.9.48. Closed 1.8.59. Demolished. Shops and offices.)

THEATRE ROYAL Peter Street. (Opened 4.9.22, reconstructed former live theatre. Taken over by Paramount 22.2.26.) Interest taken 2.6.29 (but still on lease to Paramount until c10.30) (Taken over by independent 25.6.35. Closed 19.10.35 for improvements, re-opened 11.11.35. 1943 seats. Closed 21.9.63 for Cinerama installation. Re-opened 4.11.63, 1073 seats. Closed 13.8.72. Bingo.)

DEANSGATE Deansgate. (Opened 1.14, 870 seats. Closed 18.10.30 for reconstruction, architect: G. Allen Fortescue, and re-opened 17.11.30. 866 seats.) Taken over 5.7.59, leased to 20th Century-Fox until closed 7.5.60 for modernisation and Todd-AO installation. Re-opened 4.9.60, 697 seats. Renamed ABC c1961. Former cafe converted to ABC 2 from 15.3.71, 167 seats. (Renamed Cannon. Both closed 9.8.90. Derelict.)

MANOR PARK Northeast London

CORONATION High Street North (site of earlier Coronation). (Opened 5.21, architect: Clifford A. Aish, 2000 seats.) Taken over 10.29. Closed 23.11.68. (Bingo. Snooker hall.)

MANSFIELD Nottinghamshire

GRAND THEATRE Leeming Street. (Opened c1915, former live theatre.) Taken over c1930. 1179 seats. Renamed ABC c1963. Front rebuilt in 1960s. Closed 7.1.78 for tripling. Re-opened 23.3.78, 390 & 369 & 171 seats (third in former stage area). (Renamed Cannon. Open.)

MARBLE ARCH London

see London West End

MARKET HARBOROUGH Leicestershire

RITZ Northampton Road. Opened 22.5.39 by ABC (Union), architect: William T. Benslyn with Ernest F. Tulley, 1109 seats. Partweek bingo in 1960s. (Taken over by Star 1.7.69.) Taken back 2.3.75. Closed 25.4.78. (Fulltime bingo. Closed 7.82. Supermarket.)

MERTHYR TYDFIL Mid Glamorgan

THEATRE ROYAL Pontmorlais. Taken over 11.32. (Leased to Regent 5.33 to 1935.) 1217

seats. (Taken over by independent c1939. Bingo.)

CASTLE SUPER High Street. (Opened 11.2.29, architect: O. P. Bevan.) Taken over 11.32. 1696 seats. Renamed ABC c1963. (Taken over by Star 2.7.72. Split into bingo hall and Studios 1 & 2, opened 12.10.72, 98 & 195 seats.) Taken back 2.3.75. (Taken over by independent 20.3.77. Twinned. 98 & 198 seats. Open as Flicks.)

METHIL East Fife

GAIETY High Street. Part of original circuit, from SCVT. (Taken over by independent c1929. Renamed Palace c1930. 1000 seats. Taken over by Milne 1.47.)

MIDDLESBROUGH Cleveland

SCALA Newport Road. (Opened 17.5.20, conversion of chapel, 800 seats.) Taken over 12.35. Closed 22.4.40. (Taken over by independent. Closed 1957. Demolished.)

ELITE Linthorpe Road and Borough Road. (Opened 7.23, architect: James Forbes, 1900 seats.) Taken over 12.35, 1843 seats. Closed 27.6.64 for internal reconstruction. Re-opened 27.11.64 as ABC, 1203 seats. Closed 19.1.74 for tripling. ABC 1, 2 & 3 opened 6.5.74, 490 & 289 & 268 seats. Closed 26.2.83. (Bingo.)

MILE END Northeast London

PALLADIUM 370 Mile End Road. (Opened c4.14, 1000 seats.) Taken over 21.10.35, 1332 seats. Closed 3.4.38.

EMPIRE 95 Mile End Road. (Former music hall, cinema by 11.23. Taken over by United Picture Theatres 1.28. Sold to independent 1934.) Taken over c1936. 2000 seats. Closed 3.4.38. (Demolished for new Empire.)

EMPIRE 93/95 Mile End Road (site of old Empire). Opened 12.6.39 by ABC, architect: W. R. Glen, 1974 seats. Renamed ABC 1961. Closed 25.8.73 for tripling. ABC 1 opened 9.9.73, 759 seats. ABC 2 & 3 opened 4.11.73, 213 & 211 seats. (To Cannon. Taken over by Coronet from c10.86, renamed Coronet. Closed 3.89. Derelict.)

MILES PLATTING Manchester

PLAYHOUSE Oldham Road, Queens Road and Hulme Hall Road. (Opened 7.19.) Taken over

1.7.29. 1827 seats. (Taken over by Star 1.4.69. Closed 6.6.70. Bingo. Closed. Derelict.)

MITCHAM South London

MAJESTIC 1 Upper Green. (Opened 6.10.33, architect: S. B. Pritlove, 1511 seats.) Taken over 30.4.34. Closed 25.11.61. (Bingo. Demolished. Supermarket.)

MONTROSE Tayside

KING'S Hulme Street. (Opened c1919 by SCVT, former live theatre.) Part of original circuit. 781 seats. (Taken over by independent 30.3.58. Closed 1963. Bingo.)

MOSELEY ROAD Birmingham

ALHAMBRA Moseley Road. (Opened 26.12.28, architects: Satchwell and Roberts, 1662 seats.) Taken over 1.4.30. (Leased to Regent from 5.33 to 1935.) Closed 31.8.68. (Asian cinema. Demolished. School.)

IMPERIAL 516 Moseley Road, corner of Clifton Road. (Opened 1913, 531 seats. Closed 5.27 for extension plus addition of balcony, architects: Satchwell and Roberts. Re-opened 14.11.27, 950 seats.) Taken over 10.36. Closed 13.4.63. (Asian cinema, Liberty. Closed 3.3.83. Re-opened as Imperial, showing mainstream films. Taken over by Council as community centre with some film shows.)

MOSS SIDE Manchester

CLAREMONT Claremont Road. (Opened c2.23.) Taken over 21.1.29. 1581 seats. Closed 8.2.58. (Demolished 1974.)

MOTHERWELL Strathclyde

LA SCALA Brandon Street. (Opened c2.20.) Part of original circuit, from SCVT. 930 seats. Closed 11.7.59. (Supermarket.)

NEW CENTURY THEATRE. Taken over 11.29. Closed c1932. (Largely demolished for Rex.)

REX 165 Windmill Street (site of Century Theatre, parts retained). Opened 17.8.36 by ABC, architect: C. J. McNair, 2031 seats. Renamed ABC c1972. Closed 12.6.76.

MUIREND Glasgow

TOLEDO 380 Clarkston Road. (Opened 2.10.33, architect: William Beresford Inglis of Weddell and Inglis, 1598 seats.) Taken over 7.10.34. Renamed ABC 20.7.70. Closed 9.1.82 for tripling. ABC 1, 2 & 3 opened 25.2.82, 482 & 208 & 92 (video) seats. Video screen closed. (Renamed Cannon. Listed building. Open.)

MUSWELL HILL North London

RITZ The Broadway. Opened 21.12.36 by ABC, architect: W. R. Glen, 1997 seats. Renamed ABC 1962. Closed 28.1.78. (Demolished 7.80.)

NEASDEN Northwest London

RITZ 277 Neasden Lane. Opened 25.3.35 by ABC, architect: W. J. King, 1872 seats. Closed 18.12.71. (Demolished.)

NEATH West Glamorgan

GNOLL HALL. (Leased from South Wales Cinemas by Union 3.37.) Taken over 10.37, part of Union circuit. 763 seats. (Taken back by South Wales Cinemas 1.10.39. 1076 seats. Closed c1960. Demolished.)

WINDSOR Windsor Road. (Opened 25.5.36, 1700 seats. Leased from South Wales Cinemas by Union 3.37.) Taken over 10.37, part of Union circuit. (Taken back by South Wales Cinemas 1.10.39. Taken over by Jackson Withers. Taken over by Rank 11.76. Closed 11.6.77. Taken over by independent: stalls area into nightclub 1979 with cinema in old balcony, 470 seats. Renamed Talk of the Abbey. Cinema closed 8.85. Re-opened 15.3.91 as Windsor. Closed 12.92.)

NEWBURY Berkshire

CARLTON Cheep Street. (Opened 4.20 as Central, conversion of brewery. Rebuilt and re-opened 1931 as Carlton. Taken over by Union 1933.) Taken over 10.37, part of Union circuit. 560 seats. Closed 29.5.50 by fire. (Demolished. Part of shopping mall.)

REGAL Bartholomew Street. (Opened 1931, 1290 seats. Taken over by Union 1933.) Taken over 10.37, part of Union circuit. Closed 20.4.63. (Demolished. Offices.)

FORUM Park Way. (Opened 1939.) Taken over 30.8.43, part of Mayfair circuit. 1114 seats.

Renamed ABC 1964. Closed 29.7.72 for splitting into bingo and smaller cinema. Re-opened 26.10.72, 484 seats. (Renamed Cannon. Bingo closed. Cinema open.)

NEWCASTLE-UNDER-LYME Staffordshire

SAVOY High Street. Opened 10.2.13 as King's Hall, 1000 seats. Renamed Savoy 28.2.27.) Taken over c1932. Closed 11.4.64. (Bingo. Circle opened 4.12.75 as Savoy, 200 seats. Closed 9.4.86. Re-opened. Closed 2.91.)

NEWCASTLE-UPON-TYNE Tyne and Wear
see also Benwell

GRAINGER 26-28 Grainger Street. (Opened 1.12.13, conversion of shop, architects: Percy L. Browne and Glover, 775 seats.) Taken over c1930. Closed 31.7.37. (Taken over by independent and reconstructed, architects: Marshall and Tweedy. Re-opened 2.12.37 as Grainger News Theatre, 733 seats. Called Grainger 28.3.38, feature film policy. Closed 26.3.60. Shop.)

EMPIRE 10-12 Grainger Street West. (Opened 2.4.13, shop and warehouse conversion, 600 seats. Taken over by Favourite Cinemas, part of original circuit. Closed 11.11.33. (Furniture shop. Demolished. Part of Newgate Shopping Centre.)

HAYMARKET Haymarket. (Opened 21.12.33, architects: Dixon and Bell, 1280 seats.) Taken over 6.9.35. Closed 5.36 for enlargement, architects: Dixon and Bell, and re-opened 31.8.36, 2006 seats. Renamed ABC 17.8.72. Closed 20.9.84. (Demolished. Car park.)

OLYMPIA Northumberland Road (site of Ginnett's Circus). (Opened 20.12.09, architect: J. Shaw, decorators: W. T. Gibson/Frediani Brothers, 1500 seats. Taken over by Union 1936.) Taken over 10.37, part of Union circuit. 1112 seats. Closed 8.4.61. (Warehouse. Demolished.)

ABC 1 & 2 Westgate Road, corner of Thornton Street. (Opened 29.8.38 as Essoldo, architect: William Stockdale, decorators: Alexander & Sons, 1720 seats. Closed 23.1.71 for twinning. Essoldo 1 & 2 opened 29.7.71, 650 & 390 seats. Taken over by Classic 2.4.72 and renamed Classic 1 & 2.) Taken over 31.3.74 and renamed ABC 1 & 2. (Renamed Cannon. Closed 11.1.90. Demolished.)

NEWPORT Dyfed

OLYMPIA. (Opened 14.5.13, 1000 seats. Enlarged c1915.) Taken over 22.7.29. 1570 seats. Closed 4.7.64. (Demolished.)

ABC Bridge Street (site of Lyceum Theatre). Opened 28.11.68 by ABC, architects: C. J. Foster and Alan Morgan, 1322 seats, stadium plan. Triple from 4.12.80, 530 & 200 & 140 seats. (Renamed Cannon. Open.)

NEW SOUTHGATE North London
see Bowes Road

NEWTONARDS Co. Down

RITZ. (Opened pre-1917 as Picture Palace. Taken over by Union 9.36, reconstructed, architect: R. Sharpe Hill, and re-opened 1.3.37 as Ritz, 713 seats.) Taken over 10.37, part of Union circuit. Closed 16.7.66. (Shopping arcade and health studio.)

NORBURY South London

REX London Road. Opened 4.1.37 by ABC, architect: Douglas Harrington, 1504 seats: 960 stalls & 544 balcony. Closed 17.2.62. (Bingo. Demolished. Radnor House office block.)

NORRIS GREEN Liverpool

REGAL Broadway. (Opened 27.1.30, architect: Kenmure Kinna, 1756 seats, one floor.) Taken over 1935. Closed 6.8.55 for extensive alterations. Re-opened 10.10.55, 1416 seats. Part-week bingo from 1963. Closed 10.10.64. (Bingo, with some children's film shows for a while.)

NORTH HAMMERSMITH West London
see Acton

NORTHAMPTON Northamptonshire

MAJESTIC 83 Gold Street and Horsemarket Street (now Bell's Corner). (Opened 17.8.12, former Palace of Varieties, 778 seats.) Taken over 2.3.31. Closed 26.6.37. (Bell's fireplaces showroom. Demolished. New Bell's building.)

SAVOY Abingdon Square. Opened 4.5.36 by ABC, architect: W. R. Glen, 1954 seats: 1258 stalls & 696 balcony. Renamed ABC c1961. Closed 8.12.74 for tripling. ABC 1, 2 & 3 opened

26.12.74, 1018 (balcony & front stalls) & 263 & 208 seats. (Renamed Cannon. Open.)

NORTH HARROW North London

EMBASSY Pinner Road and Imperial Drive. (Opened 10.29, architect: T. Ovenston of Emden, Egan, 1642 seats.) Taken over 14.5.36. Closed 11.5.63. (Demolished. Bowling alley and supermarket.)

NORTH KENSINGTON West London

ROYALTY 105/9 Lancaster Road. (Opened 4.2.29, architect: J. Stanley Beard, 1288 seats.) Taken over 19.2.35. Closed 19.11.60. (Bingo and gaming club from 14.4.65. Demolished.)

NORWICH Norfolk

REGENT Prince of Wales Road. (Opened 3.12.23, architect: G. Duncan Fitt with J. Owen Bond, 1800 seats.) Taken over 16.7.29. Closed 12.8.39 for alterations and re-opened 25.9.39. 1523 seats. Renamed ABC c1961. Closed 3.2.73 for tripling. ABC 1 opened 19.4.73, 524 seats. ABC 2 & 3 opened 21.5.73, 343 & 186 seats. ABC 4 (video) opened 6.8.78 in adjacent café, 74 seats. ABC 4 closed c10.85. (Open as Cannon. ABC 4 re-opened as Cannon 4 using film 8.89, 105 seats.)

HIPPODROME St. Giles Street. (Opened 1930, former Grand Opera House with some films.) Taken over c1932. 1600 seats. Closed c1942. (Theatre. Demolished 1966.)

NOTTINGHAM Nottinghamshire
see also Sherwood

NEW EMPRESS St. Ann's Well Road. (Opened 29.10.28.) Taken over c10.29. 1491 seats. Closed 12.11.60. (Bingo – overflow hall from adjacent club. Demolished c1988.)

ELITE 33 Upper Parliament Street. (Opened 15.8.21, architects: Adamson and Kinns, decoration: Fred A. Foster, 1477 seats. New decorative scheme introduced in 8.29.) Taken over c10.35. Closed 12.3.77. (Bingo. Listed building. Closed 1985. Converted to shops and offices 1993.)

CARLTON Chapel Bar and Mount Street. Opened 16.10.39 by ABC, architect: W. R. Glen, 2077 seats: 1294 stalls & 783 balcony. Renamed ABC 14.12.59. Closed 24.8.74 for tripling. ABC 1 opened 4.11.74, 797 seats. ABC 2 & 3 opened

2.12.74, 440 & 282 seats. (Renamed Cannon. Renamed MGM 21.5.93. Open.)

NUNEATON Warwickshire

HIPPODROME Bondgate/Bond Street. (Former Prince of Wales live theatre. Cinema. Reconstructed, architects: Satchwell and Roberts, and re-opened 20.3.26.) Taken over 1.29. 1170 seats. Closed temporarily by fire 11.34. Re-opened after wartime closure 8.7.41. Closed 22.12.56. (Part demolished 9.68. Rest demolished c1988. Offices and shops.)

EMPIRE Leicester Road. It appears that this music hall, though never operated as a cinema, may have come under ABC control before being taken over by an independent for variety use in April 1939.

RITZ Abbey Street and Newtown Road. (Opened 22.7.37 by Union, architects: Verity and Beverley, 1652 seats.) Taken over 10.37, part of Union circuit. Renamed ABC 13.11.61. (Taken over 30.10.77 by independent and renamed Ritz. Twinned from 23.12.79, 1250 front stalls/balcony & 200 rear stalls. Closed 6.84. Bingo.)

OATLANDS Glasgow

HIPPODROME Rathingler Road. (Opened 9.29, former live theatre.) Taken over 1931, redecorated and re-opened 21.9.31 as RITZ. 1555 seats. Closed 18.2.61. (Demolished. Houses.)

OLDHAM Greater Manchester

PALLADIUM Union Street. (Opened 9.13.) Taken over c1935. 1841 seats. Closed 1.11.58 for modernisation and re-opened 23.2.59 as ABC, 1456 seats. Closed 1.10.77. (Bingo. Re-opened as cinema 12.85, 420 seats. Closed 5.6.86. Bingo. Demolished c1990.)

OLD KENT ROAD Southeast London

REGAL 810 Old Kent Road, corner of Gervase Street. Opened 18.1.37 by ABC, architect: W. R. Glen, 2474 seats. Renamed ABC 29.11.63. Closed 9.2.74. (Bingo. Demolished 11 & 12.81.)

OLD SWAN Liverpool
see Knotty Ash

OLD TRAFFORD Manchester

TRAFFORD PICTURE HOUSE Talbot Road.

(Opened 5.22.) Taken over 27.5.35. 1129 seats. Closed 29.11.58. (Car auction room. Closed. Derelict.)

OPENSHAW Manchester

NEW ROYAL Ashton New Road. (Opened 1914.) Taken over 1.7.29. 1445 seats. Closed 31.3.62. (Bingo.) Re-opened 27.8.62. Renamed ABC c1965. Closed 25.1.69 by Compulsory Purchase Order.

QUEEN'S Ashton Old Road. Taken over c1932. 1205 seats. (Taken over by independent c1945. Taken over by Star. Bingo.)

OSWALDTHISTLE Lancashire

PALLADIUM Union Road. Taken over c1934 from Regent. 1027 seats. (Taken over by independent 5.40. Re-opened after fire 22.12.44. Closed c1968. Bingo.)

OXFORD Oxfordshire

see also Botley and Cowley

ELECTRA PALACE Queen Street. (Opened 25.3.11. Front widened 1913. Extended c1920. Taken over by Union 6.31.) Taken over 10.37, part of Union circuit. 1078 seats. Closed 23.8.58. (Annexed by adjacent Co-Op store. Demolished c1980. Marks and Spencer store.)

PALACE Cowley Road. (Taken over by Union c1932.) Taken over 10.37, part of Union circuit. (Taken over by independent c1938. Closed. Offices of Blackwell's, publishers.)

SUPER Magdalen Street. (Opened 1.1.24 as Oxford Super, architects: Frank Matcham and J. C. Leed, 1300 seats. Taken over by Union 6.31. Known as Super. 1251 seats.) Taken over 10.37, part of Union circuit. Closed 10.7.71 for "luxury lounge" treatment. Re-opened 25.7.71 as ABC MAGDALEN STREET, 853 seats. (Renamed Cannon. Renamed MGM 9.4.93. Open.)

RITZ George Street (site of George Street Cinema). (Opened 20.4.36 by Union, architect: Robert Cromie, 1654 seats.) Taken over 10.37, part of Union circuit. Renamed ABC c1962. Closed 4.63 by fire. Re-opened c10.63. Closed 27.9.75 for tripling. ABC 1 opened 16.11.75, 612 seats. ABC 2 & 3 opened 14.12.75, 210 & 141 seats. (Renamed Cannon. Renamed MGM 9.4.93.)

PADDINGTON Liverpool

NEW COLISEUM City Road. (Opened 1910 as Coliseum, 650 seats, former music hall. Enlarged and re-opened 18.11.26 as New Coliseum.) Taken over c8.35. 978 seats. Closed 1.12.56. (Demolished.)

PAISLEY Strathclyde

REGAL 95 High Street and Lady Lane. Opened 26.11.34 by ABC, architect: C. J. McNair, 2054 seats. Renamed ABC c1963. (Taken over by Caledonian Associated Cinemas 28.8.78 and renamed Regal. Closed c1982. Bingo.)

PARKHEAD Glasgow

PICTURE PALACE 49 Tollcross Road. (Opened 7.21, 1200 seats. Taken over by SCVT.) Part of original circuit. Closed 19.8.60 by fire. (Demolished.)

PENZANCE Cornwall

RITZ Queen Street. (Opened 27.7.36 by Union, architect: A. H. Jones, 1000 seats.) Taken over 10.37, part of Union circuit. (Taken over by Mecca 28.6.65. Closed 17.7.65. Bingo. Open.)

PETERBOROUGH Cambridgeshire

EMBASSY Broadway. (Opened 1.11.37, architect: David E. Nye, planned for film and live use. Live theatre only, then cinema from 28.6.53 with some stage shows.) Taken over 4.4.65, 1484 seats. Renamed ABC c1965. Some live shows. Closed 24.1.81 for tripling. ABC 1, 2 & 3 opened 14.5.81, 668 & 290 & 150 seats. (Renamed Cannon. Closed 25.11.89. Disused.)

PINNER North London

LANGHAM Bridge Street. (Opened 9.1.36, architect: T. C. Ovenston of Emden, Egan, 1502 seats.) Taken over 14.5.36. Renamed ABC c1963. Closed 27.5.67 for conversion of stalls into "luxury lounge". Re-opened 26.8.67, 1124 seats. (Taken over by independent 30.1.77 and renamed Mayfair. Taken over by Shipman and King 4.2.79 and renamed Langham. Closed 19.9.81. Demolished. Supermarket.)

PLYMOUTH Devon

PLAZA Exeter Street. (Opened 2.34, architect: H.

J. Hammick, 933 seats.) Taken over 3.6.35. (Taken over by Star 1.4.69. Renamed Studio 7 9.12.69. Taken over by Shipman and King 28.3.76 and renamed Plaza. Closed 4.10.81. Arcade/snooker hall/restaurant.)

ROYAL Union Place (site of Theatre Royal). Opened 15.7.38 by ABC, architect: W. R. Glen, 2404 seats: 1564 stalls & 840 balcony. Renamed ABC c1960. Closed 30.10.76 for tripling. ABC 1, 2 & 3 opened 5.5.77, 578 & 367 & 122 seats (plus bingo hall). (Renamed Cannon. Renamed MGM 22.5.92.)

POPLAR East London

HIPPODROME East India Dock Road. Taken over c1930. 1732 seats. Bombed 1942. (Demolished. Housing.)

PORTSMOUTH Hampshire

see also Cosham and Southsea

VICTORIA HALL Commercial Road. (Opened c1.14. Taken over by Union 8.28.) Taken over 10.37, part of Union circuit. 1407 seats. Renamed VICTORIA by 1939. 1247 seats. Closed 7.3.60. (Demolished. Office block.)

SAVOY 335 Commercial Road and Fitzherbert Street. Opened 17.7.37 by ABC, architect: W. R. Glen, 1911 seats: 1212 stalls & 699 balcony. Renamed ABC c1961. Triple from 29.4.82, 542 & 253 & 196 seats. (Renamed Cannon. Open.)

PORTSWOOD Southampton

BROADWAY Portswood Road. (Opened 6.30, architect: W. H. Masters, wall paintings: Fred Stafford.) Taken over 16.12.35, 1562 seats. Closed 26.10.63. (Bingo.)

POTTERS BAR Hertfordshire

RITZ Darkes Lane, corner of Byng Drive. Opened 8.10.34 by ABC, architect: W. J. King, 1170 seats. (Taken over by W.J. King c3.35. Leased to various groups. Closed 1.7.67. Demolished. Tesco supermarket.)

PRESTON Lancashire

STAR Corporation Street. (Opened 1921.) Taken over c1929. (Leased by independent c1933. Sold by ABC 7.35. 829 seats. (Closed 1959. Demolished. Preston University, ex-Polytechnic.)

THEATRE ROYAL Fishergate. (Opened pre-1914, former live theatre.) Taken over 11.29. 1160 seats. Closed 3.12.55. (Demolished for new ABC.)

ABC Fishergate, corner of Theatre Street (site of Theatre Royal). Opened 14.3.59 by ABC, architect: C. J. Foster, 1487 seats. Closed 7.4.73 for Painted Wagon pub to be constructed in rear stalls. Re-opened 6.5.73, 637 seats in old balcony. Closed 11.9.82. (Demolished 10/11.86.)

PURLEY South London

REGAL 92-98 Brighton Road. (Opened 26.2.34, architect: Harold S. Scott, 1578 seats.) Taken over 11.6.34. Closed 16.2.74. (Bingo. Open.)

PUTNEY Southwest London

HIPPODROME Felsham Road. (Opened c5.24, former live theatre. Taken over by United Picture Theatres c11.28.) Taken over 7.35. (Taken over by independent c1938. 1420 seats. Closed 12.40. Taken over by Odeon and re-opened 17.2.41. Closed 14.1.61. Demolished 1975.)

REGAL High Street. Opened 8.11.37 by ABC, architect: W. R. Glen, 2540 seats: 1651 stalls & 889 balcony. Renamed ABC 3.9.61. Closed 11.12.71. (Demolished for redevelopment including new ABC.)

ABC 1 2 & 3 25 High Street (in redevelopment on site of former ABC and Odeon.) Opened 14.9.75 by ABC, architect: Alan Morgan, 432 & 312 & 147 seats. (Renamed Cannon. Renamed MGM 23.4.93.)

READING Berkshire

see also Caversham, Tilehurst and Whitley

CENTRAL Friar Street. (Opened c25.3.21 as Central Picture Playhouse, architect: George Gardiner, 1400 seats.) Taken over c1931. 1588 seats. Closed 29.7.67 for conversion of stalls into "luxury lounge". Re-opened 15.11.67, 814 seats. Renamed ABC 30.7.71. ABC 2 opened 14.10.71 in former café area, 118 seats. ABC 1 closed 12.3.77 for twinning. Re-opened 12.5.77 as ABC 1 & 2, 534 & 226 seats, former ABC 2 renumbered ABC 3. (Renamed Cannon. Renamed MGM 4.6.93. Open.)

GRANBY 108 London Road, Cemetery Junction. (Opened 2.9.35, architect: Edgar Simmons, 1177

seats.) Taken over 30.8.43, from Mayfair circuit. Renamed ABC LONDON ROAD c1965. Modernised 1969. Closed 27.11.82. (Demolished 1987.)

RICHMOND Southwest London

RITZ Sheen Road. Opened 19.5.38 by ABC (Union), architect: Sam Beverley of Verity and Beverley, 2150 seats: 1456 stalls & 694 balcony. Renamed ABC 1961. Closed 11.12.71. (Demolished. Office block: Spencer House.)

RIDDRIE Glasgow

REX 650 Cumbernauld Road and New Edinburgh Road. Opened 7.12.31 by ABC, architect: C. J. McNair, 2336 seats. Renamed ABC c1961. Closed 29.9.73. (Demolished.)

ROCHDALE Greater Manchester

REGAL The Butts. Opened 16.5.38 by ABC, architect: Leslie C. Norton with W. R. Glen, 1901 seats: 1208 stalls & 693 balcony. Renamed ABC c1962. Closed 7.1.78 for tripling. ABC 1 opened 23.3.78, 538 seats. ABC 2 & 3 opened 30.4.78, 281 & 199 seats. (Renamed Cannon. Closed 8.10.92. Bingo.)

ROMFORD Northeast London

RITZ 180 South Street. Opened 7.11.38 by ABC, architect: W. R. Glen, 2019 seats: 1269 stalls & 750 balcony. Closed 9.2.59 by fire. Re-opened 27.3.59. Renamed ABC 1962. Closed 14.11.70 for tripling. ABC 1, 2 & 3 opened 15.7.71, 652 & 496 & 248 seats. (Renamed Cannon. Open.)

ROSYTH Fife

PALACE Queensferry Road. (Opened 26.12.21. Booked by SCVT.) Part of original circuit. (Taken over by independent c1930. 838 seats. Closed in 1970s.)

ROTHERHAM South Yorkshire

EMPIRE High Street. (Opened 2.5.21, former music hall extensively altered.) Taken over c1929. (Taken over by independent 9.9.39. 1228 seats. Taken over by Essoldo c1954. Renamed Essoldo c1956. Taken over by Classic 2.4.72 and renamed Classic. Modernised 1974 with circle and balcony closed off, 510 seats. Twin from 26.8.78, 314

seats in old balcony & 294 in rear stalls. Closed 22.2.90.)

WHITEHALL High Street. (Opened 7.1.24, architects: George W. Knapton and James Totty, 771 seats. Taken over by Union 2.12.35.) Taken over 10.37, part of Union circuit. Closed 25.6.60. (Demolished 1960.)

ROTHERHITHE Southeast London

HIPPODROME 34/36 Lower Road. (Opened 5.9.27, some earlier cinema use.) Taken over 10.30. 1313 seats. Closed 4.31 for redecoration. Re-opened 11.6.31, 1200 seats. Leased to Regent 5.33 to 1935. (Taken over by independent 31.8.41. Variety theatre from 20.9.43. Demolished 6 & 7.55.)

RUSHOLME Manchester

CASINO Wilmslow Road. (Opened 1916. Re-opened 3.22.) Taken over 1.7.29. 1420 seats. Closed 19.10.60 by fire.

ST. GEORGE Bristol

PARK Church Road. (Opened 1911. Balcony added 1925, architect: W. H. Watkins.) Taken over 12.32. 1000 seats. Leased to Regent 5.33 to 1935. (Taken over by independent 10.40. Taken over by Mayfair. Taken over by independent c1947. Closed 5.64. Demolished.)

ST. HELENS Merseyside

CAPITOL Capitol Corner, Duke Street and North Road. (Opened 3.10.29, architects: Gray and Evans, 1550 seats.) Taken over c1931. Closed 9.12.78. (Sports centre.)

SAVOY Bridge Street (site of old Savoy). (Opened 25.3.35, architect: George E. Tonge, 1515 seats.) Taken over 27.2.36. Renamed ABC c1961. Closed 16.9.78 for tripling. ABC 1, 2 & 3 opened 14.12.78, 494 & 284 & 179 seats. (Renamed Cannon. Open.)

ST. LEONARDS East Sussex

REGAL London Road. (Opened 8.8.32, architect: John B. Mendham, 1570 seats. Taken over by Union c1935.) Taken over 10.37, part of Union circuit. Closed c1940 by war conditions. Re-opened 3.6.46. Closed 8.9.56. (Demolished. Office block.)

SALE Great Manchester

SAVOY Tatton Road. (Opened c10.13. Modernised & re-opened 8.29, 1300 seats. Taken over by Union 7.36.) Taken over 10.37, part of Union circuit. 1369 seats. Renamed ABC c1963. Converted to "luxury lounge" 7,73, 580 seats, stalls only. Closed 2.3.74. (Re-opened 1.11.75 by independent as Savoy, balcony only. Closed 26.2.77.)

SALFORD Manchester
see Higher Broughton

SALFORD QUAYS Manchester

CANNON Quebec Drive, Trafford Road. Opened 18.12.86, architects: Howard and Unick, 1904 seats in 8 auditoria: 265 & 265 & 249 & 249 & 231 & 231 & 177 & 177. (Renamed MGM 28.8.92. Open.)

SALISBURY Wiltshire

REGAL Endless Street. Opened 22.2.37 by ABC, architect: W. R. Glen, 1608 seats: 964 stalls & 644 balcony. Renamed ABC c1963. Closed 25.1.69. (Bingo.)

SALTLEY Birmingham

ORIGINAL SALTLEY PICTURE THEATRE 20 Alum Rock Road. (Opened 1911, architect: A. Hurley Robinson.) Taken over c10.29. Closed 1932. (Nightclub. Re-opened 6.10.79 as cinema. Closed c1981. Nightclub.)

SCUNTHORPE Humberside

RITZ Doncaster Road. (Opened 27.2.37 by Union, architect: Robert Cromie, 1063 seats, one floor.) Taken over 10.37, part of Union circuit. Renamed ABC c1960. Closed 12.1.74. (Disco/nightclub.)

SELLY OAK Birmingham

THE OAK Bristol Road. (Opened 26.3.23, architect: Harold Scott, 1111 seats. Re-opened 1929, 1093 seats.) Taken over c3.35. Closed 9.35 for extension of stage end and enlargement of balcony, architect: Harold Scott. Re-opened 16.12.35, 1506 seats. Renamed ABC c1965. (Taken over by independent 16.4.78 and renamed The Oak. Closed 3.11.79. Demolished for road and Sainsbury's supermarket development.)

SHAFTESBURY AVENUE Central London
see London West End

SHAWLANDS Glasgow

PICTURE HOUSE Pollokshaws Road, Shawlands Cross. (Opened c1915 by SCVT.) Part of original circuit. Closed 30.8.30. (Top Hat Ballroom. Geneen's. Part of Co-Op supermarket complex.)
WAVERLEY Shawlands Cross. (Opened 25.12.22.) Taken over c9.29. 1320 seats. Renamed ABC c1965. Closed 31.3.73. (Bingo. Listed exterior.)
CAMPHILL PICTURE HOUSE. (Opened 1911.) Taken over late 1929. Enlarged, 1200 seats. Closed 22.4.31, almost totally destroyed by fire.

SHEFFIELD South Yorkshire

HIPPODROME Cambridge Street. Opened 20.6.31 by ABC, former variety theatre redecorated with new projection box, 2445 seats. (Taken over by independent 25.7.48. Closed 2.3.63 by Compulsory Purchase Order. Demolished. Grosvenor Hotel, shops and offices.)
ABC Angel Street. Opened 18.5.61 by ABC, architects: C. J. Foster and R. J. Westaway assisted by Peter Parks and D. Berry, 1327 seats, stadium plan. ABC 2 opened 21.9.75 in former café/lounge area, 94 seats. (Renamed Cannon. Closed 28.7.88. Demolished 1989.)

SHERWOOD Nottingham

METROPOLE Mansfield Road. (Opened 2.8.37, architect: Reginald W. Cooper, 1500 seats.) Taken over 1943. Closed 27.10.73. (Bingo. Supermarket.)

SHIRLEY Southampton

ATHERLEY Shirley Road. (Opened 14.9.12.) Taken over 12.35, 1130 seats. (Taken over by independent c1938. New ceiling installed 7.50. Closed 15.11.75. Bingo.)

SHOREDITCH North London

OLYMPIA 203/4 High Street. (Former live theatre, cinema from 11.26. 2834 seats.) Taken over c1930. 1546 seats. Closed 5.39 for new ABC and largely demolished by 1.40 (scheme stopped by War and never completed).

SIDCUP Southeast London

REGAL High Street. (Opened c1914 as King's Hall, former concert hall. Enlarged, architect: Robert Cromie, and re-opened 31.10.32 as Regal. Taken over by Union c1935.) Taken over 10.37, part of Union circuit. 1228 seats. Renamed ABC c8.63. Closed 23.10.65 for modernisation. Re-opened 18.12.65. Closed 17.9.77 for twinning. ABC 1 & 2 opened 1.12.77, 516 & 303 seats. (Renamed Cannon. Open.)

SLOUGH Berkshire

ADELPHI THEATRE Bath Road. (Opened 17.2.30, architect: E. Norman Bailey, 2042 seats. Re-opened 29.5.33 by Southan Morris. Taken over by Union c1933.) Taken over 10.37, part of Union circuit. (Taken over by independent 1.2.53. Taken over by Granada 1954. Closed 21.1.73. Bingo.)

SMETHWICK West Midlands

BEACON Brasshouse Lane. (Opened 30.9.29, architect: Harold Scott, 962 seats. Taken over by County 11.32.) Taken over 30.8.43, from Mayfair circuit. Closed 15.2.58. (Asian cinema.)

SOUTHALL West London

DOMINION The Green. (Opened 14.10.35, architect: F. E. Bromige, 1852 seats.) Taken over 10.2.36. Closed 27.1.62. (Nehru Hall – Asian films. Closed. Demolished 1982/3.)

SOUTHAMPTON Hampshire
see also Portswood

FORUM Above Bar. Opened 22.6.35 by ABC, architect: W. R. Glen, 1909 seats. Closed 1941 for several months following bomb damage. Renamed ABC c1960. Closed 12.6.71 for twinning. ABC 1 & 2 opened 25.11.71, 688 & 439 seats. ABC 3 (video) opened 1981 in former lounge bar, 83 seats. (Renamed Cannon. Cannon 3 closed 1989. Cannon 1 & 2 closed 21.2.91. Disused.)

SOUTHEND-ON-SEA Essex

RIVOLI 22 Alexandra Street. (Opened 17/31.5.20, former Empire Theatre improved, architects: Adams & [George] Coles, 1555 seats. Taken over by Union 1935.) Taken over 10.37, part of Union circuit. Modernised and re-opened

7.6.62 as ABC, 1226 seats. Closed 1.3.80 for twinning. ABC 1 & 2 opened 22.5.80, 710 & 498 seats. (Renamed Cannon. Open.)

SOUTHGATE North London
see Bowes Road

SOUTHPORT Merseyside
REGAL Lord Street. Opened 5.12.38 by ABC, architect: W. R. Glen, 1632 seats. Renamed ABC c1962. Closed 1.9.84. (Demolished. Retirement flats.)

SOUTHSEA Portsmouth
GAIETY Albert Road. (Opened 12.2.24, architect: A. E. Cogswell and Sons, 1050 seats. Extended c1.26, 1380 seats.) Taken over 8.31. Leased to Regent 5.33 to 1935. (Taken over by independent 8.38. Closed 31.1.59. Supermarket.)
COMMODORE 137 Fawcett Road. (Opened c10.11 as Southsea Electric Theatre. 763 seats. Renamed Fawcett Picture House 1926. Renamed Capitol c7.29. Enlarged and re-opened 24.5.30 as Commodore, 1000 seats.) Taken over c12.32. (Taken over by independent 1938, reconstructed, architect: F. E. Bromige, and re-opened c7.38 as State. 1000 seats. Closed 1940. Store. Embassy Ballroom. Store. Demolished. Flats – Embassy Court.)
APOLLO 42 Albert Road. (Opened 6.4.12, 500 seats. Enlarged 1916, 900 seats. Enlarged 1920, 1250 seats. Closed 5.36. New entrance hall added on adjacent property and balcony rebuilt, architect: R. A. Thomas, and re-opened 1.8.36, 1455 seats.) Taken over 26.12.37. (Taken over by Essoldo 27.12.49. Renamed Essoldo c1950. Taken over by Classic 2.4.72 and renamed Classic. Closed 29.11.75. Demolished. Shops and flats.)

SOUTH SHIELDS Tyne and Wear
SAVOY Ocean Road. Opened 12.12.38 by ABC, architect: Percy L. Browne and Son, 1708 seats: 1038 stalls & 670 balcony. Renamed ABC 17.1.63. Closed 4.12.82. (Taken over by independent and re-opened 11.1.84 with live shows and films. Closed 31.12.84. Demolished 1988. Vacant site.)

SPARKBROOK Birmingham
PICCADILLY Stratford Road and Poplar Road

(site of Picturedrome). (Opened 22.5.30, architects: Satchwell and Roberts, 1902 seats.) Taken over 22.10.36. Closed 2.3.74. (Bingo. Asian cinema, called Dreamland. Bingo.)

SPRINGBURN Glasgow
PRINCE'S Gourlay Street. (Opened 1914.) Part of original circuit, from SCVT. 998 seats. Enlarged and re-opened 8.11.37, 2050 seats. Closed 27.7.68. (Bingo. Demolished.)

STAINES Surrey
REGAL Clarence Street. Opened 20.2.39 by ABC, architect: W. R. Glen, 1613 seats: 1103 stalls & 510 balcony. Closed 30.5.70 for twinning. ABC 1 & 2 opened 11.3.71, 586 (above) & 694 seats (below). ABC 2 closed 11.11.72 for twinning. Re-opened 22.1.73 as ABC 2 & 3, 361 & 174 seats. (Renamed Cannon. Renamed MGM 16.4.83.)

STAMFORD HILL Northeast London
SUPER Clapton Common. (Opened 26.12.25 as the Cinema, architect: George Coles, 1800 seats, one floor. Taken over by United Picture Theatres 2.1.28. Renamed Super 1947.) Taken over 4.1.48. Closed 7.11.59. (Bowling alley. Demolished.)

STEPNEY East London
PALASEUM 226 Commercial Road. (Opened 3.12, former Fienman's Yiddish Theatre, 920 seats. Taken over by United Picture Theatres c5.28.) Taken over by Regent circuit 1934. Taken over c1935. 920 seats. (Taken over by Southan Morris 26.3.49. Taken over by Essoldo 26.8.54. Closed 19.3.60. Re-opened 18.10.61, renamed Essoldo. Closed 1.9.66. Asian cinema, renamed Palaseum. Closed 10.85. Demolished.)

STEVENAGE Hertfordshire
ABC 1 & 2 The Forum, St. George's Way. Opened 18.11.73 by ABC, 340 & 182 seats. (Renamed Cannon. Open.)

STIRCHLEY Birmingham
EMPIRE Pershore Road. (Opened c1912.) Taken over c1932. Leased to Regent 5.33 to 1935. Closed c1943. (Garage.)

PAVILION Pershore Road. (Opened 28.11.31, architect: Harold S. Scott, 2250 seats.) Taken over c1934. Renamed ABC c1962. Bowling alley added alongside, renamed ABC Cine-Bowl. Cinema closed 28.12.68. (Bingo. Closed.)

STIRLING Central Scotland
REGAL Maxwell Place. Opened 3.10.32 by ABC, architect: Charles J. McNair, 2208 seats. Closed 16.3.68 by Compulsory Purchase Order. (Demolished for new road.)

STOCKBRIDGE Edinburgh
SAVOY St. Bernard's Row (site of St. Bernard's Picture Palace). (Opened 28.3.21 by SCVT, architect: P. R. McLaren, 900 seats.) Part of original circuit. Closed 16.7.60. (Taken over by independent, re-opened 25.7.60 as Tudor. Closed c1964. Bingo. Printing works.)

STOCKPORT Greater Manchester
HIPPODROME St. Petergate. Taken over c1931. 998 seats. (Taken over by independent 1.38. Live theatre. Re-opened as cinema 3.12.51, renamed Astor. Closed 4.60 by fire.)
RITZ Duke Street and St. Petersgate. Opened 3.1.38 by ABC (Union), architects: Verity and Beverley, 2343 seats: 1627 stalls & 716 balcony. Renamed ABC c1961. Closed 28.11.70 for stalls conversion to "luxury lounge". Re-opened 27.12.70. (Taken over by independent 2.4.78, renamed Ritz. Closed 12.82. Demolished.)

STOCKTON-ON-TEES Cleveland
EMPIRE High Street. (Opened 1914, former Castle Theatre.) Taken over 12.35. 1031 seats. Closed 25.3.61. (Bingo. Closed 1963. Demolished.)
GLOBE High Street. (Opened 1.36 as variety theatre on site of old cinema, 2500 seats. Closed 3.4.37.) Taken over and re-opened as cinema 5.4.37. 2429 seats. Much live use. Renamed ABC c1967. Closed 15.6.74. (Live theatre. Bingo.)

STOKE NEWINGTON North London
SAVOY 11-15 Stoke Newington Road. Opened 26.10.36 by ABC, architect: W. R. Glen, 1900 seats. Renamed ABC c1961. (Taken over by independent 13.3.77 and renamed Konak.

Renamed Ace 3.82. Closed 16.2.84. Snooker hall.)

STOKE-ON-TRENT Staffordshire
see also Hanley and Longton

MAJESTIC Campbell Place. (Opened pre-1917, 1000 seats.) Taken over 12.29. 881 seats. Closed 30.11.57. (Demolished. Tesco supermarket and Majestic Chambers.)

STOURBRIDGE West Midlands

SAVOY Lower High Street. (Opened 1920 as Scala, architect: Joseph Lawden, 1100 seats.) Taken over 20.9.43. 1021 seats. Renamed ABC c1968. Closed 6.11.82. (Supermarket – Dhillons in 1993.)

STRATFORD East London

REX High Street, corner of Bridge Road. (Opened 5.11.34, former Borough Theatre, interior entirely reconstructed, architect: George Coles, 1900 seats.) Taken over 9.35. Closed 11.1.69. (Bingo. Closed 6.4.74. Derelict.)

STREATHAM South London

GOLDEN DOMES 130/4 High Street. (Opened 12.9.12 as Streatham Picture Theatre. Renamed Golden Domes c1915. Enlarged and re-opened 7.10.29, architect: J. Stanley Beard.) Taken over 8.35. 1010 seats. Closed 12.11.38. (Supermarket.)

REGAL 5 High Road. Opened 14.11.38 by ABC, architect: W. R. Glen, 1962 seats: 1232 stalls & 730 balcony. Renamed ABC 16.10.60. Closed 9.1.77 for tripling. ABC 1, 2 & 3 opened 7.4.77, 630 & 432 & 231 seats. (Renamed Cannon. Open.)

SUNDERLAND Tyne and Wear

RITZ Holmeside and Park Lane. Opened 1.3.37 by ABC, architect: W. R. Glen, 1906 seats. Renamed ABC c1961. Closed 27.4.74 into two cinemas and Painted Wagon pub. ABC 1 opened 14.7.74, 534 seats. ABC 2 opened 12.8.74, 212 seats. (Renamed Cannon. Open.)

SUTTON COLDFIELD West Midlands
see also Wylde Green

EMPRESS The Parade. (Opened 1922. 1510

seats.) Taken over 31.8.43, part of Mayfair circuit. Renamed ABC c1963. Closed 26.6.71. (Demolished for shopping precinct.)

SWANSEA West Glamorgan

CARLTON Oxford Street. (Opened 31.1.14. architect: Charles Tamlin Ruthin. Leased from South Wales Cinemas by Union 3.37.) Taken over 10.37, part of Union circuit. (Taken back by South Wales Cinemas 1.10.39. 929 seats. Taken over by Jackson Withers. Taken over by Rank 1.11.76. Closed 29.10.77. Listed building. Derelict.)

PICTURE HOUSE High Street. (Leased from South Wales Cinemas by Union 3.37.) Taken over 10.37, part of Union circuit. 750 seats. (Taken back by South Wales Cinemas 1.10.39. 942 seats. Closed c1942. Demolished.)

ALBERT HALL Craddock Street. (Opened 8.22, conversion, architect: Charles Tamlin Ruthin, of two former concert/reading halls occasionally used for films, 2000 seats. Leased from South Wales Cinemas by Union 3.37.) Taken over 10.37, part of Union circuit. (Taken back by South Wales Cinemas 1.10.39. Taken over by Jackson Withers. Taken over by Rank 1.11.76. Closed 3.12.77. Bingo.)

SWINDON Wiltshire

SAVOY 39/41 Regent Street. Opened 15.2.37 by ABC, architect: W. R. Glen, 1770 seats: 1130 stalls & 640 balcony. Renamed ABC c1961. Closed 3.3.73 for tripling. ABC 2 opened 21.5.73, 410 seats. ABC 1 & 3 opened 18.6.73, 606 & 148 seats. (Renamed Cannon. Closed 26.3.91. Derelict.)

TANKERTON Whitstable

TROCADERO Marine Parade. (Opened 9.2.31, former skating rink.) Taken over c1932. (Leased to Regent from 5.33 to 1935.) Advertised as TROC. (Taken over by independent 29.5.38. 1380 seats. Closed 9.12.38 by fire. Half of building re-opened 19.6.39, 750 seats. Closed 1947. Film studios. Re-opened 3.1.49 as Embassy. Closed 20.8.50. Re-opened 11.50. Closed 1952. Warehouse.)

TEDDINGTON West London

SAVOY High Street. (Opened 6.12 as Picture House. Closed 7.12.29 for alterations. Re-opened 6.8.30 as Savoy. 600 seats.) Taken over 14.10.35. Closed 11.1.37. (Demolished for new Savoy.)

SAVOY High Street (including site of old Savoy). Opened 29.11.37 by ABC, architect: W. R. Glen, 1574 seats: 1068 stalls & 506 balcony. Closed 22.2.58. Re-opened 11.5.58. Closed 23.4.60. (Demolished. Office block.)

TEMPLE FORTUNE North London

ORPHEUM Finchley Road. (Opened 11.10.30, architects: Yates, Cook and Darbyshire, 2800 seats.) Taken over c1932. (Taken over by County 3.34. Taken over by Odeon 8.39. Renamed Odeon c1945. Many live shows. Closed 27.4.74. Demolished c5.82. Flats.)

TILEHURST Reading

REX 836 Oxford Road. (Opened 20.9.37, architect: E. Norman Bailey, 1090 seats, stadium plan.) Taken over 30.8.43, from Mayfair circuit. Closed 18.10.58. (Offices: Lockhart House. Car showroom.)

TIPTON West Midlands

REGENT Owen Street. (Opened 7.10 as Tivoli, conversion of market hall by architects Scott and Clark. 1400 seats. Closed 1.1.20. Reconstructed and re-opened 16.8.20 as Regent, 1500 seats.) Taken over c1.31. Leased to Regent from 5.33 to 1935. (Taken over by independent c1942. Renamed Regal 28.6.54. Closed 3.12.60. Demolished. Shops.)

TONBRIDGE Kent

RITZ The Botany. (Opened 30.7.37 by Union, architects: Verity and Beverley, 1250 seats.) Taken over 10.37, part of Union circuit. (Taken over by independent 21.2.39. Taken over by Shipman and King 8.55. Closed 14.3.78. Freezer store. Former restaurant area re-opened by independent 8.78 as Carlton, 98 seats. Closed c6.82.)

TOOTING South London

MAYFAIR Upper Tooting Road. (Opened 15.2.32, architect: Harold S. Scott, 1998 seats.) Taken over 15.5.33. Renamed ABC 1963. Closed 29.5.71 for modernisation and insertion of Painted Wagon pub in rear stalls. Re-opened 6.6.71, front stalls only. Circle later re-opened to increase seating. (Taken over by independent 27.7.76 and renamed Mayfair. Closed 13.1.79. Bank in part of foyer, snooker in stalls.)

TORQUAY Devon

BURLINGTON Union Street. (Opened c1.20.) Taken over 26.2.31. (Leased to Regent from 5.33 to 1935. (Taken over by independent 7.39. 470 seats. Serious fire 9.44. Closed 12.53. Demolished.)

REGAL Castle Street (Castle Circus). Opened 30 or 31.7.33 by ABC, architect: W. R. Glen, 1600 seats. Renamed ABC c1961. Closed 24.5.78. (Bingo in holiday season. Closed 1986. Re-opened as cinema 14.8.87 by independent, renamed Regal, balcony seats only. Closed c11.87. Demolished 4.89.)

TRANMERE Birkenhead

REGENT Church Road. (Opened 1926.) Taken over c8.35. 1091 seats, one floor. Closed 1.12.56. (Demolished. Shops.)

TRING Hertfordshire

REGAL Western Road. (Opened 10.9.36, architect: Harold S. Scott, 514 seats.) Taken over 30.8.43, from Mayfair circuit. Closed 15.2.58. (Re-opened by independent 6.4.58. Closed 19.3.60. Sold by ABC on 20.9.61. Re-opened as Masque Theatre 20.11.65. Demolished. Flats: Regal Court.)

TROWBRIDGE Wiltshire

REGAL. (Opened 1.11.37, architect: Harold S. Scott, 1010 seats.) Taken over 30.8.43, from Mayfair circuit. Closed 19.11.60. (Demolished.)

TUEBROOK Liverpool

CARLTON Green Lane and West Derby Road. (Opened 11.6.32, architect: A. Ernest Shennan, 1948 seats.) Taken over 12.6.35. Renamed ABC 23.12.62. Closed 22.1.72 for modernisation and conversion of rear stalls to Painted Wagon pub. Re-opened 27.3.72, 658 seats, balcony only. (Taken over by independent 10.7.80 and renamed

Carlton. Closed 4.12.82. Pub open, cinema derelict.)

TURNPIKE LANE North London

see Harringay

TWICKENHAM West London

REGAL London Road, corner of Amyand Park Road. Opened 9.10.39 by ABC, architect: W. R. Glen, 1760 seats: 1258 stalls & 502 balcony. Closed 20.8.60. (ABC TV rehearsal studios. Demolished. Regal House office block and Rugby Tavern pub.)

UPTON PARK East London

CARLTON Green Street. (Opened 29.10.28, architect: George Coles, 2177 seats, semi-stadium plan.) Taken over 2.35. Closed 27.1.45 by rocket bomb damage. Re-opened 10.8.53 with new entrance and foyer, 1755 seats. Renamed ABC 17.9.61. (Taken over by independent 11.2.79 and renamed Ace. Closed 23.3.83. Derelict.)

URMSTON Greater Manchester

EMPRESS Higher Road. (Opened c1929. 900 seats. Enlarged, architects: Drury and Gomersall, and re-opened 5.8.35, 1228 seats. Taken over by Union 29.6.36.) Taken over 10.37, part of Union circuit. Closed 11.10.58.

UXBRIDGE West London

SAVOY 1 High Street. (Opened 1922, 1014 seats. Taken over by Union 1935.) Taken over 10.37, part of Union circuit. Closed 18.6.60. (Bingo. Closed 1982. Demolished. Offices and shops.)

REGAL 233 High Street. (Opened 26.12.31, architect: E. Norman Bailey, 1610 seats, stadium plan. Taken over by Union 1935.) Taken over 10.37, part of Union circuit. Closed 4.11.77. (Listed building. Nightclub. Closed.)

WAKEFIELD West Yorkshire

REGAL Kirkgate, corner of Sun Lane. Opened 9.12.35 by ABC, architect: W. R. Glen, 1594 seats. Renamed ABC c1962. Triple from 11.11.76, 532 & 236 & 170 seats. (Renamed Cannon. Open.)

WALHAM GREEN Northwest London

REGAL 396-400 North End Road. Opened 2.8.35

by ABC, architect: W. R. Glen, 1929 seats. Renamed ABC 9.7.62. Closed 12.2.72. (Dickie Dirts jeans emporium. Demolished.)

WALLASEY Merseyside

CAPITOL Liscard Corner. (Opened 4.9.26.) Taken over c1930, 1372 seats. Closed 5.9.59 for modernisation. Re-opened 9.11.59 as ABC. 1181 seats. Closed 23.2.74. (Bingo.)

WALLINGFORD Oxfordshire

REGAL St. Martin's Street. (Opened 7.3.34, architect: Harold S. Scott, 492 seats. Taken over by Union c1936.) Taken over 10.37, part of Union circuit. (Taken over by independent 16.6.57. Closed 17.3.73. Demolished.)

WALLSEND Tyne and Wear

RITZ. Opened 15.5.39 by ABC, architects: Percy L. Browne, Son and Harding, 1622 seats. Closed 8.9.62. (Bingo.)

WALNEY ISLAND Cumbria

WALNEY Natal Road. (Taken over by Union 8.36.) Taken over 10.37, part of Union circuit. 786 seats. (Taken over 20.3.48 by Essoldo. Closed c1959. Demolished c1983.)

WALSALL West Midlands

HER MAJESTY'S Town End Bank. (Former live theatre.) Taken over 31.3.36. 1050 seats. Closed 12.6.37. (Demolished for Savoy.)

GRAND Park Street. (Former live theatre.) Taken over 31.3.36. 630 seats. Closed 11.38. (Leased to independent for music hall use. Destroyed by fire 6.39.)

PALACE The Square/Old Square. (Opened 12.4.10, architects: Hickton and Farmer, 1000 seats. Enlarged with balcony and re-opened 3.4.20, 1500 seats.) Taken over 31.3.36. 1600 seats, later reduced to 1165 seats. Closed 29.9.55. (Demolished.)

IMPERIAL Darwell Street. (Opened pre-1914.) Taken over 1.4.36. 1130 seats. Closed 3.5.68. (Bingo.)

SAVOY Town End Bank (site of Her Majesty's Theatre). Opened 3.10.38 by ABC, architects: W. R. Glen and Hickton & Medley, 2169 seats: 1358 stalls & 811 balcony. Renamed ABC c1962.

Closed 7.7.73 for tripling and insertion of Painted Wagon pub. ABC 1 opened 30.9.73, 506 seats. ABC 2 & 3 opened 16.11.73, 278 & 143 seats. (Renamed Cannon. Open.)

WALTHAMSTOW Northeast London

DOMINION Buxton Road (site of Prince's Pavilion). (Opened 22.12.30, architect: Clifford Aish, 1685 seats, stadium plan.) Taken over 30.3.31. Closed 15.3.58. (Wrestling.) Re-opened 6.10.58. Closed 4.3.61. (Bingo.)

WALTON Liverpool

see also Kirkdale and Paddington

COLISEUM City Road. (Opened 7.12.22.) Taken over c1935. 978 seats. Closed 1.12.56. (Football supporters club.)

ASTORIA Walton Road, corner of Furness Street. (Opened 21.7.30, architects: Gray and Evans, 1586 seats.) Taken over 9.35. Renamed ABC 12.63. Closed 23.2.74. (Derelict. Nightclub from 9.11.84. Closed.)

WALTON-ON-THAMES Surrey

REGAL New Zealand Avenue. (Opened 26.3.38 by Lou Morris, architect: C. Edmund Wilford, 1590 seats.) Taken over 30.8.43, from Mayfair circuit. Renamed ABC c1963. Closed 11.12.71. (Demolished. Shops.)

WANDSWORTH Southwest London

SAVOY 262 York Road. Opened 22.2.32 by ABC, architect: W. R. Glen, 2166 seats: 1158 stalls & 1008 balcony. Closed c1.45 by damage from rocket bomb. Re-opened 7.1.46. Closed 8.3.58. (Wrestling.) Re-opened 18.5.58. Closed 6.6.59. (Demolished 4.60.)

WARRINGTON Cheshire

GRAND Bridge Foot. (Opened 13.11.22, 1300 seats.) Taken over 12.30. (Taken over by independent and re-opened 19.8.40. Closed 3.52. Demolished for bridge.)

RITZ Barbauld Road & Arpley Station Approach/ Bridge Foot. (Opened 23.8.37 by Union, architects: Owen Bond and Son, 1928 seats.) Taken over 10.37, part of Union circuit. Renamed ABC c1960. Closed 19.8.72 for splitting into bingo and smaller cinema. Re-opened 7.12.72. 472 seats in

former balcony. ABC 2 opened 11.80 in former café, 90 seats. Both closed 23.10.82. (Nightclub: Mr. Smith's.)

WARWICK Warwickshire

COUNTY. (Opened c1921, former live theatre.) Taken over 22.10.36. 699 seats. Closed 31.10.51, licence not renewed. (Car showrooms. Pickford's depository. Demolished c1990 – ceiling saved.)

WATFORD Hertfordshire

EMPIRE Cassio Road. (Opened 6.11.13, 900 seats. Modernised 1952. Modernised 1966. 531 seats. Taken over by Shipman and King 19.12.76. Modernised 4.78. Closed 31.5.80 for twinning. Empire 1 & 2 opened 21.8.80, 363 & 204 seats.) Renamed ABC 1 & 2 24.5.85. (Renamed Cannon. Open.)

WEDNESBURY West Midlands

RIALTO Earp's Lane. (Opened c1918 as Borough Theatre, former live theatre, 600 seats. Renamed Rialto c1927. Closed for nearly complete reconstruction, architects: Satchwell and Roberts). Taken over and re-opened by ABC 9.31, 917 seats. Leased to Regent 5.33 to 1935. (Taken over by independent, enlarged and re-opened 15.8.38, 950 seats. Closed 30.3.57. Re-opened 12.57. Closed 8.7.61. Bingo.)

WELLINGBOROUGH Northamptonshire

LYRIC Midland Road. (Opened 14.12.36, architect: Edgar Simmons, 1424 seats.) Taken over 30.8.43, from Mayfair circuit. Renamed ABC c1965. Closed 9.4.69. (Bingo. Demolished for Arndale shopping centre.)

WEMBLEY Northwest London

REGAL Ealing Road. Opened 8.2.37 by ABC, architect: W. R. Glen, 2017 seats: 1300 stalls & 717 balcony. Renamed ABC 1962. Closed 4.12.76. (Taken over by independent and re-opened 12.11.78 as Asian cinema, Milan. Closed. Demolished early 1987.)

WESTBOURNE Bournemouth

GRAND Poole Road. (Opened 18.12.22, 1000 seats. Taken over by Savoy Cinemas.) Part of

original circuit. Leased to Regent 5.33 to 1935. (Taken over by independent 21.12.53. Closed 8.10.75. Partweek films from 27.3.76. Closed 8.10.77. Fulltime bingo.)

WEST BROMWICH West Midlands

PLAZA Paradise Street. (Opened 1927, former Kennedy's Empire Theatre, 1100 seats.) Taken over c1.29. (Taken over by independent 9.37. Live theatre 1948 to 25.1.57. Re-opened 11.3.57 as King's cinema. Closed 28.4.73. Demolished for new King's.)

TOWER High Street, Carters Green. (Opened 9.12.35, architect: Harry Weedon, 1922 seats.) Taken over 22.10.36. Renamed ABC 3.7.61. Closed 28.12.68. (Bingo. Closed.)

WEST HARTLEPOOL Cleveland

FORUM Raby Road. Opened 27.2.37 by ABC, architects: Percy L. Browne and Son, 1932 seats: 1160 stalls & 772 balcony. Renamed ABC c1963. (Taken over by independent 16.2.76 and renamed Fairworld, 787 seats. Closed 1.5.83. Derelict.)

WHITLEY Reading

SAVOY 265 Basingstoke Road. (Opened 20.3.36, architect: E. Norman Bailey, 1027 seats.) Taken over 18.1.37. Closed 12.8.61. (Demolished. Supermarket.)

WHITLEY BAY Tyne and Wear

NEW COLISEUM. (Opened c1924.) Taken over 23.12.29. 1299 seats. (Taken over by independent 22.11.70. Closed 1.5.71. Bingo.)

WIGAN Greater Manchester

RITZ Station Road. Opened 7.3.38 by ABC (Union), architects: John Fairweather and Son, 2560 seats. Renamed ABC c3.62. Closed 28.5.77 for tripling and bingo in former stalls area. ABC 1 2 & 3 opened 27.10.77, 485 & 321 & 106 seats. Closed 5.3.83. (Re-opened 4.1.85 by independent, renamed Ritz. Open.)

WILLESDEN Northwest London

HIPPODROME High Street. (Former music hall. Taken over 3.9.27 by Bernstein Theatres. Re-opened 12.9.27 as cinema. Taken over by Abrahams.) Taken over c8.30. 1900 seats.

Closed 9.38. (Reverted to music hall, films on Sundays. Bombed 1940. Demolished 1957.)

WIMBLEDON Southwest London

ELITE 144 Broadway. (Opened 7.2.20, architect: Lt. Col. James E. Adamson. Closed 2.6.28 for enlargement of balcony, architect: Robert Cromie. Re-opened 9.28. Taken over by Lou Morris 2.30.) Taken over 10.35. 1264 seats. Auditorium entirely reconstructed, architect: C. J. Foster, re-opened 12.9.64 as ABC, 1030 seats. Closed 26.2.83. Demolished c4.85.)

WINCHESTER Hampshire

RITZ Middle Brook Street. Opened 29.4.40 by ABC (Union), 1470 seats: 1035 stalls & 435 balcony. (Closed 19.11.60. (Bingo.)

WINCHMORE HILL North London

CAPITOL 794 Green Lanes. (Opened 26.12.29 by Lou Morris, architect: Robert Cromie, 1929 seats.) Taken over c12.30. Closed 11.7.36 for renovation. Re-opened 3.8.36. Closed 22.2.58. Re-opened 11.5.58. Closed 5.12.59. (Demolished 1960. Office block: Capitol House.)

WINDSOR Berkshire

REGAL 113 Peascod Street. (Opened 1.13 as the Windsor. Renamed Regal c1931. Largely reconstructed and re-opened by Southan Morris 2.35. Taken over by Union c1935.) Taken over 10.37, part of Union circuit. 739 seats. Closed 4.1.69. (Bingo.)
ROYALTY. (Taken over by Union c1935. 783 seats.) Taken over 10.37, part of Union circuit. 658 seats. Some live use. Closed c1938.
PLAYHOUSE 59-60 Thames Street. (Opened 26.12.28 by Lou Morris, architect: Robert Cromie. Taken over by Southan Morris 26.6.30. Modernised and re-opened 1.5.33. Taken over by Union c1935.) Taken over 10.37, part of Union circuit. 1460 seats. Renamed ABC c1961. Closed 20.3.71 for conversion of stalls to "luxury lounge". Re-opened 11.4.71, 528 seats, stalls only. (Taken over by independent 11.82, renamed Carousel. Closed 16.1.83. Demolished 7.84.)

WISHAW Strathclyde

PLAZA. (Opened c1927 by SCVT.) Part of original circuit. 1074 seats. Closed 26.7.56 as unsafe (threat of subsidence).

WOKING Surrey

RITZ Chobham Road, corner of Church Street East. (Opened 12.4.37 by Union, architects: Verity and Beverley, 1518 seats.) Taken over 10.37, part of Union circuit. Renamed ABC c1962. Closed 8.4.72 for smaller cinema and bingo. Re-opened 13.7.72, 495 seats (former balcony). ABC 2 (video) opened 27.8.78 in former café, 83 seats. Both closed 4.9.82. (Bingo. Demolished 1988.)

WOKINGHAM Berkshire

SAVOY 10 Broad Street. (Opened c1913, conversion of shop. Taken over by Union c1936.) Taken over 10.37, part of Union circuit. (Taken over by independent c1942. Closed 1.51.)
RITZ Easthampstead Road. (Opened 29.5.37 by Union, architect: E. Norman Bailey, 716 seats, semi-stadium.) Taken over 10.37, part of Union circuit. (Taken over by Star 30.6.69. Taken over by independent 1.11.77. Closed 10.11.79. Bingo. New cinema opened 3.81 in front extension. Second cinema opened 1986 in half of old balcony, 200 seats. One cinema closed 8.90. Other cinema closed 10.1.91. Bingo continued.)

WOLVERHAMPTON West Midlands

NEW THEATRE ROYAL Bilston Street. (Opened 15.6.31, former live theatre.) Taken over c1932. (Taken over by Clifton 20.6.38 and renovated. 1073 seats. Renamed Clifton 19.9.48. Taken over by Star 13.2.66. Closed 19.2.66. Bingo. Demolished.)
SAVOY Garrick Street and Bilston Street. Opened 20.12.37 by ABC, architect: W. R. Glen, 1777 seats: 1155 stalls & 622 balcony. Renamed ABC 12.60. Closed 27.4.74 for tripling. ABC 1, 2 & 3 opened 13.5.74, 590 & 127 & 94 seats. (Renamed Cannon. Closed 17.10.91. Disused.)

WOLVERTON Buckinghamshire

EMPIRE Church Street. (Opened 21.11.32, former toy factory and theatre, 650 seats. Taken over by Union.) Taken over 10.37, part of Union circuit. (Taken over by independent 1939. 620 seats. Closed 5.69. Post Office extension with front rebuilt.)

WOODFORD Northeast London

MAJESTIC 60/64 High Road. (Opened 5.11.34, architect: S. B. Pritlove, 1724 seats.) Taken over 5.8.35. Closed 4.11.72 for tripling. Re-opened on 5.2.73 as ABC 1, 2 & 3, 592 & 201 & 133 seats. (Renamed Cannon. Open.)

WOOLWICH Southeast London

HIPPODROME Wellington Street, corner of Lower Market Street. (Opened 1924, former live theatre. Taken over by United Picture Theatres.) Taken over 7.35. Closed 1939. (Demolished for new Regal.)
REGAL Wellington Street, corner of Lower Market Street (site of Hippodrome). Opened 19.9.55 by ABC, architects: C. J. Foster, S.E. Woodyear, G. MacFarlane and P. Turner, 1524 seats. Renamed ABC c1963. Closed 20.11.82. (Nightclub.)

WORTHING West Sussex

PLAZA Rowlands Road and Eriswell Road. (Opened 14.12.33 by Lou Morris, architect: Harry Weston, interior designers: Mollo and Egan, 2005 seats.) Taken over 5.2.36. Closed 11.12.68. (Bingo.)

WYLDE GREEN Sutton Coldfield

PAVILION Chester Road and Gravelly Lane. (Opened 10.10.31, architect: Harold S. Scott, 2270 seats.) Taken over 11.1.34. 2128 seats. Closed 3.9.60. (Bowling alley. Demolished. Houses.)

WYTHENSHAWE Manchester

FORUM 456 Palatine Road, Northenden. (Opened 22.11.34, architect: Charles Hartley, 1904 seats.) Taken over 15.4.36. Renamed ABC 2.64. Closed 23.2.74. (Forum live theatre.)

YARDLEY Birmingham

TUDOR Haunch Lane and May Lane. (Opened 30.3.29, architect: Harold S. Scott, 1322 seats.) Taken over c1934. Closed 17.3.62. (Bingo. Demolished 7.90.)

YARMOUTH Norfolk

see Great Yarmouth

YIEWSLEY West London

MARLBOROUGH. (Opened 1923. Remodelled and redecorated, architect: H. Scott Willey, and re-opened 18.9.33. Taken over by Union.) Taken over 10.37, part of Union circuit. Closed 2.6.56. (Taken over by independent and renamed Ritz 26.8.56. Closed 16.4.60. Store. Demolished.)

YORK North Yorkshire

REGAL Piccadilly. Opened 25.9.37 by ABC, architects: W. R. Glen and Penty & Thompson, 1720 seats: 932 stalls & 788 balcony. Renamed ABC 1.61. Closed 2.9.72 for conversion of rear stalls to Painted Wagon pub. Re-opened 27.11.72, 680 seats in former balcony. Closed for tripling. ABC 1, 2 & 3 opened 2.10.80, 653 & 259 & 176 seats. Closed 18.6.86. (Demolished 1989. Marks and Spencer homeware store.)

Bibliography

One of the reasons for undertaking this book was the shortage of information about ABC, so the following list is brief.

Book

Golden Hill to Golden Square. By W. 'Bill' Cartlidge. (New Horizon, Bognor Regis, 1982). Career and personal reminiscences of a man who spent most of his working life with ABC as manager and executive.

Booklets

The Associated British Picture Corporation. (Undated brochure issued in 1960/61 describing the activities of the various branches of the company.)

B.I.P. (Booklet dated July 1930, issued by British International Pictures principally to describe the company to its shareholders.)

Magazines/articles

ABC News. (1947-   ). In-house publication full of staff news and photographs.)

Focus on Film: "Union Cinemas" by Allen Eyles, no. 37 (March 1981). (History of the circuit which was taken over by ABC.)

Picture House (The Magazine of the Cinema Theatre Association): "Hippodrome Blackpool" by Gordon Coombes, no. 6 (Spring 1985), pages 12-14 (recalls the author's various contacts with the theatre while working for ABC); "ABC in North West London" by Gordon Coombes, no. 8 (Spring 1986), pages 26-31 (recalls the author's experiences as district manager in the immediate postwar period); "With ABC in Scotland" by Gordon Coombes, no. 12 (Autumn 1988), pages 7-15 and 24 (recalls the author's experiences as district manager for Scotland North, 1951-52).

Videos

The ABC of ABC. 1989 three-hour video compiled by John Fernée (One Farm Way, Burgess Hill, West Sussex RH15 0JX), relating the history of the circuit in colour and black-and-white images with some specially shot video material.

Union Cinemas + Shipman & King Cinemas. (Part two of *The ABC of ABC.*) 1990 three-hour video by John Fernée.

Book references

Curtains!!! Or a New Life for Old Theatres.. Edited by Iain Mackintosh and Michael Sell. (John Offord [Publications], 1982.)

The Dream Palaces of Liverpool. By Harold Ackroyd. (Amber Valley Typesetting Services, Birmingham, 1987.)

Kinematograph Year Book 1941. (Kinematograph Publications, London, 1940.)

Mr. Rank. A Study of J. Arthur Rank and British Films. By Alan Wood. (Hodder and Stoughton, London, 1952.)

Silver Screen in the Silver City – A History of Cinemas in Aberdeen, 1986-1987. By Michael Thomson. (Aberdeen University Press, Aberdeen, 1988.)